Brief Counselling in Schools

Brief Counselling in Schools

Working with Young People from 11 to 18

Dennis Lines

SAGE Publications
London • Thousand Oaks • New Delhi

© Dennis Lines 2002

First published 2002

SAGE Publications Ltd
6 Bonhill Street
London EC2A 4PU

SAGE Publications Inc
2455 Teller Road
Thousand Oaks, California 91320

SAGE Publications India Pvt Ltd
32, M-Block Market
Greater Kailash - I
New Delhi 110 048

British Library Cataloguing in Publication data

A catalogue record for this book is available from
the British Library

ISBN 0 7619 7354 0
ISBN 0 7619 7355 9 (pbk)

Library of Congress Control Number available

Typeset by SIVA Math Setters, Chennai, India
Printed and bound in Great Britain by Athenaeum Press,
Gateshead

CONTENTS

ACKNOWLEDGEMENTS

Without the sharing of minds the individual's thought becomes sterile and unimaginative: I have benefited enormously from theoreticians and practitioners whom I have consulted. A number of colleagues have supported me in the composition of this book. First, I am grateful to Janet Bellamy and Bill O'Connell, my tutors in training, for their insistence on academic rigour and for their patience and imagination when nurturing my counselling skills; particularly Bill in pointing me forward to where brief counselling is moving. I acknowledge also the inspiration and encouragement of Ron Best, an academic I have never met personally, but with whom I have corresponded frequently. I am grateful also to Alison Poyner, Commissioning Editor, and the rest of the team at Sage, for their encouragement in steering me through this project and for giving me an opportunity to put into writing all that I have learned in brief school-based counselling. To all my teacher colleagues who have taught me so much in adjusting my idealism to the practicalities and constraints of a school-based setting, I remain grateful. I acknowledge especially Marie Woods and Wendy Oldfield-Austin for their suggestions on early drafts of chapters. I acknowledge also my former headteacher and current headteacher who, along with the Birmingham LEA, have supported the provision of counselling in school and who thereby have given weight to the need to support the emotional literacy of pupils. I thank also Deirdre Barber for her painstaking work in correcting early proofs.

Finally, and more importantly, I express my gratitude to my daily tutors of life's rich experience: the pupil-clients who come forward for counselling. I have learned from them more than I can express and every problem presented in the counselling room has been a means of developing my practice and refining my technique. One 15-year-old pupil once presented a series of paintings through which she articulated her stormy relationship with her father. Through brief art therapy, we explored her world and this was one of the most poignant contacts I have ever made with a young client. Regretfully, she would not grant me permission to publish her story or reproduce her paintings. I remember feeling sad about this because the material would have contributed something to this book but obviously I have respected her wish. It struck me afterwards that the learning I had acquired was being absorbed in my practice almost imperceptibly with further clients. It seems that each client adds something to the counsellor that has the potential to develop practice if the practitioner can remain intuitive to what the client is saying and feeling on different levels.

Dennis Lines
August 2001

INTRODUCTION

This book is written for counselling practitioners who work with young people in school. Principally, they are school counsellors, teacher counsellors, educational social workers, social workers, educational psychologists and careers advisers. The book is written from a practitioner's perspective to broaden the skill-base of those already involved in counselling youngsters in the closing years of compulsory education and in colleges of further education. It is not, therefore, a counsellor skills training manual, or an introductory text on counselling. The reader is assumed to have a theoretical and working knowledge of basic counselling. Students on counselling courses will find the book of assistance in broadening their understanding of brief counselling practice in an educational setting.

As a full-time residential school counsellor in a large comprehensive school, I serve a community comprised both of young people who are socially deprived and of those who are socially advantaged, and I therefore have referred for counselling the whole range of client difficulties. In this book, I wish to illustrate ways of working with troubled young people through models that integrate goal-centred approaches with aspects of traditional methods applied briefly.

The first three chapters set the context of counselling in school. Chapter 1 covers the beginning and development of school counselling. Although well behind the United States and marginally behind Australia, there are encouraging trends that counselling in schools is growing in England and Wales. The chapter covers different orientations of school counselling and explores the limitations of carrying out counselling in school. Chapter 2 covers the professional and ethical boundaries of counselling in a setting among colleagues who are *in loco parentis*. The developmental process of the targeted client-group is taken up in Chapter 3, where the impact of puberty and the process of individuation as it affects young people transferring from children to adults are addressed. Teenage culture in Britain is judged by surveys as being in a state of crisis with regard to alcohol, drugs and sexual behaviour. Britain currently has the highest rate of teenage pregnancy, and comes out top of European countries for having the highest numbers of teenagers experimenting with drugs and binge-drinking of alcohol. Chapter 3 closes, therefore, with a discussion on parenting styles that foster healthy adolescent development.

Chapter 4 outlines the theory and practice of brief counselling. After reviewing the research evidence that validates time-limited work, the chapter moves on to examine the merits and limitations of traditional approaches within the constraints of the school setting. Brief therapy refers to counselling contracts of fewer than 20 sessions, which in school would not be considered as 'brief'. I was tempted to entitle this book *Brief, Brief Counselling in School* to make my point that effective therapy in a school setting has to acknowledge the stretched resources of time and the practicalities of a school environment. When the practitioner attempts to integrate his personal style, he has to acknowledge the limitations of the setting and the targeted client-group. Consequently, I have found goal-centred models that have a future orientation, and which are solution-focused, to be particularly effective. Equally effective are elements of narrative therapy integrated within an Egan framework, so long as therapy is not considered an end point but as a supportive means of helping youngsters on their way.

The closing seven chapters cover the whole range of teenage difficulties. Each chapter is a unit in itself and the reader may select at random. Most chapters begin with a short review of the research and theoretical perspectives that cover the particular area. Case studies are written concisely in order to get the main point over, but are composed with the assumption that the practitioner fills in the gaps from his own experience. As such, the writing passes over the reflective listening discourse, the feelings evoked and other finely tuned resonating of counsellor and client in order to present for readers what might be new, and what might be incorporated into their own practice. In promoting new methods of working briefly, I am not denying thereby the essential core counselling conditions – empathy, congruence and unconditional positive regard – or the therapeutic relationship for bringing about change. I hope the reader will take this as read.

All case studies are composite characters taken from real practice, but which have had identifying features removed in order to preserve client anonymity. This is important ethical practice, since I judge that the majority of my clients are not able to give 'informed' consent for publishing their material. All names are pseudonyms. Case discourse is written grammatically though youngsters rarely speak in sentences. The symbol ~ denotes a break in transcript. Often in writing on psychotherapy there is an inference that all counselling (no less youth counselling) moves smoothly towards satisfactory outcomes. This is not always the case, and I would not pretend otherwise. While practitioners should evaluate their work through genuine client feedback, sometimes counsellors get 'stuck', or fail to meet their client's needs – hence the need for supervision.

Chapter 5 looks at the worrying rise in depression in young people and closes with models for supporting those who have been sexually abused. School bullying is the focus of Chapter 6, in which brief approaches are presented in countering bullying by working with groups of pupils and individually with bullies and victims. Name-calling behaviour is given particular emphasis in this chapter. Chapter 7 illustrates supportive models that I have found effective with young people who face parental separation, or who are facing conflict among step-parents within altered family compositions. I serve a socially deprived area and it is common to counsel youngsters who do not live with their biological parents. There is a pressing need, therefore, to address this situation in school, since the experience for the teenager of his or her parents splitting up is not dissimilar to that of bereavement, which is covered in Chapter 8. Counselling pupils and students who have lost their parents or close loved ones is deep therapeutic work. Every teacher is aware of the effects of loss and how it impacts on learning and student wellbeing, and when youngsters become distraught in class the public display of grief requires someone set apart from the class to hold and support them. The chapter highlights what can be achieved with brief approaches, particularly by utilizing other peers in the healing process. Chapter 9 covers sexual inclination and illustrates various brief models of supporting teenagers over their first sexual experience. The primary focus is on counselling those who discover their sexual orientation to be homosexual. Chapter 10 covers smoking, drugs and alcohol, and in this chapter I illustrate a means of supporting young people briefly with a model that is placed within their mind so as to serve as a template to motivate them towards sobriety and self-regulation. Finally, in Chapter 11, spiritual issues are covered. This is a particularly important area to cover in counselling, as in education. I sometimes wonder whether the general malaise among some young people, which is revealed in sexual promiscuity, drug addiction and alcohol misuse, is an indicator of spiritual emptiness in a world of shifting values. This chapter covers brief spiritual counselling from an inclusive stance through a single case study.

The interface of education and counselling holds open an exciting future. They serve different aims, but have certain similarities. Education in Britain has become highly competitive, as opposed to being collaborative and co-operative. The wellbeing of pupils and students has been displaced by an exclusive focus on academic achievement, but there are encouraging signs of change. I remain optimistic that counselling in schools may soon be given a high priority. Education has to integrate citizenship and more extensive personal, social and moral education (PSME) into its subject-led curriculum, to be more inclusive of the child's social, emotional and moral world. The British Association for Counselling (BAC) included psychotherapy in its title in 2000 to become BACP. There is in this move an interest in becoming less exclusive in what is understood by the terms 'counselling' and 'psychotherapy' in order that the whole profession may benefit. Both education and counselling are in transition.

Much of my work carried out in school I would describe as counselling, rather than psychotherapy (I don't wish to enter a polemic turf war here), but I still see my involvement as therapy. I use the term psychotherapy when referring to in-depth, longer-term work. Although I come from an eclectic counselling background, I use the term integrative in place of eclectic, simply because much of my work involves a careful blending of different models and approaches to suit client needs.

I alternate between masculine and feminine pronouns when describing the counsellor, which is done to preserve anti-discriminative practice and to avoid the cumbersome repetition of 'he or she'; I do similarly with the gender of my clients. The client-group represents young people from the ages of 11 to 18. By 'pupils', I mean those attending school from the ages of 11 to 16, and who are in years seven to eleven, whereas by 'students' I mean those in full-time education from 16 to 18, years eleven to thirteen.

In England, Wales, parts of Scotland and Australia, pupils and students in full-time education attend secondary or comprehensive schools. In the United States and other parts of Scotland they are called high schools, sometimes academies or colleges. In order to be inclusive, I simply use 'school' to encompass all educational settings attended by pupils from 11 to 18 years.

1

SCHOOL COUNSELLING

The move from local 'tradition-centred' communities over the last two millennia to the larger, labour-orientated masses of the industrial cities presented less support for the old, sick, poor and insane (McLeod, 1993). Factories drew youngsters from the home to work in depersonalized institutions, and schools followed suit. Collectively, these developments reduced the supportive structures in society. Not only was the concept of the 'nuclear family' beginning to fragment, but also the sense of community was changing. The role of the priest as the listener and emotional supporter was taken over by the doctor, and 'mental illness' became a 'condition' that was diagnosable (such as 'hysteria') and, perhaps, treatable by means of hypnosis and mesmerism. These treatments led to a scientific approach to medicine and to the acknowledgement of the 'unconscious mind'. The apparatus was therefore in place for twentieth-century psychotherapy.

While offering 'education' more broadly than vocational learning in cottage industries, the social implications of early schooling, whether village or factory schooling, was beginning a trend of state cohesion, rather than that of the family. In previous decades, 'children were seen and not heard', and were not expected to have social or emotional difficulties, were not 'individuals' as such, and were not likely to be 'depressed'. Psychological and psychiatric provision was for adults not children, for the latter were juvenile and were expected to get on with things without fuss. Many of the older generation therefore look back on their schooldays with disdain and bitterness, for they were generally not happy times.

DEVELOPMENT OF SCHOOL COUNSELLING

Counselling in British education grew out of what was loosely termed 'guidance' in the early 1900s. Guidance in education traditionally covered three distinct activities. There was child guidance, which was often provided by the medical service, then there was careers or vocational guidance provided by the new Careers Service, and thirdly there was educational guidance.

The first two received generous funding, but neither was steered towards the provision of individual counselling in schools. Career guidance for long-term employment and independent living was the focus of work, but individual counselling over sensitive relationship issues was not generally undertaken. In spite of the Careers Service giving pragmatic advice and information, this was not complemented by emotional support (Thomas, 1990). It is hardly surprising therefore that, with the modified title of careers adviser, there was no brief to offer contracts of counselling.

The School Psychological Service provided educational guidance in the main (Milner, 1980). While resources have been forthcoming from educational funding with the Psychological Service – largely through Acts of Parliament (1910) and statutory regulation – there have not been many educational resources put into child guidance. Although clinics for child guidance have existed since 1921, their service from inception has been geared towards children of 'normal intelligence' whose behaviour is disruptive or non-conforming. School counselling emerged not from education, then, but from the medical service, principally the National Association for Mental Health, at a conference held in 1963. Courses set up at the universities of Reading and Keele from 1965 onwards promoted the writings of Carl Rogers and offered skills training in person-centred and non-directive counselling.

This trend sat comfortably with modern approaches in education that were moving from an authoritarian, didactic style towards pupil-centred learning. Out of this training, a support group was formed called the National Association of Educational Counsellors, which was renamed the National Association of Counsellors in Education (NACE). It established a professional code of ethics and endorsed the dissemination of ideas and research findings. NACE currently exists as a sub-division of the British Association of Counselling and Psychotherapy (BACP).

EXTENT OF COUNSELLING PROVISION IN SCHOOL

There were 351 counsellors working from two orientations in schools in England and Wales according to research published in 1977, but a decade later in 1987 there were only 90, a 75 per cent reduction (Mabey and Sorensen, 1995). In comparison with North America, where the trend has been in the opposite direction, these figures are dispiriting. But the tide has recently turned.

Counselling in schools in England and Wales

Summarizing the current state of school counselling in England and Wales, and exempting those authorities that provide 'drop-in counselling centres' outside school (some of which are staffed by volunteers), provision generally appears to be growing (Capey, 1998). The Association of Teachers and Lecturers (ATL) unanimously adopted a resolution in 1996 in favour of the employment of school-based counsellors. All chief education officers were written to, asking for their policies on the role of such counsellors and what advice and support they could offer schools in this respect. Sixty replies were received and were published in the ATL's journal, *Report*, in early 1997. This was followed by a report published by Educational Management Information Exchange (EMIE), which had been commissioned to extend the research. Overall, 90 authorities replied to ATL or EMIE (89 in England and Wales, and 1 in Northern Ireland), providing information about counselling services for pupils at school and young people generally. This represented 58 per cent of all LEAs in England and Wales.

Screening the received data carefully, EMIE established that most of the provision was through outside services or through the services of the educational psychologists, the educational social workers or through the behaviour support agencies of the LEAs (Capey, 1998). I have summarized the report elsewhere (Lines, 2000), but the salient points are as follows.

Regarding the appointment of professional counsellors in schools, 22 LEAs (24 per cent of the replies) reported that they had a policy on such appointments. Thirty-three LEAs reported that they had appointed one or more professional counsellors in one or more schools. Bexley, Bristol, Cheshire and Sheffield could offer support and guidance, and much advice was available to schools in Devon, Hertfordshire, Brighton and Hartlepool. Devon has had an established support for counselling since the 1960s and has 17 full- or part-time counsellors in their schools, and at the time of writing intends to increase counselling provision for school pupils. Hertfordshire reports 'a number' of trained counsellors in post in schools. Brighton and Hove have an innovative 'Drugs Prevention Project' that provides on-site counselling facilities in three schools. In addition, the authority could boast that seven out of ten secondary schools and two out of six special schools could offer a counselling service. Hartlepool reported that the 'authority is aware that some [schools] are developing counselling services', and that they are concerned by 'the unreasonable expectations that may be placed on those involved in "peer counselling"' (Capey, 1998: 14). Besides myself – a full-time residential school counsellor – three part-time counsellors are employed in secondary schools in Birmingham, although 27 schools profess in a survey to provide counselling through pastoral staff (D. Williams, Health Adviser, Birmingham LEA).

One LEA has a more generous policy. The Dudley LEA has employed counsellors for the last 25 years, enlisting the support of a peripatetic team of seven full-time school counsellors to provide a therapeutic service of one day/week for 22 secondary schools, and for over 80 primary schools within its authority. Being an 'external' provision for schools, the team can provide counselling for children's needs which is often viewed as less enmeshed in school issues. Parental consent is normally required before counselling, but exceptions occur when an assessment reveals that the client is 'Gillick competant'.

LEAs in England and Wales offering counselling support via non-educational agencies include Brighton and Hove, Newham, and Swindon, albeit on a very small scale. External agency support is provided by the Catholic Children's Society's Counselling Service in three dioceses covering South London, Hampshire, Surrey, East and West Sussex and Kent, where four qualified counsellors have worked in ten schools. Several comprehensive schools in Birmingham enlist 'Open Door Youth Counselling Service' on a part-time basis. Croydon is supported by a counsellor/training agency and registered charity called 'The Place to Be'. In Bristol, the NSPCC's 'Counselling in School' service is a project involving a partnership between the Society and local secondary schools. The Health Authority in Kent financed three counsellors for the Canterbury and Thanet School Counselling Service. Finally, the 'One to One' counselling service for young people in the schools and community of Beddau in Wales was set up in Rhondda Cynon Taff offering nine counsellors to serve four comprehensive schools in the area.

Counselling in Australian and Scottish schools

Education authorities in Australia appear more favourably inclined towards counselling in school than do those in the UK. The majority of state-funded secondary schools in Australia have a school counsellor on site, and many have implemented a peer counselling (support) service (Reid, 1996). This is the result of the Australian Education Council in 1989, which instructed education authorities to enhance performance through attending to the student's personal wellbeing and self-esteem. The issues being addressed in Australian secondary schools are in regard to professional practice, particularly over levels of confidentiality, rather than whether the counselling provision is under-resourced.

Scotland, similarly, has more counselling provision proportionally than England and Wales, but the counselling practitioner is termed a 'guidance teacher'. Guidance teachers form a self-standing department (for approximately 130/140 pupils) within the school and have non-contact periods (around one-third timetable) for individual 'counselling' and a range of responsibilities that fall alongside their teaching role. Guidance is attending to the personal difficulties of pupils and helping them to make choices and decisions, according to the Scottish Education Department (SED, 1968). Theoretically, at least, the guidance teacher compensates for parental inadequacy and provides each individual with counselling support, but in practice the distinctive role of counselling, as opposed to discipline, has not been worked out. With growing demand in Scottish secondary schools since the inception of guidance, individual support has had to be prioritized. With the subsequent legislation (SED, 1976) from the early 1970s, abolition of corporal punishment in schools has not addressed these issues (Simpson, 1995) to produce a comprehensive therapeutic provision for many of the emotional and social difficulties of youngsters.

In referrals to guidance teachers, it is clear that boys are over-represented, largely to do with the imposition of sanctions. One local study (Simpson, 1995: 34) found that only 6.4 per cent of referrals were for 'personal reasons', which compares with 82 per cent for misbehaviour or non-conformity, listed as 'abusive language', 'behaviour', 'graffiti', 'fighting', 'truancy', 'inappropriate dress', 'bullying' and 'racism'. The SED (1976, para. 4.15) recognizes that guidance teachers should attend to problems which may have underlying causes – such as irregular attendance, prolonged absence, repeated misbehaviour, late-coming, bullying and victimization. It is wondered, however, where the counselling role fits in with conventional pastoral responsibilities, which in England and Wales are dealt with by Heads of Year or the like. As Simpson (1995) concludes, these roles are a difficult blend in the same person (as with teacher-counsellor), and this lack of role clarity is intensified through unrefined policy. Divergent expectations of referring teacher colleagues, who find that the above behaviours represent an intrusion into the learning process and school routine, lead again to role conflict. Given the fact that guidance in Scottish schools is given such status, it is regretted that the counselling role is not made more explicit in both policy and practice.

TEACHERS ACQUIRING COUNSELLING SKILLS

From the mid-1970s, there has been a decline in provision of psychiatric and psychological services to children in the UK. Already overburdened pastoral teachers recognize that the need outweighs their personal resources. There can be little doubt that many school pupils would benefit from counselling, and that all schools would welcome funding to set up regular counselling provision.

Research carried out in 1975 estimated that 14 per cent of children in school had symptoms of emotional disturbance and maladjustment, with 1–2 per cent of these having severe psychiatric disturbance that warranted psycho-medical attention (Mabey and Sorensen, 1995). Much higher numbers of pupils are currently seeking regular help with less intensive social-emotional difficulties. Teachers have traditionally taken up the slack of pupil need by taking an interest in individual pupils (Biddulph, 1998; Lines, 2000), by building self-esteem and by broadening their social horizons by personal involvement. But such personal investment is becoming a rare commodity, as institutional changes have the effect of discouraging teachers from this level of association. Child protection protocol and safe caring practice promote cautious engagement for professionals with individual pupils.

In 1989, the Elton Report was anticipating the current situation by recommending the need for teachers to acquire counselling skills:

> We are convinced that there are skills which all teachers need, involved in listening to young people and encouraging them to talk about their hopes and concerns before coming to a judgement about their behaviour. We consider that these basic counselling skills are particularly valuable for creating a supportive school atmosphere. The skills needed to work effectively with adults, whether teachers or parents, are equally crucial. We regard such skills as particularly important for all senior pastoral staff (deputy heads, heads of house and year). (Elton Report, 1989: 111)

Successive governments in the UK have not responded with resources for counselling provision but have instead formalized Special Educational Needs legislation. The Code of Practice places pupils with emotional behavioural difficulties within a collective framework of registration, which carries an inference that remedies can be found within the school or the LEA. Psychiatric services have begun to use drug regimes (ritilin) and to diagnose behavioural disorders with clinical labels: Attention Deficit Hyperactivity Disorder (ADHD), Dyspraxia, Atypical Autism, Asperger's Syndrome, Autistic Spectrum Disorder (ASD) and Semantic Pragmatic Disorder (SPD).

Rather than helping, this administrative change has added to the sense of powerlessness among teachers, as well as leaving professionals divided. On the one hand teachers are encouraged to work more therapeutically with pupils who turn to them for help, and on the other they feel de-skilled by recent psycho-educational changes, and the pressure of time. The use of ritilin for behaviour modification and control is currently under review by medical authorities.

Such is the pressure of teaching in the modern competitive climate that many older teachers are going off sick through stress and are not able to get counselling for themselves, let alone for their pupils. Younger teachers are being trained to register their pupils' emotional-social deficits, and training courses have begun to offer counselling skills modules within teacher training. Although there has been no wholesale commitment from central government to Lord Elton's recommendation, there is evidence to suggest that resources are being committed from schools' own budgets to counselling skills training, as shown by the numbers of teachers subscribing to counselling courses and receiving partial or full INSET funding.

OPEN- AND SYSTEM-ORIENTATION SCHOOL COUNSELLING

While there are many different approaches to school counselling nationally, each can be broadly categorized under two general orientations of 'individual' or 'open-orientation', and 'system-orientation' (Mabey and

Sorensen, 1995). Open-orientation school counselling inadvertently offered pupil-clients the opportunity to oppose the demands of the school system, thus reflecting the individualism of the 1960s. System-orientation school counselling, where the counsellor role was acting on behalf of the organization, normally used behavioural modification programmes, token economies and biofeedback (Herbert, 1978), thus reflecting the political ethos of Thatcher's Britain that opposed individualism in favour of a sense of community responsibility. In a dwindling job market, attitudes that favoured rebellion against the school establishment became tantamount to a refusal to take on adult responsibility. Counselling models which were targeted at getting pupils to conform became more popular than those which encouraged personal autonomy. Counsellors with abilities to work with socially disruptive pupils became popular in school.

Each counselling orientation has its own distinctive boundary issues. School counsellors based at the school are system-oriented, while those coming in from outside agencies tend to be open-oriented. The role of the counsellor is implicit in each orientation, but it is arguably less clear for the counsellor working under a system-orientation. It is doubtful whether the counsellor is able to remain completely impartial and independent of a headteacher who serves as her line manager under a system-orientation. This is more problematic for the pupil-centred approach than for one with cognitive or behaviourist leanings. If the counselling practitioner has a teaching commitment, it is questionable whether these two roles can be combined effectively, particularly if the teacher has a pastoral (disciplinary) duty, or is in regular communication with parents. Pupils' perceptions of true allegiance may become confused.

A further difficulty with the system-orientation lies in parity of status for a counsellor who, where forenames are not used, will be viewed as a member of staff – 'Sir', 'Miss' or 'Ms' hardly foster an alliance of equals – and where psychological distance will be expected. Confidentiality might be compromised among teaching staff who are used to sharing information about pupils, and where teachers are held by the law to act *in loco parentis*. In addition, there is the related difficulty of the counsellor's files, or notes. Should they be accessible to parents upon request in the same way as pupils' pastoral files are by law?

Apart from geographical factors that may impose easy access, there are some disadvantages to open-orientation school counselling. With open-orientation school counselling it is a prerequisite that parental permission is sought before an appointment is arranged. But this imposes considerable restrictions for pupils who have a 'right' to receive counselling but who wish their parents/guardians not to know, particularly if parental home factors are part of the problem.

If pupils are permitted to make self-referrals, then there are issues concerning headteachers fulfilling their responsibility *in loco parentis*. If parental permission is obtained prior to counselling, there is still a controversial issue for the headteacher who is indirectly legitimizing confidential discussions by virtue of enlisting a counsellor on site, without having very much idea of what is said behind closed doors. One local headteacher of a maintained school disclosed to me his decision to terminate the contract of one counsellor whom the governors had agreed to fund for twelve months. This was because of some disquiet that the counsellor was privy to information that he felt bordered on child protection. This example illustrates the tension between an open-orientation service and the headteacher's legal position *in loco parentis*, which is discussed in the next chapter.

Researchers point to three benefits of having a therapeutic counsellor operating a system-orientation within the school (Mabey and Sorensen, 1995). First, having the counsellor on site removes the difficulty of deciding whether or not to refer to an outside agency in the first instance. Second, parents, unsure of referrals to outside psychological clinics, may feel it more acceptable to speak to someone within the school. Third, labelling can be minimized to some extent, since a counselling practitioner will speak with many pupil-clients over a broad diversity of problems, including many trivial difficulties. Labelling can occur among teachers, likewise. Resistance of teachers who may resent 'advice' given by 'outside professionals' who do not have to cope with the 'difficult pupil-client' within the 'class group context' can be minimized. Such behaviours might be played out in exhibitionism on the blind side of the visiting counsellor, yet shared more confidently with the teacher-counsellor or resident school counsellor. The residential school counsellor may avail herself of an opportunity to view at a distance the group dynamics of the classroom, or fall back on the experience on which she may have initially cut her teeth before becoming a school counsellor.

There are two further benefits. One is personal job satisfaction (and thereby personal efficacy). A peripatetic school counsellor spoke (in personal correspondence) of his sense of alienation at not being part of the school community that made his personal fulfilment and job satisfaction lower than it might otherwise have been. A school creates a corporate ethos for teams of staff as well as pupils, and this has great psychological appeal.

But more importantly, the school provides a rich and diverse series of peer groups, which not only reflects society in microcosm, but also offers an enormous and grossly under-used resource. The counsellor can work more readily and more efficiently within a cognitive behavioural approach with pupils and their parents within the context in which the behaviour is manifested. This offers more potential for change. In addition, the presence of various peer groupings offers considerable resources for supporting pupils of low self-esteem and with low befriending abilities, for bringing into school pupils who have a phobia about entering crowded playgrounds first thing in the morning, for group approaches to a number of presented problems, for the development of social skills in group settings and for peer support. Peer support ideally requires a trained counsellor to be the manager, which, quite obviously, would put considerable (perhaps impractical) demands on an outside trainer that would not apply to a system-oriented school counsellor.

Role conflict arises in both system- and open-oriented school counselling when a pupil-client discloses information that borders upon child protection issues. Since the school is under obligation to report the matter to social services, the school counsellor must breach the code of confidentiality. These boundary difficulties apply as much for peripatetic counsellors visiting the school as for counsellors in residence, for the former may still be perceived by pupils as being an extension of the system while maintaining some degree of independence. These issues are explored more fully in Chapter 2.

LIMITATIONS OF COUNSELLING IN SCHOOL

There are significant limitations in counselling pupil-clients in the school setting, and while this may check the fervour of those promoting (commendably) a more expansive provision (McGuiness, 1998), they need to be addressed. As these are outlined, I am conscious of highlighting the negative aspects and frustrations of my own practice. But as I speak with counselling colleagues, it becomes apparent how widespread and general my practice limitations are. Perhaps we school counsellors tend to be too defensive and accept too readily political and school management constraints in which therapeutic support is regarded as an ancillary aspect of school life. Leaving politics aside, to offer a professional counselling service for young people in school, a range of factors need careful thought:

- the type of setting for pupils to feel safe to discharge their feelings
- counselling aims which are in keeping with the setting
- resources for counselling
- planning and sustaining counselling programmes
- counselling styles with which pupils feel comfortable
- particular techniques which are appropriate in school

Counselling setting

The provision of a 'contained' setting in which pupils may experience catharsis and have an opportunity to explore deep issues cannot be guaranteed in school. Whatever preparations are made, like detaching telephone lines and asking receptionists to secure no interruptions, school buildings are a hive of activity during the school day. Counselling boundaries are imperative in school, but pupils nevertheless regularly seek me out while I am in session with clients, irrespective of my wishes. Pupils arrive late in school and, rather than going straight to lessons, they may approach me to arrange an appointment. Pupils enter the counselling room for trivial reasons – asking for a classroom key, asking the whereabouts of a teacher, asking what lesson they may have, etc. – principally because I am approachable and usually not tied up with teaching. They approach me because they are being bullied, and refuse to go to the next lesson because the perpetrator will be in the class. This is because they have not understood the difference between the counselling role and the disciplinary one, and because the Head of Year is teaching or otherwise engaged. Interruptions occur because a pupil has become distraught in class and the teacher has sent him or her down with a note or with an accompanying pupil for consolation. Occasionally, teachers send upset pupils to me two at a time, and it seems that however much the counselling boundaries are publicized, interruptions will still occur. Teachers send pupils, or accompany pupils, with concerns that matters are troubling them, or that family problems are affecting them in school, feeling under pressure and saying, 'Can I leave Robert with you, I have a class to teach?'

Some pupils storm to my room to protest over a teacher's (perceived) professional misconduct, or to complain that they have been sent out of class unjustly. In these situations, I generally deny them immediate audience but offer them a later appointment to discuss the matter. This gives them space to calm down and reflect, and supports teacher-colleagues who might feel that the counsellor favours the pupil and is incapable of impartial judgement; the policy also dissolves the unconscious manipulative ploys of avoiding responsibility for misbehaviour. Having maintained professionalism among colleagues and earned a degree of integrity among teachers and pupils, I can mediate in personality conflicts. But this represents a possible intrusion in neatly programmed sessions of contracted work.

School bells, fire alarms, and the delivery of administrative documents similarly present occasional interruptions that thwart focused in-depth therapy. The counsellor working in other settings will have a privileged arena in which to work where it is guaranteed no interruptions will occur, and may well be surprised by such practice conditions, but these are the realities of counselling in school.

Counselling aims

Counselling aims need to be in keeping with the school setting, to some degree. Encouraging pupils to become self-assertive or self-expressive, or to become individuals, may not go down well in school among teachers who constantly insist on behavioural conformity, standards of silence and community responsibility. A pupil may need to set a goal of standing up for himself after being continually bullied, and may misinterpret 'standing up for himself' as 'beating up the aggressor', and thereby become excluded for fighting. Counselling goals which are designed to foster individuation may not be perceived by parents as being helpful if they are struggling to maintain control, are threatened by enmeshed relationship bonding, or are attempting to regulate peer affiliations that are judged as having inherent risks. I am not advocating that such goals should be discouraged, but I am saying that their social implications need weighing up.

Group therapy requires lesson interruptions for a number of pupils who are often in different classes, and in spite of structured pre-planning, this can go wrong when pupils are absent or cannot be found. Alternatively, a significant member of the group may have forgotten, or may not be released by the teacher, or may prefer to be in a lesson.

Counselling resources

There are considerable resource implications of school counselling, even for residential full-time practitioners. Serving a large school community in a designated social priority area will at times involve prioritization of referrals. Resources have to be appropriately apportioned if the counsellor has other roles and responsibilities that engage his time (which is the norm in resident school counselling).

The counsellor working within a school timetable must adjust appointment setting to match lesson changeovers. This will mean that he can offer only five sessions at most each day if he counsels every lesson slot, and lessons last for 50 minutes. With half-sessions of 25 minutes, more counselling can be fitted in, with a further slot of 20 minutes during form period or assembly time. The school counsellor will have to give time to pre-arranged sessions for parents, meetings with teaching staff, policy meetings with senior teachers, and possibly case conferences or consultations with social workers, educational social workers, or educational psychologists. Counselling notes have to be written, letters of referral typed up and telephone calls made, often at set times of the day. Cumulatively, even if no other roles and administrative responsibilities take precedence, these tasks cut into counselling time and require a carefully planned day.

In my practice, there are normally three quality counselling sessions each day, with three to four brief engagements with pupils – largely to provide information or brief option-exploration over minor difficulties. In a given week, therefore, I may offer quality counselling in 15 appointments (occasionally two per week for one individual) for 1,700 pupils from 11–18 years. Given stretched resources, counselling sessions require self-audit and prioritization.

Programme planning

It follows that the planning and the sustaining of counselling programmes in school will be problematic on occasion, not only because of resource implications and the higher likelihood of interruptions than would exist in off-site therapy, but because of the clientele. Young people are novices in self-planning. Pre-pubescent and younger adolescents tend to live for the moment, lack organizational skills and live in a 'dreamy-state' of consciousness. Being essentially egotistic, they see themselves as the centre of the universe, have fleeting interests and are prone to seek immediate rather than suspended gratification. These traits are exaggerated in disorganized or dysfunctional families. While adolescents will put their trust in a counsellor they respect, or one having a reputation of being respected, to commit themselves to a programme of work that does not have a transparent outcome requires a higher degree of faith. They generally need to see the pay-off from a commitment to a programme where the outcome is not clearly understood.

From the 1970s, when school counselling in England and Wales focused largely on behavioural programmes, pupil support has become more therapeutically orientated and much more comprehensive in scope. Teachers generally have become more accepting of the need for school counselling as a further branch of pastoral support, yet counselling practitioners need to foster good relations with teachers in Britain, many of whom are threatened on occasion by counsellor–client alliances in school.

Pupils can be manipulative, and counsellors in an educational setting need to be aware of teacher pressure as well as pupil pressure, particularly with volatile youngsters who are prone to fly off the handle and storm from the classroom when being corrected. Consequently, I choose not to give appointments on spontaneous demand. Whatever my personal views on the large-scale practice of sending pupils out of the classroom for misbehaviour, I do not give youngsters an immediate audience when they wander down to the counselling room. Counsellors in the past developed a negative reputation for supporting the pupil against the teacher, a stance that reinforced avoidance behaviour. Flexibility is required in cases where the emotional charge is high or if I know the circumstances of the youngster as a current or former client.

Counselling styles

Pupil-clients in counselling are used to teaching methods and classroom stimuli that are structured, fast moving, objectively measured in terms of newly learned skills and 'entertaining'. Quality teaching results in quality learning, which is measured through rigid assessment and data recording. In brief, this means that youngsters are not used to sitting still and discussing issues solely about themselves in a wholly focused manner. In the main, pupils are motivated by teachers who project energy into leader-led activities, and are stimulated by didactic styles that can skilfully manage group interactions in debate, discussion and drama that does not result in a breakdown of control or in chaos. Pupils expect to be taught and are used to being told what to do, or to receive advice on what they should do to improve their situation from an adult's perspective. Non-directive counselling, or exploration of the client's options may be empowering, but it is not the normal experience of youngsters in educational settings where teachers are *in loco parentis*.

There are exceptions, of course, for some pupils suffer a distinct lack of stimulus, interest and attention shown to them in the home. With such, there are risks of over-dependency as pupils thrive on the one-to-one highly focused attention that they have rarely experienced. The counselling style, therefore, must not lead to confused boundaries where the client misinterprets the purpose of therapy and seeks from the counsellor a substitute parenting relationship in place of one of personal empowerment.

Counselling techniques

Pupils moving from the pre-pubescent stage through adolescence become increasingly self-conscious. From a stage in the early years of secondary schooling where youngsters can be exhibitionists, they become reluctant to do anything they perceive as 'showing them up' or pushing them forward, or becoming assertive among peers. Whatever they say in therapy, therefore, they will not attempt to do very challenging things in practice.

Measuring intelligence and skills in articulation of some pupil-clients is essential with wholly rationally based therapeutic interventions. Conversely, the emotional vulnerability, or low ego-strength of some clients needs assessing more particularly in school settings than in outside counselling clinics. In school, the client will not be granted the space for recovery after challenging work, but will have to attend the next lesson shortly after the session. Paradoxical techniques can lead to confusion for some youngsters. Finally, the majority of pupils who self-refer will be unsure of the level of confidentiality to which they have a right until they have experienced it in practice, particularly in cases where teachers are in regular contact with parents. Techniques that encourage deep reflection about highly personal, or possibly abusive, material will need careful assessment.

CONCLUSION

The history and development of school counselling has been chequered, both nationally and internationally. While the majority of schools in the UK have virtually no formal counselling provision, there are signs that the tide is turning in that education authorities may follow the lead of Australia and financially support counselling in schools. The presupposition of campaigning for counselling for pupils in school is that happy and contented pupils perform better than those who are worried or traumatized. The Australian experience suggests that school counsellors are generally under-qualified and in need of better supervision. Australian practice falls behind that of North America, particularly over boundaries of confidentiality.

The recommendations of the Elton Report made in 1989, and the resolution of the Association of Teachers and Lecturers in 1996, have never been significantly implemented in the UK. There are signs, however, that many more teachers are entering counselling courses than was the case a decade ago, and more headteachers are enlisting part-time counsellors from their school budgets. Recent funding has become available centrally for local initiatives, and mounting pressure of pupils with emotional and social difficulties is tempering the hardened spirits who resist counselling in school. Providing counselling for pupils in school is only part of an evolving process, for institutional factors impose a range of limitations on practice that call for careful planning and decision.

The first decision is whether to opt for system- or open-orientation school counselling. Then, the constraints of time-tabling and rooming have to be considered in respect of the type of setting for pupils to feel safe. Other considerations when structuring therapeutic provision include: counselling aims that are in keeping with the setting; counselling resources; session programming; counselling styles; and techniques that are appropriate in school. These constraints have been highlighted in this chapter. In Chapter 4, limitations are reviewed again to determine which counselling models and approaches best meet the requirements of an educational setting.

2

PROFESSIONAL AND ETHICAL BOUNDARIES IN SCHOOL COUNSELLING

Counsellors offer their clients almost absolute confidentiality, a code that pledges to safeguard their personal material, yet absolute confidentiality is unrealistic in the counselling of young people in educational settings (DFEE 2000). The school counsellor is expected to be professional and work within the law, but the law cannot be prescriptive in regulating every ethical dilemma. Added to which, some laws and regulations, far from solving dilemmas, create further ones, dilemmas that call for discretion. Professional and ethical issues are discussed in this chapter with reference to the particular boundaries that surround school counselling. Confidentiality and the access to records, the possibility of suicide, the abuse of restricted drugs, delinquency, sexual conduct and child protection all impose constraints upon the practitioner working in school that do not apply as much in other settings.

CONFIDENTIALITY AND THE LAW

There is no statutory protection to safeguard information shared in counselling during a hearing, as Casemore recognizes: 'No counsellor legally has the total privilege of confidentiality, unimpeachable by law' (1995: para. 1). This has proved so difficult for counsellors working in schools and youth centres that the Children's Legal Centre has seen fit to run a daily national advice line on issues relating to children and the law. Under pressure, the Centre has produced a booklet entitled *Offering Children Confidentiality: Law and Guidance*. The booklet outlines the legal position of counselling work, since counselling practitioners are not entirely sure of the legal boundaries of confidentiality when working among teachers who serve *in loco parentis*. But judges are, nevertheless, sympathetic to codes of confidentiality in practice:

> There is no statute currently in existence in England and Wales which *protects* a
> confidential relationship, but English common law recognizes the concept of a
> confidential relationship, and remedies are available if information received in
> confidence is disclosed or misused. (Hamilton and Hopegood, 1998: 2)

There are other laws that have relevance to the rights of the police to
collect files on clients. Part II of The Police and Criminal Evidence Act
(PACE) 1984 empowers the police to seize 'relevant evidence' to assist in
the detection of crime, and counselling records could constitute 'relevant
evidence' in certain circumstances. However, counselling and advice
records are exempt and are generally protected under section 11(1) of
PACE. The following section (12) defines personal advice records and
counselling documents as those which relate to the following:

a) physical and mental health,
b) spiritual counselling, and
c) counselling and advice voluntarily given by a person responsible for a
   client's welfare, or which is given by a person responsible for supervision
   of an order of court.

Under section 9, The Police and Criminal Evidence Act 1984 provides counselling records with protection by requiring a search warrant, signed by a
circuit judge rather than by a magistrate, permitting police access to records.

Parents of children below the age of 16 may apply for access to their
child's records under Regulations 4(1)(b) and 6(1) of the Education (School
Records) Regulations 1989, but counselling records relating to the child
should be regarded as confidential. They should not be filed within the
pupil's school record or with any other records that are accessed by anyone
other than those for whom they were compiled. Communicating with other
responsible parties should be on a need-to-know basis, ethically with the
permission of the client where appropriate. Information on pupil-clients
stored on computerized records or network systems is legally available to
young people where the Registrar General is satisfied that the young
person understands the nature of the request (Data Protection Act 1984).

A counsellor's personal notes, kept as an *aide-memoire*, or details of the
counselling process completed for reasons of supervision, remain the personal property of the counsellor and are not for broader disclosure, even
if kept on computer.

In practice, counselling supervision necessitates the sharing of a client's
personal information for very good professional reasons. All professional
counsellors have reached a level of competence through training and
experience, and should therefore receive regular supervision as a matter
of course in adherence with the BACP *Code of Ethics and Practice*:

> Counsellors must have achieved a level of competence before commencing
> counselling and must maintain continuing professional development as well as
> regular and ongoing supervision. (BACP, 2000a: B.6.1.1)

Not all practitioners using counselling skills in schools will receive regular supervision, but for those who attempt in-depth therapy it is imperative. Supervision should not be provided by managers of the agency and should be independent of the organization (BACP, 2000a: B.6.3.2). It should be a formal arrangement conducted by an experienced practitioner at regular intervals as befits the volume of work – conventionally one and a half hours of individual supervision for each month's counselling (BACP, 2000a: B.6). Supervision is necessary for maintaining the professional conduct of counsellors, for helping them to examine their own feelings of countertransference, and for providing a quality service for clients. Supervision is aimed at ensuring ethical practice, in both protecting the client and supporting the counsellor, at revealing blind spots and the sense of being 'stuck' in the therapeutic process, and at exploring the counsellor's sense of 'self' in the relationship. But this process cannot be conducted without a partial disclosure of the client's material. Supervision is essentially an exposure of information shared in confidence. During supervision – whether individual or group supervision is undertaken – the client's material is presented in a fairly detailed form for exploration, and all but the client's name becomes the means of evaluating the counsellor's practice.

Furthermore, training courses, books and journals that serve to promote counselling skills and research theory require case-study material that is drawn from authentic practice. So, although the client's anonymity is preserved in such publications, the transcript interviews are available for any reader (BACP, 2000a: B.3.5.4).

CODES OF CONFIDENTIALITY WITH PUPIL-CLIENTS IN SCHOOL

Her Majesty's Inspectors (HMIs) early on exercised the right to sit in with school counsellors and clients during counselling sessions, but the BAC sought barrister opinion and was successful in overturning this requirement. The contest was won on grounds of a violation of the particular nature of the counselling relationship and the resultant damage to the therapeutic provision of the school. The result is that the Office of Standards in Education Department (OFSTED) may inspect the management of the counselling service and measure its contribution to the overall ethos of the school, but inspectors are not permitted to sit in on sessions as a means of evaluation and assessment of the service. The rights of a headteacher and OFSTED inspector have therefore given way to the rights of children and young people to receive confidential counselling.

Some school counsellors are appointed on teaching contracts and conditions of service. As such, there is a legal right for the headteacher to insist on being given information about pupils gleaned through counselling in the school (Casemore, 1995, para. 2). However, headteachers recognize that an over-use of this legal requirement would diminish the effectiveness of the counselling service. The headteacher has to balance the legal right of parents to know what their child is saying with the code of confidentiality afforded to that child by the counsellor under her employ. In addition, counsellors may elect to refer their clients to other counselling agencies or psychological/psychiatric services. This presents no legal difficulties so long as parental permission has been sought. However, if counsellors refer pupils to alternative services *within* the school day, yet *without* parental consent, this is another matter.

In cases where an adolescent is persistent in wanting to speak with social services during the school day (without parental consent), it is prudent to give out only contact details without personally making the referral on the pupil's behalf, thus serving only as an information provider. Such legal difficulties can be avoided by a public display of information in the counselling waiting room and other public areas around the school. In spite of parental over-control in some cases, children still have rights to confidential counselling if they are mature and consenting, even if they are under the age of 16. If counselling is acknowledged and consented to by parents, this does not give them the right to know of the content of such counselling sessions if the client does not wish it (Hamilton and Hopegood, 1998: 4).

Young people from 16 to 18, generally, are by statute regarded as competent and able to consent to their own medical treatment (Family Law Reform Act 1987, section 8). The House of Lords ruling in the case of Gillick (Gillick, 1985, 3 All ER 402) permitted doctors to provide medical treatment for children under the age of 16 without parental consent. The Gillick decision of 1985 gave general practitioners the right to give contraceptive advice to young people under the age of 16 without parental permission, if the child wished it. The only requirement was that the doctor should strike a balance, when arriving at a judgement, between the protective wishes of the parent and the considered consequences of *informed consent* – measured by the age, intelligence and maturity of the individual. Such a child was termed a 'Gillick competent child'. These newly developed rights to grant individual contraceptive advice upon request have been extended to counselling:

> Similarly young people requiring counselling, who have sufficient understanding and intelligence, do not have to consult their parents, nor does the counsellor have to inform their parents that counselling has taken place. (Mabey and Sorensen, 1995: 95)

Counsellors were influenced by this legislation when devising their codes of confidentiality for young people.

The absolute rights of parents have since then given way to the increasing rights of children and young people. Pupil rights and a general sense of empowerment have been a modern trend in British education.

Given the legal parameters of the counsellor's code of confidentiality, the particular applications of the code are influenced by one other legal constraint, that of being *in loco parentis*. The school counsellor employed on a teaching contract and conditions of service will be under tension to respond and behave towards the child within school as would befit a 'reasonable parent', but this working condition would impose professional and ethical difficulties in many counselling dilemmas, as will be outlined.

PUPILS AND STUDENTS HAVING SUICIDAL TENDENCIES

Some life-threatening issues brought up in therapy oblige the counsellor to report matters to family members or to other professionals who have the responsibility and capacity to protect people from their own self-destructive impulses.

> The management of confidentiality is inextricably linked to decisions about when to act in order to attempt to preserve life and when to remain silent out of respect for a client's autonomy. (Bond, 1994: 4)

The adolescent phase is the movement from childhood dependence to adult autonomy, and some independent judgement will be called for when deciding whether or not to disclose the contemplation of suicide, revealed in counselling. It is unlikely that broad latitude can be granted in school to suicidal young people under the age of 18. Few counsellors can risk their professional integrity by not reporting to general practitioners the possibility that a suicidal client may indeed take their own life, whatever code of confidentiality formed the basis of the original contract (BACP, 2000a: B.3.4.3). Most counsellors assess their client's situation before arriving at a judgement on whether or not to preserve confidentiality over a suicidal wish, but in school the counsellor cannot grant this measure of independent decision-making and latitude to young pupils.

In view of these factors, many counsellors see fit to explain clearly their ethical boundaries and to publicize at the outset the extent of the confidentiality that is offered (BACP, 2000a: B.4.2.1). The BACP *Code of Ethics and Practice* recognizes the need to outline the limits of confidentiality and the tensions that arise through such conditional codes of confidentiality:

> Confidentiality is a means of providing the client with safety and privacy and thus protects client autonomy. For this reason any limitation on the degree of confidentiality is likely to diminish the effectiveness of counselling. (BACP, 2000a: B.3.1)

> Counsellors must ensure that they have taken all reasonable steps to inform the client of any limitations to confidentiality that arise within the setting of the counselling work.... (ibid.: B.3.3.1)

> Exceptional circumstances may arise which give the counsellor good grounds for believing that serious harm may occur to the client or to other people.... (ibid.: B.3.4.1)

> Counsellors hold different views about the grounds for breaking confidentiality, such as potential self-harm, suicide, and harm to others. Counsellors must consider their own views, as they will affect their practice and communicate them to clients and significant others e.g. supervisor, agency. (ibid.: B.3.4.3)

When counselling students over 18, more latitude in decisions to report their client's suicidal tendencies is called for. Decisions will be based upon the following principles:

- the degree of risk of suicide (Bond, 1993)
- the decision being rational and autonomous, well planned out rather than prompted by mental illness or drugs
- a realistic means of prevention
- the legal issues centring upon breaches of confidentiality (Bond, 1994: 4).

THE LEGAL AND MORAL DUTY TO DISCLOSE INFORMATION OF 'OFFENDING'

A range of ethical dilemmas occurs in school counselling over issues of the possession and abuse of illegal substances and delinquent acts of adolescents, such as theft, burglary, physical assaults and motor vehicle offences – theft, driving and riding in stolen cars. Some of these dilemmas call for the practitioner to reflect on her conduct that prescribes the *moral* duty as much as on her *legal* duty. There is no general duty in criminal law to disclose information that criminal offences have been committed, but, as the Children's Legal Centre recommends, professionals working with delinquent youths should be careful to avoid doing something which might constitute aiding and abetting the committing of an offence (Hamilton and Hopegood, 1998: 5).

There are many nagging questions of a moral rather than a legal nature that confront counsellors in educational settings. There is the question of how the school counsellor is expected to operate among professionals who work within the legal framework of serving *in loco parentis*. If the school counsellor is part of the teaching team, then disclosures about infringement of school rules are likely to present some difficulties. On balance, a counsellor would not be expected to breach confidence, but this might pose a difficulty for those having no separate identity from the organization or for those having to find a compromise between dual roles.

Further, there is the question of how to respond with care, empathy and understanding in cases where the law is at best ambivalent or at worst set against the interests of individual welfare. If the law is ambivalent, there is room for manoeuvre. There is not so much room for manoeuvre where the law is clear, even if it is judged to conflict with individual morality, say where societal needs (as decreed by Acts of Parliament) clash with individual ones (as delineated in counselling).

A controversial question arises here, namely whether the professional course *always* requires the strict observation of the laws of the land, Acts of Parliament, or the rules of the organization to which the professional is committed. Reconciling the counsellor's role of, on the one hand, offering a measure of confidentiality with, on the other, an expectation to serve *in loco parentis* is never easy when dealing with older pupils in school. Pastoral teachers and school counsellors sometimes become privy to information that involves a pupil flouting rules, or openly breaking the law. Most commonly, teenagers buy and smoke cigarettes when under-age. Similarly, they purchase and consume alcohol. In such cases, apart from when there is a significant health issue, school counsellors may not feel obliged to violate the necessary trust essential to resolve other more serious problems, by reporting such behaviour to the youngster's parent or guardian. If the adolescent smokes cannabis, then the decision is less clear. In spite of the illegality of both the possession and consumption of cannabis, a counter-balancing factor will be the tolerance threshold of the school, its ethos and the prevalent attitudes within the school community over cannabis use. In the case of other substances, such as ecstasy, crack cocaine, heroine or solvents, then counsellors may be more sure of their professional course of action:

> If a young person has disclosed that drugs are being sold in the youth club and the youth worker takes no action, this could amount to aiding and abetting. Under the Misuse of Drugs Act 1971, it is illegal to allow premises to be used for the smoking of cannabis or opium or the illegal consumption and supply of controlled drugs. (Hamilton and Hopegood, 1998: 5)

What applies for the worker in the youth club, is even more the case for the practitioner in school. The professional course for a counsellor who discovers that young people have become drawn into dealing in and profiteering from illegal substances is totally unambiguous. There is no alternative but to report such intelligence to the police with or without the client's consent: 'Counsellors must take all reasonable steps to be aware of current law as it applies to their counselling practice' (BACP, 2000a: B.1.6.1). Here, the welfare of a client in preserving an absolute code of confidentiality is set too high and does not take into consideration the welfare of others who would no doubt suffer as a direct result of the client's indifference and immoral profiteering.

Delinquent behaviour disclosed in counselling is another grey area. Most professional counsellors working in independent agencies when asked how they should respond to such disclosures would probably reply that it all depended on what the client had done. Rash reporting of minor infringements of the law is likely to jeopardize the therapeutic relationship, but failure to report a case has two disadvantages apart from putting therapists in a compromising position. First there is the principle of learned behavioural patterns through social reinforcement. Repeated delinquent behaviour is self-reinforcing when not detected, and thus consolidates a learning principle that 'crime pays', encouraging the adolescent to take unmeasured risks for short-term gains that have unforeseen dire consequences of a life in crime. The habit of offending is soon formed through getting away with it, and by a rewarding pay-off for criminal offending.

Second, there develops an unclear boundary issue whereby the counsellor becomes over identified with those of the youngster's criminal network, rather than remaining neutral. Some delinquent pupils may be on court supervision orders that require professionals to report breaches of supervision, bail or curfew. In such cases, the school counsellor is advised to safeguard her role as distinct from a senior pastoral teacher colleague who might more suitably carry out the conditions of the supervision. If an adolescent discloses information gradually through successive counselling sessions, ending up with details of a serious crime, then the counsellor is working as an accessory to a criminal offence by an act of collusion – unless she becomes proactive in altering the conditions of confidentiality (BACP, 2000a: B.3.4.1).

The law is technically inflexible, and ill-judged decisions may lead to negative perceptions of the counsellor's role and responsibility by other would-be pupil-clients as well as by parents and professional colleagues. Although there is no statutory obligation, there is a moral obligation for the counsellor working in schools to report serious crime to the police. The professional counsellor will clearly outline his legal accountability before counselling begins, so as to avoid inconsistency and to maintain integrity. There are occasions when teenagers abscond from home and are put at risk, particularly when adults unknown to the parents offer the child a refuge at a time when the police are anxious to establish his or her whereabouts. The counsellor who becomes privy to such information has difficulty justifying withholding such information under any pretext of confidentiality.

THE LEGAL POSITION ON UNDER-AGED SEXUAL BEHAVIOUR

Teachers generally do not see a student's (that is, those over 16) private sexual conduct to be their area of responsibility. Their overall duty is to educate and protect pupils in cases of immaturity and exploitation, and it makes good sense for all practitioners and educators to advise on safer sex for both homosexuals and heterosexuals in the light of the risks of AIDS. This is not illegal and is a national curriculum requirement. If a pupil receives *individual contraceptive advice* from the schoolteacher, as she might from a nurse or the GP, however, then there is a breach in law.

Disclosed sexual behaviour can be problematic for counsellors wishing to work ethically and professionally in balancing the moral and the legal duty to pass on confidential information. When clients come for support the counsellor cannot predict fully the outcome, but during the counselling process there will often be the need to consider afresh the issues that best meet each particular need. Professional and ethical behaviour is expected of school counsellors in every context when dealing with young people, particularly where the guidelines are not clear. Agreed codes of conduct and the procedural guidelines of the agency essentially tie the counsellor's hands and limit choice. But the professional course or guiding principle is less clear in cases where the law is not specific or is silent.

A number of anomalies and dilemmas surround the legal position of youth counsellors working with pupils and students in the area of sexual conduct. It is known, for example, that a significant number of heterosexual youngsters are sexually active well before the legal age of consent, though few 'offences' are brought before the judicial system. It remains an open question to what extent the counsellor is expected to disclose to parents information revealed under confidential agreement about such matters as under-age sexual intercourse – apart from extreme cases that border on rape. Counsellors working in independent agencies will have no contact with the parents of young people who refer themselves. If parents refer their adolescent son or daughter to an agency for counselling, the ethical dilemma of to whom the counsellor is accountable is normally agreed at the contracting stage, usually in favour of client allegiance and confidentiality. The school counsellor's role is closer to that of the teacher of being *in loco parentis*, but not as far as being the parent *in absentia*.

'Age of consent' for homosexuality

A homosexual 'offence' is not comparable to rape, murder, abuse, or terrorism (BACP, 2000a), yet still falls under control of criminal law. A custodial sentence of two years maximum can be issued in England and Wales for the 'offence' of under-age homosexuality, yet rarely do 'offences' come to court. There is no comparable law that regulates sexual relations for lesbians. There is no valid reasoning for this gender discrimination other than an ignorant presumption that under-age lesbian relationships do not exist. While the law appertaining to consent for homosexuals should help clear the ground, in practice it tends to compound the difficulty because of widely differing opinions.

British law regarding homosexuality has been notoriously conservative in comparison with other countries. The political debate and general softening of entrenched views in some quarters have not yet brought about unanimity of opinion. In Britain, the law permits two consenting heterosexuals to have sex at 16, while consenting homosexual men had, before the end of June 1998, to wait until they were 18. Previously, the age of consent for gay men in Britain was 21, and was the highest in Europe. The gay community was aggrieved that it took so long to reduce the age to 18, and at the time of writing are campaigning to bring down the age of consent to 16, as for heterosexuals. In some countries the age of consent is the same for both orientations: in Ireland the age of consent is 17, it is 14 in Albania, Iceland, Italy and Russia, and 13 in Japan.

There is evidence that such conservatism was the result of prejudice, since the reduced age of consent to 15 or 16 in Scandinavian countries has not led to an increase in homosexuality, 'perversity' or AIDS.

Parliament under the previous Conservative administration brought the age of consent down from 21 to 18, voting against legal parity for the age of consent for straight and gay couples. Under the Labour government, the House of Commons voted in the Crime and Disorder Bill, of reduced legal consent, but with no amendments to guard against the exploitation by older men of boys of 16 committed to their care in institutional settings. However, the House of Lords, under Baroness Young, succeeded in blocking the Bill, arguing the need for amendments to safeguard young men in institutions – a requirement that, strangely, does not appear to have been considered already covered by child protection legislation.

A further legal debate currently causing a stir is Clause 28 of the Local Government Act, which states:

> A local authority shall not: (a) Intentionally promote homosexuality or publish material with the intention of promoting homosexuality; (b) Promote teaching in any maintained schools of the acceptability of homosexuality as a pretended family relationship.

This clause not only prohibits any teaching on homosexuality in schools, but it has checked much counselling provision for gay and lesbian young people in school (Mason, 2000).

It is perhaps regrettable that British criminal law still holds a mandate to legislate on private morality, but since it does the counsellor has no choice but to work within or around the law as it stands. If the law is held to be an ass, then the question that remains is whether the counsellor has any ethical legitimacy to work or advise above the law in seeking the wellbeing of the client. Looking at the law in operation in other countries does not help but unfortunately heightens the conflict between the counsellor's ethical stance and her professional action when dealing with student homosexuals, in that there is no universal agreement on the age of consent.

In deciding upon an ethical course, the counsellor must assess what intervention is appropriate for the wellbeing of the pupil-client. The advice of LEAs in England and Wales to teachers about informing parents of a child's under-age, albeit *private*, sexual conduct is confusing and contradictory. In places there is a responsibility for the senior teacher to inform the headteacher (who might enlist a counsellor) and the parent, but only if the person is judged to be 'at moral or physical risk or in breach of the law' (DFE, 1993).

This leaves unclear the appropriate course of action for the senior teacher and school counsellor in cases where it is judged that the pupil is not at moral or physical risk but whose sexual conduct may still be in breach of law. There may be cases where adherence to the law *puts* the child at 'moral or physical risk' – such as in families where violent corrective measures that border upon physical assault and child abuse are meted out to children. In such cases, there must be room for discretion in balancing the code of confidentiality and the rights of autonomy with the legal requirement of having to inform parents.

Whatever ambiguity exists within LEA guidelines on heterosexual (inferred) misconduct, there is simply no guidance for homosexual orientations, not even in the most recent circular on sex education within personal, social and moral education (DFEE, 2000). In fact, to date, the DFEE has issued no specific direction for headteachers or school counsellors on procedural conduct for disclosures of a homosexual nature made by school pupils in England and Wales.

Ethical codes for counselling homosexual pupils

The BACP *Code of Ethics and Practice* (2000a, B.1.6.1) stipulates that counsellors should work within the law. Clearly this is unequivocal in the maintenance of professionalism (and personal integrity) and the protection of all parties (school pupils) who could suffer loss or harm. But it is ambiguous over private morality, particularly regarding sexual matters in cases where all involved parties may be consenting, age-appropriate, and fully aware of what they are doing ('Gillick competent'). In such cases, other parts of the code appear to override:

B.2.1   Counsellors work with clients in ways that *affirm* both the common humanity and the *uniqueness* of each individual. They must be sensitive to the *cultural context* and world view of the client, for instance whether the *individual*, family or the community is taken as central.

B.2.2   Counsellors are responsible for working in ways which *respect and promote the client's ability to make decisions* in the light of his/her beliefs, values and context.

B.3.1   Confidentiality is a means of providing the client with *safety and privacy* and thus protects client *autonomy*. For this reason any limitation on the degree of confidentiality is likely to diminish the effectiveness of counselling. (My italics.)

Counsellors generally need to understand 'the broad ethical, moral and value considerations that inform and underpin the statements made in formal codes' (McLeod, 1993: 174), but some codes and laws are in competition with ethical and moral principles. The above rulings assume there to be no tension, yet the converse is often the case over individual sexual morality. 'Affirming' the 'uniqueness' of the homosexual 'individual' and providing 'safety and privacy' in order to 'respect and promote' the client's 'ability to make decisions' in protecting 'autonomy' seems to me to be the crucial counselling aim.

In cases of physical and sexual abuse, there is a statutory obligation upon the school counsellor and all teachers to report matters to outside authorities.

CHILD PROTECTION AND CODES OF CONFIDENTIALITY

The Children Act 1989 gave unclear ruling on the rights of children to confidentiality in counselling, and the concern has been recognized by the Children's Legal Centre. This matter is as yet unresolved. The ruling on child protection, however, has no ambiguity. Section 47 of the Children Act 1989 compels social services to investigate referred cases of child protection.

Counselling organizations that are bound by local authority rules are expected to liaise and co-operate fully with the investigating bodies, seeing their course prescribed and regulated under an inter-agency perspective (DFEE, 1995; DH, HO and DFEE, 1999). Although co-operation is encouraged by the Children Act – both in the spirit and letter of the law – the legal requirement, says Tim Bond (1993), only applies to an *inquiry* being conducted. There is no stipulation that counsellors should share information that is *not requested*. The Act is quite specific in outlining this legal injunction:

S. 47.9   Where a local authority is conducting enquiries under this section, it shall be the duty of any person mentioned in subsection (11) to assist them with those enquiries (in particular by providing relevant information and advice) if called upon by the authority to do so.

S. 47.10 Subsection (9) does not oblige any person to assist a local authority when doing so would be unreasonable in all the circumstances of the case.

S. 47.11 The persons are –
a)   any local authority
b)   any local education authority
c)   any local housing authority
d)   any health authority; and
e)   any person authorised by the Secretary of State for the purposes of this section.

As Bond points out, for an Act of Parliament to have gone through such an extensive and complex series of consultations, including a Law Commission, it is surprising that the law does not make information-sharing a statutory obligation. The initiative to pass on child protection information rests wholly with the professional to whom the disclosure is made. In practice, therefore, a counsellor working in a voluntary agency, and privy to information that borders upon child protection, is *not compelled* to refer the case to social services or to conform to the child protection procedures. This is because such action may violate the agreed code of confidentiality that is the basis of counselling contracts. If information is *requested* by social services when making an *inquiry* over a matter that may threaten a child's wellbeing, or which puts them at significant risk, then the counsellor is compelled to put that code above the honouring of his client's confidential agreement (Mabey and Sorensen, 1995). If the same counsellor becomes privy to the same child protection information he is not in breach of law by choosing not to pass on the same to social services automatically if no request has been made. In cases where the court subpoenas a counsellor to disclose material that has been divulged in confidence, again there is no choice but for the counsellor to comply with a court order, or risk the consequences of contempt of court. The exception clause (section 47.10) is so imprecise as to be impractical to implement.

The counsellor working within an educational setting has no such latitude, whether employed by an educational authority or enlisted by an individual school from its own budget, but must report cases of child abuse to the headteacher or the person responsible for child protection. More latitude may exist in higher education where students are above 16 and are 'Gillick competent'. A strong case can be argued on the rights of the counsellor to decide when or if ever to report abuse to social services (or more anonymously to the NSPCC) if during counselling the client has expressed explicitly that this is neither what has been asked for nor been the reason for seeking counselling (Daniels and Jenkins, 2000). BACP has seen fit to supplement the guidelines on confidentiality for college counsellors in further education and sixth-form colleges (BACP, 2000b).

CHILD PROTECTION POLICY IN PRACTICE

Conventionally, the headteacher, or a designated senior teacher (DST) delegated by the head, is the person who has the statutory responsibility for implementing child protection procedures. All teachers and school counsellors, however, have a direct responsibility for child protection until the case has been referred to the DST. Experience has shown how abused pupils and their families find the procedures and their aftermath problematic.

> Within the past two years in my own school four pupils were interviewed some time after the procedures had closed. They were each asked a question designed

to elicit from them – the victims – the quality of service the various social workers and child protection WPCs had provided. They were each asked individually, 'If the same thing happened to you again, or something similar, do you think you'd report the matter a second time knowing what you know, knowing how the case would be dealt with?' Each of the respondents answered in the negative. When asked why, they said, variously, 'It's not worth the hassle, not worth all the trouble it causes.' They each wanted the abuse to stop (of that there was no doubt), but they didn't want the offender (normally some-one known to the abused) to get into trouble. It appears that the procedures are not capable of halting the abusive activity without thereby causing the victim to experience a high level of guilt for having the case reported to official bodies.

Families appear to close ranks – in giving tacit acceptance to the abuser – as soon as officials withdraw. If the parent or step-parent is the abuser, an injunction that he or she leaves the family home has economic implica-tions that put the rest of the family under financial hardship. The other parent (who is not implicated) is thereby forced to make a choice of sup-porting/protecting the victim or taking a pragmatic course of keeping their partner (possibly the one employed) within the family. Siblings (who are generally not privy to all the details of the abusive allegations) often blame the innocent brother or sister for 'saying something' (telling lies?) that sends dad or mum out of the house. It can be a very lonely and trau-matic experience to report abuse, therefore, and it is little wonder that young victims choose to report matters only long after the event(s), at the point, in fact, when they have become economically independent of their parents or guardians.

> One girl in school had an opportunity to disclose that she had become her father's sexual partner in place of her mother. She was approached by social workers after they had received three anonymous letters. She turned down the opportunity for disclosure even though she abhorred the way her father was abusing her. Not only was she scared, but she felt no one would believe her, and was keenly aware of the social and economic implications of her disclosure. Two years later she rang Child Line and felt prepared to go through with the procedures that eventually put her father in prison. Though the family eventu-ally believed her, this did not prevent her from having to leave the home and from experiencing intense guilt for engaging in something in which she had no control or choice. There can be little doubt that a victim like this will need counselling to help her to come to terms with such an experience.

If a parent is the abuser in a case of sexual abuse or inappropriate sexual conduct, then it is rare for that parent to make contact with the school after the procedures have closed in order to assert their integrity, argue their defence, or re-establish what they presume will be a marred reputa-tion with pastoral staff. Similarly, parents lie low out of embarrassment, or pretend that nothing has actually occurred, in cases of alleged sexual abuse within the family. In spite of the investigating parties recom-mending the need for the victim to receive counselling in order to come to terms with the trauma of the event, or of the ensuing procedures, parental indifference is common.

Cases of neglect have shown evidence of large-scale parental ignorance of 'normalcy' within family patterns. Low economic factors, or alcohol misuse, reduce the quality of living to the poverty level.

Physical abuse, or 'over-correction', is easier to manage in the aftermath, since there is generally not the same stigma attached to physical violence towards a youngster as there is to sexual violence. Parents may put up their hands, confess to having gone too far, and admit fault under a perception that the school shares the same view that the adolescent's behaviour is sufficiently challenging to warrant physical maltreatment. This combined evidence suggests that the procedures are not quite right, but until such time as they are changed there is little alternative but for all parties to adhere strictly to them.

There is an issue of a victim's perception of the counsellor who attends a child protection case conference, or a strategy meeting, prior to an investigation, and who first learns of the abuse from such a meeting. School counsellors need to establish and communicate clearly their role at such meetings if requested to attend, in order that future work is not thwarted by confused allegiances. Attendance at such meetings has mixed advantages and disadvantages. With or without previous involvement, the counsellor may find that their role becomes confused with that of a social worker, but there is a gain by presence at such meetings. Pupil-clients may have a great burden lifted from their shoulders by becoming aware that the counsellor is privy to information shared at such conferences. The person-centred counsellor does not require such detail in order to address the client's feelings, but cognitive and solution-focused models are more effective with a broader knowledge of the client's problematical situation, which in the case of child abuse is not easy for an adolescent to have to recount.

The implementation of child protection procedures is problematic for all counsellors. It has been argued above that no counsellor can offer complete confidentiality within an educational setting. Voluntary counsellors enlisted by the school, or employed by the school on a part-time basis, are under the responsibility and jurisdiction of the LEA and are subject to child protection policies as set out in the authority's guidelines. Whatever conditional confidentiality forms the basis of contracted counselling, if a pupil discloses an incident which threatens her, or puts her at risk of significant harm, then every counsellor in a school setting must be professional. She is expected to halt the session, explain why the disclosed event(s) cannot be kept in confidence, break the code of confidentiality and report the matter to a third party whose responsibility it is to share the information with those who have to carry out a statutory investigation. It takes little awareness of the counselling relationship to see how such an action will mar the therapeutic alliance and affect future work.

A pupil may be aggrieved when the counsellor informs him that his disclosed material must now be passed on to another person who will inform social services. Further tension arises when the statutory referral stage is conducted in the absence of the client. It may give rise to a sense of betrayal when the counsellor speaks about the client's material with the DST behind closed doors, or even in her presence. The DST will probably see the need to interview the pupil further thus taking over the matter from the counsellor. In this case, the pupil is forced a second time to disclose material that has been the cause of much distress, and to a person who at best is unknown to him, or at worst a person with whom he has had previous fractious dealings. Part of the child protection procedure is the requirement not to over-interview the victim, but merely to elicit an outline narrative of what happened in order to assess whether or not it is a child protection matter. Even so, re-disclosure is still a painful experience to have to undergo.

Counsellors, as with all pastoral teachers, should hold the wellbeing of all their pupil-clients in the forefront of their minds, and this involves essentially the issue of protection from power-abusing adults. If a youth counsellor argues that spurious forms of confidentiality override the cardinal rule of respecting a young person's wellbeing, then the values and logic at play have not been thought through enough, given the evidence of long-term harm that results from physical and sexual abuse. Mabey and Sorensen (1995) outline a set of guidelines designed to marry the conflicting principles of statutory reporting and client confidentiality, arguing that the procedure should include:

1. Clear direction relating to when consultation should take place with a supervisor and/or the co-ordinator of the service in order to decide the best way to proceed.
2. If the young person is at risk, the original contract should be reviewed and if necessary renegotiated with a view to the client retaining as much autonomy as possible in the circumstances.
3. If confidentiality is to be breached, this should be discussed and if possible agreed with the young person. In circumstances where this is not possible and the young person is assessed as a 'Gillick competent child', the implications of such a move should be carefully thought out with regard to that young person and their future relationship with the agency. (1995: 97)

The authors continue: 'In our experience, confidentiality can usually be satisfactorily renegotiated with a young person if there is time and if a good relationship has been built with the child protection team' (1995: 97–8). Personally, I favour anticipating the problem and acting beforehand. The following extract from my own school's child protection policy illustrates the cautionary advice for counsellors and all teaching staff over guarantees of confidentiality:

7.2   *It is important that no absolute guarantees of confidentiality are given to pupils* if teachers are approached with pre-conditioning questions like, 'If I tell you something will you promise to keep it secret?' In spite of good intentions, this collusion has several disadvantages: the hands of the teacher are tied in carrying out statutory obligations; an undue responsibility is carried for the child's welfare by the wrong person; a level of betrayal is felt by a broken promise in a worsening situation that warrants procedures being implemented. A child's trust is enhanced by 'being direct', by not offering complete confidentiality, even if the consequence is that the disclosure may be deferred (remember, a child is always free to withdraw an allegation at any point in the proceedings, so rushed disclosures are not the ideal). There is an enormous upheaval for a youngster both in preparation to disclose and in actually carrying it through. The whole family relationship dynamic is altered, often with victims feeling guilty in revealing secrets to outside agencies and made to feel the betrayers of the family. The child wishes that the abuse might stop, but the consequence of disclosure might be that one family member (often the victim) has to leave home; a result which affects all (innocent) family members.

In my practice, then, the boundaries of confidentiality with respect to child protection are clearly outlined before counselling commences. Normally, this is only done with clients wishing to engage in counselling contracts, or those suspected by referrers of harbouring family secrets of dubious goings on. The manner of communicating the boundaries of confidentiality in the introductory session will vary depending upon the age and level of comprehension of the particular client. With students over 16, the counselling boundary will be explained with something like the following:

> *Counsellor:*   I feel it's necessary before counselling begins to explain to you the limits of what you can say to me that is confidential. Although I work in school, I am not under the same obligation to share with parents what you say to me as teachers are in school. I will not speak with your parents about our conversations unless you agree that it might help. However, if you share information that puts your welfare at risk, then I may not be able to keep that confidential. If you disclose to me details, for example, that you have been abused, then I have to pass that information to social services. I'm sorry to begin this way, but I feel it's necessary to be honest and direct with you. I wonder if you'd like to respond to anything that I've said before we start?

Such an introduction may be entirely unsuitable for a younger pupil, however, for, while it may be assumed that an older student would understand what child abuse is, this cannot be taken for granted with pre-pubescent children and younger adolescents. A simplified vocabulary and explanation are called for. Taking the precaution of avoiding leading questioning for legal and therapeutic reasons, the whole issue would need a fuller introduction that might follow this form:

Counsellor:	I'd like to explain to you, Sara, that counselling is a choice. If you would like us to talk about your difficulties that's OK, and you can end counselling whenever you wish. What we speak about is confidential, and I will not be speaking with your parents unless you wish me to do so, or to any teacher, or to pupils. What is said is confidential, yet I wonder what you understand by confidentiality?
Sara:	Does it mean keeping secrets?
Counsellor:	In a sense it does, but it's more like an agreement. It's like trusting me not to tell other people your problems. Is that helpful and clear?
Sara:	Yeah.
Counsellor:	There's one exception to this that I'd like you to understand before we start speaking. I can't promise you that I can keep absolutely everything confidential. Say, for example, you told me that you were being hurt in some way. If someone was beating you hard and regularly, or if someone was doing things to you sexually, then I couldn't keep that confidential. I would have to stop counselling and telephone social services. I would still support you, but I feel you should have a clear understanding of what would happen...

This may appear an obstructive introduction to counselling, and hardly good grounds for building a therapeutic relationship. It is not the most sensitive way of encouraging pupil-clients to disclose their most sensitive feelings, but it is necessary when working with adolescents who are presumed to have suffered abuse. Ethically, the pupil-client must be informed of the boundaries of confidentiality that can be offered in educational settings. Experience has shown how difficult it can be to halt proceedings at mid-point when wholly unanticipated material of a child protection nature comes to the fore. If the counsellor is forced to renegotiate the terms of confidentiality at the very point when much resistance has been overcome in relating the details of abuse, then this can be very traumatic. Certainly, the adolescent, who is at a developmental stage where communications with adults become fraught, will have every reason to be very unsure of counselling agreements in the future.

With this open and more honest approach, the pupil-client is left with no confusion over what will happen should she choose to reveal details of abuse. For clients who have been abused, the issue over such an introduction may well be when to disclose rather than to whom to disclose. The client who is nursing no secrets of painful abuse will be temporarily bewildered, inevitably, but the legal and professional standing of the practitioner working in school makes this the most prudent course. On balance, then, the pupil-client will have confidence through being spoken with directly, with no hidden agendas or surprises at the point at which the contract has been entered upon.

In summary, the counselling practitioner's distinctive role and boundary demarcation from the pastoral teacher may be confusing to many parents. Counselling will operate in a room on the school campus, during the school day, and personnel are usually reached through the school switchboard. Practitioners may socialize with teaching staff and be in communication with all teachers, the educational social worker and the educational psychologist. The parent's perception, therefore, is to view the counselling provision as part of the school's overall pastoral system. Since all parents have direct access to school staff generally, there may be an expectation on the part of parents that they have a right to approach the counsellor to discuss the self-referral of their son or daughter. To make clear the differences of roles and responsibilities, it is politic to publicize all practice information in the school prospectus and in other induction documentation.

Having explored the professional and ethical boundaries in school counselling, and before illustrating counselling practice with various emotional, social, behavioural and spiritual dilemmas, I present a psychological analysis of pupil-clients as they pass through the developmental phase known as adolescence.

3

THE DEVELOPMENTAL
PROCESS FROM 11 TO 18 YEARS

And a woman who held a babe against her bosom said,
   Speak to us of children.
And he said:
   Your children are not your children.
They are the sons and daughters of Life's longing for itself.
   They come through you but not from you,
And though they are with you yet they belong not to you.

You may give them your love but not their thoughts,
   For they have their own thoughts.
You may house their bodies but not their souls,
   For their souls dwell in the house of tomorrow,
      which you cannot visit, not even in your dreams.
You may strive to be like them, but seek not to make them like you.
   For life goes not backward nor tarries with yesterday.
You are the bows from which your children as living arrows are sent forth.
   The Archer sees the mark upon the path of the infinite,
      and He bends you with His might that His arrows may go swift and far.
Let your bending in the Archer's hand be for gladness;
   For even as He loves the arrow that flies, so He loves also the bow that is stable.
                                                              (Gibran, 1972)

Every parent will have cause to wonder at times what makes adolescence
such a difficult and frustrating period of development. Why do most
young people become intolerable through their teens? Passing through
the years from 11 to 18, from years seven to thirteen in school, is the developmental transition from child to adult, from dependence to autonomy,
and this transition in western society is termed adolescence. But what
actually is adolescence, and is it a universal phenomenon? For while it is
instantly recognizable, it is not easily defined.

   This chapter attempts to portray this period of development as it
impacts within school, since no counselling approach, brief or long term,
can suitably address teenage difficulties without an understanding of

the internal and external world of young people. I shall examine the developmental process from 11 to 18 years through a psychodynamic theoretical framework, then review the developmental pressures brought about through puberty, intellectual development and socialization. The more nebulous aspects of spiritual development are taken up in the final chapter. Through this period, adolescents unconsciously attempt to achieve certain developmental tasks, and these will be set alongside ideal parenting conditions that are required for a satisfactory transition.

ADOLESCENCE: CHARACTERISTICS OF DEVELOPMENT

A number of characteristics identify the developmental stage of adolescence. Throughout this chapter they are identified as psycho-sexual development and its emotional effects, socialization with peers, and cognitive development as shown in individualized abstract thinking, that is, the move towards autonomy, non-conforming behaviour, rebellion, and a testing of mores and standards. These characteristics, if taken singly, would portray the teenage phase as a fragmentary condition – where particular stages could be observed and plotted upon a graph – rather than a process of transition. The analysis that follows might help in understanding the various facets that make up adolescence, but it is important to recognize that these are integrated within the young person in such a way as to make them rarely discernible as separate entities.

I shall present adolescence within a psychodynamic theoretical framework, since this approach has had the most impact upon the therapeutic understanding of troubled young people. Adolescence is presented within the construct of psychodynamic theory not because it is the only construct available, and certainly not because it can be verified scientifically, but because it provides a credible account for the particular emotional moods and behaviours that we in the west observe in adolescents.

Individuation and identity formation through adolescence

The psychodynamic view takes as a starting point the upsurge of instincts that take place at puberty. At this point, argued Freud (1937), a number of internal emotional changes occur: the personality becomes more vulnerable than at any other time since the end of childhood and is evidenced by an upset in psychic balance (Coleman, 1987).

Psychologists describe adolescent transition as individuation – a term used by Jung to describe the lifetime process of becoming whole, indivisible and uniquely that person the self was meant to be – in contrast to the constructs of others. The adolescent begins to sever powerful emotional bonds with her parents and becomes more sexually aware and drawn to look for 'love objects' outside the family. Inevitably, this instinctive breaking away results in trials of loyalty and emotional blackmail. The personality is fickle and fragile at this point and the adolescent learns to cope with this feeling of tug-of-war tension by employing defence mechanisms, unconscious devices that are mainly spontaneous and maladaptive.

Maladaptive behaviour stems from the inadequacy of psychological defences to cope with inner conflicts – a process that is very similar to that occurring at the end of the third year where the self-reliant toddler begins to explore. This accounts for adolescent behaviour that is described as regressive (infantile sulking, tantrums etc.).

> There are many similarities between this transition and the process of individuation that happens in early childhood, during which the child learns to see herself as a person physically and psychologically separate from, and yet dependent on, the mother or primary care provider. (Mabey and Sorensen, 1995: 7)

The 'ideal mother–child relationship' has been a subject of psychological papers for some time. It has been established that a *secure attachment* has enormous consequences for adolescents completing the task of separation and autonomy (Bowlby, 1952). If a mother is able only to form an *insecure attachment*, little distress from the child will be observed at separation and no register on her return, whereas a *secure attachment* is shown by the child's brief distress on parting, followed by a return to a calm state when reunited with the mother (Ainsworth et al., 1978). A *secure attachment* is the ideal relationship in preparation for autonomy and successful adult relations. During adolescence, known as the 'second individuation process', there are reactivated ambivalent, yet very powerful feelings, such as depression, emotional instability of relationships, a contradiction in thought and feeling, illogical shifts between loving and hating the same person, acceptance and rejection of a loved one, involvement and non-involvement with friends or parents.

With the expanding opportunities for freedom, adolescents can be the most loveable and at the same time the most objectionable of people. This is due to anxiety resulting from an instinct of self-exploration that is in tension with a parental control designed to keep the instinct in check. Although freedom is exciting and a goal to which the teenager aspires, it will occasion much self-doubt and insecurity – the thought of living away from home and of fighting one's own battles is a daunting prospect.

There is some disagreement among psychologists on the universality of adolescent conformity and rebellion, but there is no doubting its prevalence in western society. Psychodynamic theory sees adolescent rebellion as an aid to the disengagement process. It is said that the more old-fashioned and out-of-date the parents are, the easier becomes the task of breaking the emotional ties. If the 'generation gap' is pronounced, then, as the adolescent becomes more identified with the peer group, the emotional launch into the deep is less traumatic, there being everything to gain and nothing to lose from breaking away from parents. Beyond this general psychodynamic construct of individuation there is the theory of identity formation as proposed by Erik Erikson (1968).

Erikson has come to be regarded as *the* commentator on youth, and ranks above other psychoanalysts in that he takes into consideration the influence of social and cultural circumstances. In his classic studies he saw adolescent life as an 'identity crisis', as a series of stages during which the young person must establish a *coherent identity*, and overcome a sense of *identity diffusion* (1968). The adolescent must take major decisions at this time in almost every area of his life and each involves a crisis and the need to defeat identity diffusion. Four well-recognized features show this.

The first is the fear of *intimacy*, of being committed and fully engaged in a close personal relationship, involving a surrender of the self and the loss of personal identity. Many adolescents require a long time of courting and testing out of relationships before they will fully entrust themselves in intimacy. Adolescents lacking a strong identity of trust from early positive childhood experience are prone to form either formal relationships or the most unsuitable partnerships. They may choose to shrink from the challenge and remain in isolation through a fear of intimacy.

The second is the need to combat what Erikson calls *diffusion in time perspective*. This is where the adolescent finds it difficult to plan for the future. There is ambivalence over the possibility of a promising future: on the one hand a disbelief that time will bring change, and on the other an anxiety that change might indeed come with time.

Thirdly, there is *diffusion of industry*, in which the adolescent finds it difficult to harness resources in a realistic way, either in practical work or in study. It is a paralysed condition of lethargy and redundancy, an inability to concentrate or a preoccupation with one single activity to the exclusion of all others.

Finally, there is the appeal of forming a *negative identity*, one that is contrary to that which is preferred by the parent or significant adult. The wish to oppose is a process of finding a true identity. It is expressed as a scornful rebuttal of the role that is considered respectable and proper for the family or community. Erikson also speaks of a period of *psychosocial moratorium*, a time when decisions can be left in abeyance. Society allows, he says, indeed it encourages, the decision to delay major choices. The adolescent finds space to experiment with roles in order to discover the sort of person he or she wishes to be, which, for Erikson, is a healthy function and an opportunity for social play.

Identity confusion in healthy development is different from that of early childhood, for the peer group will now support the individual in forming a relationship of intimacy and commitment. The adolescent is much more influenced by what friends think than by what parents say. The group may appear radical and unconventional to the parents, but it is within its own terms really quite uniform in many respects. Parents and teachers often recognize that the self-expressive so-called individualism of modern youth has become diluted into a form of group-identity conservatism: 'To keep themselves together they temporarily over-identify, to the point of apparent complete loss of identity, with the heroes of cliques and crowds' (Erikson, 1963: 234–40).

Three emotional-behavioural aspects co-exist in Erikson's account of adolescence. The first is a youngster's inner conflict arising from puberty, the second is the effect of socialization, and third the impact of cognitive development that gives adolescents the apparatus and power to rebel against authority.

Impact of puberty

There are physiological growth spurts taking place concurrently with cognitive development during puberty, and those who are outside the perceived 'norms' experience anxiety (Thomas, 1990). Physical and hormonal changes occurring within the bodies of adolescents affect the way they look and feel about themselves. With the onset of puberty there occurs physical maturation: menstruation in girls and nocturnal emissions in boys. There can be anxiety and confusion in trying to understand the new urges, mood swings, sensory and psychological excitements and the opportunities for pairings. The hormone oestrogen causes menstruation for girls between the ages of 10 and 16 (the average being 13). The ovaries are producing an egg each month, the hips begin to widen and the breasts are forming. Puberty in boys, between 11 and 16 (the average being 14), is triggered by the hormone testosterone which results in the testicles producing sperm, the chest getting larger, the voice deepening and a growth in facial and pubic hair. Although in recent decades puberty has occurred earlier, the onset is variable at a time when adolescents are preoccupied with 'normalcy'. Hormonal changes and bodily alterations create deep emotional feelings that are innate and that are largely out of control.

> Dean becomes embarrassed in the pool while standing alongside the girls because his penis has become noticeably erect under his trunks. He turns his back hoping they will not comment and makes himself comfortable before diving into the water.

> Danielle was disconcerted in the changing room when seeing drops of blood on her underclothes. She had been forewarned by her mother to expect her first period, but at this time she wanted to avoid doing gym and get home for reassurance from her older sister.

Sex play and experimentation without intimacy occur much earlier, often harmlessly, among siblings within the family home. Making sense of personal sensations is not the need for intimacy at this point, but more a curiosity over the other's 'private equipment' (Thomas, 1990):

Paul entered Jessica's room shortly after his bath, and after their parents had left them in the charge of a baby-sitter. The opportunity had presented itself for each to satisfy the other's curiosity over their different sexual forms. They simulated non-penetrative sexual intercourse by copying sex scenes they had seen on television, material that their parents thought went over their heads.

Mark and his twin brother Robert engaged in sex play one night in their bedroom. This was unplanned and occurred after a wrestling match. They lay exhausted on Robert's bed wearing only their boxer shorts. Quite off-guard they each reached for the other's penis and began mutually masturbating. They both enjoyed the sensual pleasure and only ceased the stimulation after Robert quickly removed his hand when overcome by a sense of guilt. They never repeated the activity, largely through fear of what the other might say to their parents.

Personal masturbation and fantasising, both for boys and for girls, become the means by which sexual urges are satisfied during puberty. Sex drives become dominant in early adolescence and a strong yet unfulfilled desire to become engaged in sex play and procreation develops. A spirit of innocence and coyness checks such feelings until middle to late adolescence. There is more talk and boasting than action but this does not stop the body from being a cauldron of sensations.

During mid-adolescence, powerful feelings well up within the individual that can lead to obsessions about personal appearance, the image of the self, and the ability to form relationships with the opposite sex. Such obsessions can bring about over-sensitive reactions to expressed opinions and to criticism. With conforming adolescents (as are most), the satisfying of sex drives is largely deferred for reasons of inhibition, social convention, inherited mores and value-systems, or simply for the lack of opportunity. For this reason, sexual fantasy lingers on within the youngster's imagination over a longer period for western adolescents than might be the case with societies where parenthood is entered into much earlier on (Arabic and Asian cultures). As a consequence, the sexual drives of adolescents in western society are satisfied (or titillated) by sex scenes on television and the cinema, or pictures in pornographic magazines. According to some theories promulgated by Freud, deferred sex drives can be channelled into other outlets like ambition (May, 1969).

From the late 1970s onwards, evidence of earlier sexual activity among adolescents has been accumulating – 65 per cent of 16 to 19-year-olds being sexually active (HEA, 1992). Thirty per cent of boys perceive that sex is the most important thing in a relationship compared to 13 per cent of girls (Sherratt et al., 1998). Gathering data on such a topic is notoriously difficult and some findings are contradictory, perhaps showing varied experience from one geographical area to another, and across different cultures. One recent report found that the first experience of penetrative intercourse took place on average at 16 years for girls and at 18 for boys (1998).

Peer-group pressure to conform and compete requires a psychological adjustment that is not satisfied with masturbation. Middle to late adolescence is the time for experimentation and daring with the opposite sex (Conger, 1975). There is broad diversity in sexual attitudes and behaviours (petting and coitus) across gender, age, and demographic, socio-economic and social class boundaries together with a general trend in greater frequency and earlier activity in a cultural change of increased 'openness'. It is a time for fantasizing of 'trial runs for actions and feelings which are strange and frightening', and for ironing out mistakes before they happen (Noonan, 1983: 24). There is a delicate balance between being viewed as too 'prudish' and too 'promiscuous', which is far riskier for girls than for boys (Lees, 1993).

Some feel that there is a place for infidelity among young people before making serious commitments, for having sexual experience before marriage or living together (Skynner and Cleese, 1989). Researchers have suggested that the most settled relationships are those in which each partner is not hankering after fantasy sexual fulfilment or extra-marital affairs. Those who have experienced such long-term committed relationships know how difficult it is to maintain a healthy sexual compatibility. Energy is lost in fuelling fantasies, and the running of two relationships later in life with all the deceit involved is not fulfilling. Teenage promiscuity and experimentation may serve to promote more secure relationships in later life.

Clearly, sexual experimentation is a matter of personal decision and responsibility since sexual liberty is not the best course for those adolescents whose conduct is in violation of their personal morals or spiritual beliefs.

Erica came for counselling after losing her virginity one evening during an experience that bordered on rape. At 14 she was keen to keep her first experience of sexual intercourse for 'that special time when it felt right'. When she was only 11, she was very frightened when a childminder 'tried it on' with her. This left her scared of being alone and of sexual intimacy generally. In her relationships with boyfriends, however, she walked close to the wire. One evening when sitting in the back of a car with a 19-year-old male friend – a person she knew had fancied her for some time – she became so engrossed in conversation that she was unaware of what was happening. They kissed for a while, and she allowed him to fondle her breasts over her clothes. At one point she asked him to stop, though with bouts of giggling. Taking her laughter as a lead, and kissing her when she tried to speak, he held her hands behind her back and with his other hand he unzipped her trousers, pulled down her clothing and inserted his penis.

For a few minutes she felt she had to put up with what was happening, mesmerized as she was and in shock. Afterwards she dressed herself again and went home feeling 'dirty', ashamed and upset. She came for counselling the next day with a range of fears, from the possibility of being pregnant to anxiety to keep this from her mother. She felt unable to press charges of rape because he was a 'friend' of the group. Apart from understandable anger, there was heavy regret over her lost virginity – this was not 'that special time when it felt right', that magic moment she could treasure.

Rollo May (1969) is more cautious about sexually liberated attitudes and describes western culture as the 'sexual wilderness', where 'throwing off the shackles' has brought about a new puritanism. The former adolescent anxiety was *when* and *with whom* to lose one's virginity, but nowadays the different and greater anxiety is *how well to perform*. Innocence has given way to the commonplace viewing of explicit sex scenes on television and the numerous textbooks on sexual technique and the best positions in which to achieve orgasm. Sex has become a utility, an act that is wholly sensual and without feeling and reason. The body has become a mere machine for other people's gratification: 'The Victorian person sought to have love without falling into sex; the modern person seeks to have sex without falling into love' (1969: 46). It was once a sin for young people to have early unplanned sex; it is now a sin for many to say 'no'. Romance and falling in love, according to May (1969), have become confused with sex.

Teenagers may not be as fearful in society's 'free love' ambience of engaging in their first sexual experience, but they are certainly fearful of entering into psychological intimacy with a partner. The new fear is not natural inhibition, but commitment. This is the confusing world of the young. While most young people find their first sexual experience unromantic, most come through this turbulent period of sexual perplexity and develop a positive attitude towards their own sexual needs and wants.

Socialization within the peer group

Through adolescence the rapid physical development of sexual organs has *psychological implications* (Thomas, 1990). Sexual excitement, rivalry and fierce competition for pairings will take place, and many will feel awkward and out of step with the perceived norms. Slow development in puberty and late maturity will affect leadership potential and will prolong infantile behaviour, affecting the self-concept detrimentally. The degree of rebelliousness and self-assertion that is necessary for the formation of ego strength and adulthood will be held in check (Thomas, 1990). With an increase in physical strength in boys, a shooting up in height in girls, and widely varying rates of sexual development in both, there is anxiety and confusion.

Although Erikson acknowledged the importance of social factors in adolescent development, he saw society's influence mainly in terms of its effects upon internal processes. However, sociologists and social psychologists are also interested in the influence of social factors upon adolescent identity in terms of 'socialization' and 'role'. Learning and an understanding of how an adolescent role should be played out are brought about through agents of socialization, such as school, work, university, group association, etc.

From childhood, adults largely prescribe the roles for young people. Adolescence brings new opportunities through peer-group affiliations to enable role transitions, and the insecurity of becoming less dependent on authority figures has the effect of making one depend more upon the peer group for reassurance in supporting the self-concept. Role change, then, is an integral feature of adolescent development (Coleman, 1987). But social changes in postmodern culture have heightened this phenomenon of role conflict by widening the age gap, by reducing the time that adults and children spend together, by decrying traditional rites of passage into adulthood and by creating a moral and ethical climate where traditional values are viewed as little more than outdated taboos.

Social historians have long recognized that 'childhood' did not exist for the majority of the labouring poor till late into the nineteenth century (Muncie et al., 1995). The social construct of 'adolescence' is a recent designation of western industrialized cultures. The particular emotional and physical stage of development that western young people pass through, and which we term 'adolescence', is not a universal phenomenon, then, but a particularly conditioned phase of passing from childhood to adulthood.

The early studies of Margaret Mead (1928, 1930, 1949) demonstrated that adolescence does not occur in societies that draw children rapidly through the processes of assuming adult responsibility. She showed how free children were when held strictly within an extended family regime that had specified social roles, that had relaxed sexual attitudes, and that deferred marriage (1928).

Adolescence is therefore a cultural phenomenon, not an instinctive biological staging post through which each must pass in order to arrive at adulthood. 'Teenage problems' are relatively recent (Miller, 1978). Before the arrival of adolescence, and under the general maxim that 'children should be seen and not heard', it was hardly imaginable that young people would have the types of problems that beset adults. Now we see adolescents coming for counselling over such difficulties as depression and sexual problems, difficulties that were not heard of a generation or two ago.

This social trend as outlined by Mabey and Sorensen (1995) is the result of a range of political changes that have occurred since the 1950s. The optimism of post-war Britain, with widespread employment through apprenticeship schemes and clerical vocations, is contrasted with the crisis of the modern period with high-level youth unemployment and little hope of economic independence outside state provision. A 'youth culture', born after the war, rapidly spread from the United States to Britain.

The new culture was caricatured by an array of pop idols and highly influential figures. There were James Dean and Elvis in the USA, the Rolling Stones and the Beatles in Britain. Moving through the 1980s there was the punk movement with outrageous figures such as Sid Vicious of the Sex Pistols. With the rise of feminism there came the female power in Britain of the Spice Girls during the late 1990s. With such icons young people found symbols with which to identify and express their individuality. They were new voices against the political systems and ideologies of the establishment. No longer were they subject to adults. 'Come fathers and mothers throughout the land. Don't criticize what you can't understand. For your sons and your daughters are beyond your command. The times they are 'a changing', sang Bob Dylan.

The new-found freedom and liberty of the swinging sixties brought about the 'drug culture' and sexual liberation, where previously held mores began to be questioned and turned on their heads. Ideologies abounded from the 1960s through to the end of the 1980s, encompassing every conceivable philosophy, from passivity, anti-materialism, transcendental meditation and mysticism to protest, indulgence, physicalism and rebellion.

Thatcherism in Britain encouraged an 'every man for himself' [sic] mentality aimed at heightening, for the 'feckless poor', their individual responsibility to rise to greater levels of prosperity. But Thatcherism removed the economic possibilities for this to take place. It had produced a great economic divide between 'the haves' and 'the have nots'. Money was held as the passport to success and status, but unemployment was never so high. The prosperous south became indifferent to the poorer north, all under the political rubric that if you can look after the masters of economic growth then wealth will somehow magically trickle down to those on the breadline. It didn't work. The political paradigm proved false. It is little wonder then that the young had arrived in a world where the expectations were higher than the possibilities. They were left with much confusion and considerable resentment.

Poorer children are now compelled through high-pressure advertising to achieve status among wealthier peers through cosmetic gains that are beyond the pockets of their struggling parents. The marketing of designer-labelled clothes and the forces of 'consumerism' bombard those of the new millennium. Modern youngsters in run-down housing estates are growing up in a world that offers them minimal support and maximum censure. It is not easy being an adolescent within areas of high unemployment, where 'neighbours from hell' may terrorize the law-abiding. Growing up can be fraught with tension, even for healthy adolescents of middle-class homes. With the open market-place for drugs and the availability of contraceptives, young people are facing peer-group pressures that were previously unimaginable. The crossover from parent to peer-group allegiance is not easy amidst the range of contradictory attitudes that are censorious in some quarters and *laissez-faire* in others.

With the family unit beginning to crumble, relationships have become less formal, more fluid and increasingly transitory. The homogeneous family as the ideal is rapidly becoming rare in some urban communities. None of the major institutional forces of religion, politics or education appear able to restore the former pattern of the nuclear family. Not only have the media icons become blatantly hedonistic and outrageous, but the norm for many adolescents is to live in families of split parenthood or step-parents, two or three times over in some cases. In addition, high youth unemployment and increased opportunities for extended schooling have added to the tension of socialization and role conflict, by extending the time for sons and daughters to leave the family home.

The young person during adolescence must progress from childhood to adulthood, from dependence on 'mother' to grown-up dependence on 'friends', along a continuous route towards autonomy. This journey is not easy. There will be role conflict when the individual is pressured to live out two largely incompatible roles. Two sets of people make demands on the adolescent to have different attitudes, to order different priorities and to display radically different forms of behaviour. The individual is caught between two stools. High and unreasonable expectations of parents will lead to higher levels of anxiety and role conflict. As the adolescent mixes with the peer group, new confidences develop in a whole range of social situations.

For healthy adolescents who integrate well, the social norms become those of the group, and inner confusion and turmoil become shared and lessened through group discussion. Peer pressure is recognized to be increasingly influential in teenage conformity, and is shown in such codes as not 'grassing on mates' and in the habit formation of smoking, drinking, drugs, sexual behaviour and in delinquency. Peer-group pressure in school is most evident in an adolescent's appearance, fashion and dress, as the following extract illustrates:

Counsellor: Suppose, for example, your shoes had worn out and your folks had said to you, 'I've got a really nice pair of shoes from the car boot.'

Sarah: Oh no!

Naomi: Er no! That's nasty.

Simon: No!

Counsellor: One pound twenty; a really nice pair of black shiny shoes. How many of you would wear them?

Naomi: No way!

Alan: No! (*group laugh*)

Counsellor: Suppose your parents said, 'Look I'm offering you these one-pound-twenty pair of shoes. I will give you, if you like, forty pounds to spend on anything you want.'

Naomi: I'd rather go to school in something I used to wear than go to school in something me mum gives me and be picked on all the time.

Counsellor:	What is it that would stop you from making good economical sense? Everybody would want forty quid in their pocket. What would make you make that sacrifice rather than wear those shoes? Why turn it down?
John:	Because people would laugh.
Alan:	Because people would put pressure on you.
John:	Because they'd think you search around for old-fashioned shoes.
Simon:	They'd laugh at you.
Alan:	Saying, 'You can't afford a pair of shoes.'
Simon:	Yeah.
Naomi:	Pick on you for ages; all over forty pounds.
Alan:	Can't afford a pair of shoes.
Sarah:	Yeah.
John:	And you have to go to the car boot for all your shoes for one pound fifty. (*group laugh*)
Counsellor:	Suppose they were a lovely pair of ellesse shoes, right, and they were nice shoes. They were quite fashionable shoes, but the word had got around your group that your mum had got them from the car boot.
Sarah:	I still wouldn't wear them.
Simon:	I'd die!
Sarah:	I wouldn't wear them.
Counsellor:	So, it's got nothing to do with the shoes.
John:	Somebody else has probably worn them; they'll smell.
Simon:	It's that they're second-hand.
Counsellor:	What is it that makes an ordinary pair of shoes...
Simon:	You can get verrucas. (*group laugh*)
Counsellor:	You're thinking of medical reasons. I wonder if it's got anything to do with medical reasons. I'm just wondering what kids would say if they find out that you'd got these shoes from a car boot?
Alan:	Take the mick out of your mum, saying 'you're like cheap!'
Simon:	And tease you; call you names; call you 'tramp!'
Naomi:	You won't have any friends. They would all...
John:	They'd think you can't afford something.
Counsellor:	Now, that's peer-group pressure.... If my dad made me have a hairstyle that was totally unfashionable I wouldn't want to go to school, but the pressure that I was under was not anything like what you would have today. How do you see yourself then? How do you like to see yourself?
David:	Nice and tidy and clean.
Counsellor:	Tidy, clean.
Alan:	Fashionable.
John:	Good-looking.
Counsellor:	Good-looking. Is it important to you, John, that people think that you spend a lot on clothes and things like that?
Simon:	Yea, like brand-named clothes and things like that.
Alan:	No.
David:	ellesse – Nike – Puma – adidas – Rockport.
Counsellor:	So, it's important for your image that people get the idea that you spend a lot on your clothes and you wear brand names.

John:	Yea.
Sarah:	Yea.
Counsellor:	How many of you would bluntly refuse to wear something you think kids would actually laugh at? (*all hands are raised*)
Naomi:	Me.
John:	Me.
David:	I would.
Counsellor:	So, tell me what would happen if your folks were saying, 'There you are. I want you to wear that for school.'
John:	No.
Simon:	No.
Alan:	'Mom, I'm gonna stop away.'
Naomi:	I'd throw a strop and say, 'No way!'
Counsellor:	They say, 'I don't care what you say, you're still going to wear them.'
Naomi:	I'd run out the house.
Alan:	I'd just say, 'No!' (*laughs*)
John:	I'd run.
David:	I'd put my trainers in my bag, pretend to go to school and then don't go to school.
Alan:	I'd wag!
Counsellor:	So, all of you are very affected by the way you are seen by other people aren't you?
Alan:	Yea.
Naomi:	Yea.
Counsellor:	So, you're not free... (*stunned silence by the whole group*)

Anxiety about appearance can become particularly obsessive for those who find peer-group acceptance problematic. Some young adolescents are so preoccupied with other teenagers' opinions of them that it becomes for them a losing of energy and self-confidence. They live in an insular world of an imagined audience that is permanently peering at them, mocking their appearance, censoring their actions and seeking opportunities to trip them up. Such a phenomenon is wholly imaginary but pervading. It is extremely debilitating and restrictive. Although the imagined audience is unreal to the adolescent's carers, this is not the case for the individual:

Dean walks down the street continually looking round at the young people hanging about in the shopping precinct. For everyone who glances at him he wonders 'What the hell's he looking at? What's the matter with her?' He keeps checking his appearance in the shop window for creases in his trousers, for dirt on his coat or for his hair to be out of place. 'What's everyone looking at, for God's sake?'

If the imagined audience is not given up, the youngster will become paranoid and in need of psychiatric treatment. In most cases, however, it passes away with maturity and increased self-confidence.

Adolescents may acquire a personal fable – a feeling of uniqueness and invulnerability that is directly associated with the taking of risks (Geldard and Geldard, 1999). It is a time of daring and hazardous challenges – there is a naïve sense of immortality and no fear of danger. In youth some friends and I abseilled down a 120-foot gorge in the Lake District and scaled a dangerous cliff edge, while other friends walked along the handrail of a bridge above the swirling currents of the Barmouth estuary in Wales. These daredevil feats we now consider to be incredibly hazardous and, in some cases, quite mad, wondering how on earth we accomplished such deeds.

Cognitive development and challenging behaviour

Whilst it is true that the external context of the social environment is a considerable factor in psychological development, it is also true that the complex internal context of cognition has an influence upon identity and behaviour. The two go hand in hand and are complementary. We come full circle: from inner conflict arising from puberty to environmental influences, and from socialization we return to the relationship of thinking to self-identity and behaviour.

Along with significant growth spurts and chemical changes, the stage of adolescence within life-span development is a transition from 'egocentrism' to higher cognitive abilities (Thomas, 1990). It is a time of inner conflict as youngsters seek to define their identity and begin to relinquish their 'dreamlike', playful consciousness for focused attention. But they are moving towards a stage of responsibility and personal accounting in a social flux of paradox and mixed messages. Adolescents become illogical and inconsistent as they pass through this highly critical phase. They are idealistic and closed-minded, but eventually they move towards a more moderate phase of integration, a stage that is only fully reached with employment. There will be the *need* for adolescents to rebel, which, while difficult to manage and live with at times, should be viewed as the natural process in securing ego strength and identity.

Around puberty there is a significant development from a form of thinking that Jean Piaget described as 'concrete operations' to a higher form of reasoning and abstract thinking, which is termed 'formal operational' thought (Inhelder and Piaget, 1958). Earlier adolescent behaviour was determined largely by social learning through rewards and reinforcement. If a child experienced a favourable outcome or reward for a particular response, she would tend to repeat the response in order to get the reward, and the more consistently the conditions applied the more reinforced became the behaviour. At adolescence a fundamental shift occurs in cognition. The teenager becomes capable of forming propositions from abstract ideas, of forming hypotheses around possibilities, and of reasoning in deductive logic.

The adolescent's achievement of formal operational thought allows her to think about not only her own opinions, but about the opinions of others (Geldard and Geldard, 1999). To see the perspective of others while not necessarily agreeing with them brings about a different form of egocentrism, an egocentrism that is, paradoxically, different in character from that of childhood. Adolescent egocentrism is conditioned by will in a full awareness of others, whereas childhood egocentrism is more an instinctive impulse (Coleman, 1987). Thus, teenagers are quick to perceive an adult's inconsistencies and contradictions, and even quicker to point them out. On the receiving end they understandably become sensitive to criticism and ridicule. These complex cognitive changes make identity formation quite confusing. Examples are given throughout this book where the trials resulting from cognitive development have led to social upheaval both in respect of the family and friends.

Although a moderate degree of resistance and rebellion should be anticipated and, indeed, expected in healthy adolescent individuation, there are cases where this goes disastrously wrong. Unstable family factors, lax disciplinary boundaries and an over-dependence on a delinquent youth sub-culture can leave an adolescent confused and unduly affected by deviant role models that lead to criminality (Geldard and Geldard, 1999):

Gavin was a year eight pupil, 13 years old, having an attendance record of 60 per cent absenteeism in his first year and 82 per cent in the autumn term of his second. When in school, he was disaffected and totally out of the habit of conforming to school conventions: he would regularly walk in and out of class or the building when it suited him and would appear genuinely surprised if asked to account for his actions. He had developed the art of winding up his teachers for laughs from disruptive peers until confrontations resulted in him swearing and storming out of the classroom. He clearly made no commitment to his schooling, made no investment for personal progress, and engendered no friendships with his teachers. His grandparents had brought him up from a very young age because his mother could not cope with his non-conformity. He was heavily meshed into a burglary network, having links with adults who shelved stolen goods and encouraged the enterprise of a team of Fagin recruits by financial incentives. The route to 'winning him back' from delinquency was by introducing him to an active youth club with a pro-social peer group and an enterprising youth leader – with whom Gavin formed a modelling relationship.

The youngster's ability to resolve the tensions and trials throughout adolescent transition depends upon three factors, then: the strength of self-image in dealing with puberty; socialization within a supportive peer group; and a smooth transition through the rebellious phase.

But there is a fourth factor that, perhaps, is the most important, not least because it (hopefully) is the constant throughout the whole transitional phase. It is the tolerance, understanding and flexibility of those significant adults guiding the youth through. If any of these four are lacking, there will be undue confrontation and crisis. This chapter closes, therefore, with a discussion of this fourth need for healthy adolescent transition.

HOME CONDITIONS FOR HEALTHY DEVELOPMENT

Insights of non-possessive parenting so eloquently expressed in Kahlil Gibran's poem are easier to recognize than to practise. It is natural to want to possess one's child, but it can impose an emotional tie that proves restrictive to their individuation and autonomy.

In spite of many trials and much emotional turbulence, most adolescents are able to come through this stormy period relatively unscathed, so long as they have supportive carers and strong peer-relationships, and so long as they can grow in an environment that allows them to develop physically, cognitively and emotionally. There is an anomaly about quality parenting within modern society, for many parents experience difficulty because of the lack of preparation that is given for this exacting task. It is assumed that parenting is an automatic, instinctive skill, when it is clear that most parents adopt a style of leniency or strictness which is only a slight modification of their own experience of being parented.

'Good-enough' parenting

Parents will not be perfect, but may be 'good enough'. As pointed out, early secure attachment bonds are a good predictor for smooth transition through all life-stages (Holmes, 1993). There will be undue tension for adolescents living in homes that are at the two extremes of the monitoring spectrum: those where conditions are lax, or, conversely, those where the regime is regimental. Insecurity is inevitable in a family where there are no rules, yet alienation and delinquent behaviour are the risks where parental stances are inflexible (Skynner and Cleese, 1989).

Obsessive neurosis can occur where a person feels compelled to do certain things through an excessive fear of disapproval as a result of past failures. There will be a lack of confidence about launching into independence. The child will be out of control and will fear personal elements (instincts and impulses) that fly out of control and land him or her in trouble. There will be a felt need to keep checking what is done, a fastidiousness over fashion and cleanliness through fear of disapproval, and a disconnection with feelings through a compulsion to live out parental wishes. An excessively authoritarian upbringing is harmful (Biddulph, 1996), but a strict upbringing, with plenty of love as well is not in itself as much of a problem as one having fuzzy boundaries. Suitable parenting is a question of balance, but is tilted towards firmness. During adolescent growth spurts, the parent must encourage exercise and provide a balanced diet of minerals, protein and carbohydrates (Thomas, 1990). In child-raising there are three psychological necessities for developing a positive self-concept. These are affection and protection, realistic expectations, and a predictable environment (Thomas, 1990):

> Robert at 12 was deprived of all three. His mother had a learning disability, was illiterate, and was unable to show affection. His father was diabetic and was a constant worry to him. Both parents were alcoholics, which meant they could offer him no protection while they were drunk. They made inconsistent demands of him – apart from expecting him to be their 'parent'. Robert was uncertain about what he would find when arriving home. He was low in self-confidence, had a stammer and was referred for being anxious, 'bossy', and being significantly small and under-developed. There were obvious signs of serious neglect.

At the other extreme, some parents attempt to channel the adolescent to live out their own aspirations, by 'programming' them early. With such families adolescents have felt like objects of their parent's dreams, as child prodigies expected to achieve all that their parents were incapable of achieving through lack of opportunity.

Research carried out in Dallas examined a sample of healthy and successful Harvard graduates over a long period. It identified a number of factors contributing to adequate parenting. The study concluded that a healthy family is one in which both parents and children have a positive and friendly attitude that is outgoing and confident. The parents have a high degree of emotional independence which allows them both intimacy and separateness. They have a family structure that encourages a strong and equal coalition. They are prepared to lay down the law if they have to, but will always consult very fully with the children first. They are able to cultivate a very free and open communication, based on the children's sense that no feelings they experience are unacceptable or forbidden, giving a feeling of freedom and lots of fun and high spirits. They will perceive the world very clearly, based on the fact that they can accept all their own feelings and therefore don't need to project them on to their children. And, finally, all members of a healthy family can cope quite readily with change, because they enjoy an extraordinary emotional support derived from a transcendent value system (Skynner and Cleese, 1993). By contrast, some parents fail even to look after themselves, let alone their children.

Fostering supportive friends

A nurturing and mutually supportive peer group is essential in order to be able to identify with those undergoing the same experiences at a similar time (Conger, 1975). The opposing pulls and new allegiances of the adolescent bring about some degree of conflict, not only with parents, but also with all authority figures. The whole matter is unpredictable, however, for the clash of adolescent value-systems is not universal. Apart from exceptional circumstances, the wise parent or guardian will facilitate growth by adopting a positive and encouraging stance towards the friends of their children. Some parents interpret their child's group allegiance as a gesture of deliberate hostility to themselves. They do not understand the nature of group membership, the fierce loyalty that can at times become fanatical, or the need not to lose face publicly. In extreme cases, there will be head-on collisions that result in ultimatums being drawn up in a futile attempt to soften hardened wills.

Some middle to late adolescents will display 'shocking' behaviours, such as drug-taking, alcohol abuse, smoking, absconding from home and body piercing – behaviours which seem to be trying to say something that cannot be expressed in words (Geldard and Geldard, 1999). It is a means of assertion, of breaking out of closeted family relationships. For this reason, parents and teachers who choose to advise against smoking, drinking, drug experimentation and sexual voyeurism by nagging and moralizing over the physical and social threats to wellbeing, only feed into a condition which has powerful appeal. Responsible decision-making is the preferred approach (McGuiness, 1998), and the more the individual is engaged in healthy peer-group relations, the more communal group identity will be formed and the more personal uniqueness will be exchanged for similarity of experience.

Letting go of adolescents

Boys often need male companionship at critical stages of their development, particularly boys brought up by single mothers (Biddulph, 1998). Suitable male role models serve as mentors in place of older delinquents from the street.

The breaking of parent–daughter bonding, particularly, can be traumatic for some parents when boyfriends come on the scene. As their adolescent daughter moves away from the home, some parents become neurotic and over-controlling, and often go to extreme measures to halt the process. Adolescents of strongly *enmeshed* families have a traumatic route to individuation. Berkowitz (1987) suggests that parents who stand in the way of this separation process of individuation may run the risk of pathological behaviour in the child. Many borderline adolescents exhibit extreme behaviour, such as guilt, depression and suicidal anomie, in protest against parental omnipotent control. The parents will rationalize their own resistance with the argument that the world is a hostile place in comparison with the safety of the family. Danger outside – rapists, murderers, sex-abusers and drug-pushers – is highlighted and is over-exaggerated as a manipulative ploy to impede individuation. The hazards are there, of course, but adolescents need to develop the social skills to survive in the world and not avoid it altogether. An unreasonable avoidance will create phobia in the face of such risks, with a disproportionate fearfulness. Over-cautious parents point to their offspring's mistakes made along the way, to justify their precautionary restrictions.

When a daughter becomes sexually curious, or sexually active, the mother may wish to 'chain her up', or to 'vet' the boyfriend, while the father may tacitly collude in keeping her bound within the home. There is a compulsion to hold the child close, to possess the outreaching adolescent and to prevent individuation. In reality the child has no problem, but is following a natural inclination to escape a claustrophobic environment. It is the parents' neuroses that are the problem. So, rather than welcoming the fact that their daughter is moving from the nest, they refuse to see her as the centre of her own initiative.

Some parents encourage regressive behaviours and induce guilt, which limits the horizon of autonomy. Anger may be expressed disproportionately when youngsters arrive late after being out with friends. The defiance is interpreted by the parents as rejection. There will be undue reward for regressive behaviour, such as tears, cuddling and the like – all in order to keep the adolescent ever the child. These are counter-separation manoeuvres. The guilt-inducing behaviour is normally displayed covertly by parents whose relationship is likely to be dysfunctional. Often they have no friends and little social life outside a closeted family of dependants. Such parents long for earlier days when a faulty relationship could be hidden behind 'needed' parental roles (Berkowitz, 1987).

Parents of healthily developing adolescents have a range of flexible child-rearing skills that help to facilitate individuation. Such parents will not see a supportive peer group as a threat but as a resource. Rather than opposing the process, the enlightened parent will encourage the move into the larger world of opportunity.

COUNSELLING IN LIGHT OF ADOLESCENT DEVELOPMENT

Before attempting to counsel adolescents in school, the practitioner will need to understand the particular client's difficulties within the broader context of normal adolescent development. An emerging interest in sexuality and in physical differences will have its effects in inter-pupil relations, and the counsellor will need to bear in mind the rivalry and isolation that some may feel if they are marginally behind the rest in the onset of puberty. Peer-group bonding will take over earlier loyalties towards parents and teachers, and the need to create a trusting relationship with an adult in the counselling role may pose a risk of over-dependency and a threat to ongoing peer relations, if not guarded against.

Interventions that appear more interrogative than therapeutic will not foster the empowered self for which counselling should aim. The process of individuation requires an early stage of cognitive development of 'self-hood' within a social ambience that allows an adolescent the freedom to challenge and question without incurring a sense of guilt. There is a fine line between this healthy function on the one hand, and rudeness, lack of respect and discourtesy on the other, particularly in school. This will require clear denunciation at times when the border has been crossed because of immaturity. The integrative counsellor may sometimes need to mediate with fellow professionals when tempers have been roused. Finally, the practitioner may on occasion be asked to counsel parents on appropriate strategies in adolescent rearing and corrective measures. A grasp of the research evidence that points towards a pattern of ideals and 'good-enough' parenting is more than a useful grounding for counsellors and pastoral teachers using counselling skills.

4

BRIEF COUNSELLING IN SCHOOL

The massive research project carried out by Smith, Glass and Miller (1980) concluded that all psychotherapies – verbal or behavioural, psycho-dynamic, person-centred or systemic – were beneficial to clients, and were consistently effective. In spite of inherent limitations in individual and family therapy settings (Dryden, 1984; Street, 1994), many traditional approaches can be adapted within the time-pressured setting of school (Lines, 2000). While psychodynamic counselling may have limited applicability in school, the approach offers a framework for understanding young people's difficulties, which can enlighten many forms of brief therapy. Humanistic approaches (notably, person-centred) are popular in educational settings (McGuiness, 1998), along with integrative cognitive-behavioural counselling (Geldard and Geldard, 1999) and approaches that have emerged from family therapy – such as solution-focused therapy (Davis and Osborn, 2000) and narrative therapy (Winslade and Monk, 1999).

THEORETICAL COUNSELLING FRAMEWORK FOR YOUNG PEOPLE

Psychodynamic therapy is largely impractical in school because it involves in-depth self-exploration for clients over a considerable period of time. The aim in psychodynamic counselling is to help clients gain insight into their condition, to broaden awareness of the cause of disturbance, and to reveal and remove if appropriate the blocks that impede development towards mature relationships. The features of this approach include the interrelationship of external and internal worlds and the understanding of resistance and defence mechanisms. In short, the primary purpose is to help the client 'make sense of current situations' (Jacobs, 1988). School counselling in general has a much more modest aim. Psychodynamic therapy is aimed at *reconstructing* the personality (Clarkson, 1994), while school counselling is normally aimed at *enabling* the young person. There is a demand in school for approaches that 'fix people' quickly, then, in place of drawn-out therapy.

In spite of this limitation, the school counsellor may view the theoretical perspective of psychodynamic counselling as a framework for understanding teenage difficulties (Erikson, 1968), as a conceptual tool to disentangle the complex web of feelings and fantasies which exist in the client's troubled relationships. The client lives in an internal and external world, and the unconscious internal world substantially determines his feelings and actions in external relationships. This insight, when combined with the person-centred notion of the client in a state of 'becoming' (Rogers, 1967), has appeal as an overarching framework for understanding adolescent development.

As a complementary perspective, cognitive-behavioural counselling supports an image of the person that has appeal to the pragmatic mind (McLeod, 1993). Its transparent outcomes lend an air of respectability when dealing with youngsters in school who have been tutored to accept empirical forms of reality (Lines, 2000). The practical experimental-type methods and techniques of observation, measurement and evaluation mark cognitive-behavioural counselling as 'the most overtly "scientific" of all major therapy orientations' (McLeod, 1993: 45). The approach is fitting for a postmodern world that is suspicious of grand theory and ideology. Another attraction is its strong emphasis upon action. These factors go to make cognitive-behavioural counselling and related therapies popular in educational settings.

THE SCHOOL SETTING FOR TRADITIONAL COUNSELLING APPROACHES

The particular constraints of counselling in school were outlined in Chapter 1, yet these constraints point to the appropriateness of some styles in place of others. The preference for a particular approach is as much a question of what is achievable in a school setting as of what the client seeks from therapy. A setting of 'containment', for example, is for some approaches a necessity, but the degree of 'holding' the client will vary with each approach. The matching of aims with resources in counselling, and the planning and sustaining of counselling programmes are important in most approaches. The counsellor's preferred style and the selection of particular techniques have implications for young people in school that may not be as significant for adults in other settings.

A setting of 'containment'

The psychodynamic counsellor attempts to make sense of the client's projections through transference. Counsellors working extensively with adolescents are prone unconsciously to 'become parent' for the client, and through transference to receive the resentment, the frustration and rebellion that is normally bestowed upon parents for insisting on rules that appear unreasonable to adolescents. This happens when setting counselling boundaries. With some non-conforming youngsters, counsellors can experience countertransference feelings that emanate as much from their parenting encounters with their own children as from the client's projections. This can result in a strong resistance on the part of the adolescent to an unconscious manoeuvre for control, and unless there is a willingness on the part of the client, and an arena of 'containment' (Jacobs, 1988), then effective therapy is thwarted. But it is unlikely that the school can provide consistently such an arena of containment for this depth of work.

When school-based person-centred counsellors show empathy, clients can exhibit a pose of defencelessness, which stirs in the counsellor a maternal instinct to care for and protect a helpless client. The client needs holding but not smothering. The counsellor must reflect on the particular counselling role that is distinct from forms of nurturing relationships. It is liberating for clients to feel contained and to experience equality in power and status from an adult involved in helping them. But all this points to the need for more regular supervision than might be judged necessary for a pastoral teacher merely using counselling skills with less in-depth work. Young people can stir strong parental emotions in adult practitioners in school. Adults who undergo counselling have attained a measure of financial and social if not psychological independence, yet adolescents cannot be expected to have such a degree of autonomy, and many will thrive on the attention given in long-term work, attention which is ultimately an obstacle to empowerment.

The counsellor must safeguard the need of the client to be autonomous and self-monitoring, avoiding at all costs the tendency for dependency, especially when the counsellor is working with older adolescents who develop an unhelpful sense of security from being held overlong. Some pupils request appointments merely to avoid attending unpopular or difficult lessons and this, if acceded to, can affect the counsellor's image in school. Firm and precise policies of referral and boundary setting are called for here.

Goal-centred and narrowly focused counselling which is brief does not require a contained setting, since the task rather than the person becomes the object of therapy. Cognitive-behavioural methods, Egan's three-stage model, solution-focused therapy, narrative therapy and motivational interviewing (Miller and Rollnick, 1991) readily lend themselves to the time-limitations and frequent interruptions of an educational setting.

Counselling aims in-keeping with the setting

Apart from personal reflection and the ability to introspect, in-depth therapy requires from the client skill in articulation, and this rules out the majority of younger pupils in school. Those therapies that are not language-dependent will be more applicable for pupils having low intelligence, particularly in the lower years.

During the adolescent phase, a spirit of rebellion is in itself not a bad thing, for it helps the breakaway from parental attachment and fosters an identity with the peer group who are undergoing the same trials towards individuation. Through rebellion teenagers test values, attitudes, feelings and actions and so discover how *they* feel, think and assess priorities in life. Secure boundaries represent a paradox in that conflict (Noonan, 1983). The psychodynamic counsellor will not obstruct this developmental need, may indeed encourage it in some respects, but this may leave the client confused after counselling when entering the classroom and not finding the teacher as willing to permit reactionary verbal challenging.

Promoting self-responsibility is a characteristic of Gestalt, rational-emotive [behaviour] therapy (REBT), goal-centred counselling and motivational interviewing, and therefore is in keeping with what teachers continually attempt to do when pupils misbehave in school. The 'externalizing' discourse of narrative therapy (White, 1989) when applied with those clients brought up within confused boundaries can lead to the suggestion that the counsellor is promoting lax personal responsibility and the flouting of school rules. Yet these techniques are designed to create a therapeutic climate of motivation for change, and some styles which take the line of devil's advocate are really attempting to make use of paradoxical techniques to prompt the opposite behaviour to that which is described.

Person-centred approaches which discourage a sense of community or other-self responsibility in a pseudo-quest to reach the *organismic self* (Rogers, 1967), will find little sympathy among teachers in school. Critics see a problem for person-centred counsellors over delinquent behaviour, and claim that Rogers' view of the person becoming altruistic *through* finding the self is naïve and untested. Cognitive-behavioural therapists view the fully functioning human as hedonistic, with a limited sense of caring and responsibility for the plight of others. To this objection, Rogers held steadfastly to a belief that 'the human organism, when trusted, longs for relationship with others and for opportunities to serve and celebrate the wider community' (Dryden, 1984: 112). The practitioner in school must balance the wish to find the client's *self* with the need to survive and thrive in the competitive culture of modern education and peer-group pressure, and may need to think about counselling aims more broadly than individual actualization and aggrandizement.

The Gestalt model has been criticized by some practitioners for being too dismissive of the moral values necessary for the functioning of society, which is an inevitable consequence of discouraging the client's adherence to 'shouldism' behaviour (Perls et al., 1972). It is felt that the excessive emphasis upon self-responsibility promotes a sense of ultra-individualism that ignores the place of social obligations and collective responsibility in the ethos and social expectations of life in school. These objections do not apply to the task-centred and problem-solving therapies that follow, which include social integration as part of the counselling aim.

Counselling tailored to resources

There are two major handicaps in applying the psychodynamic model in school: the resource implications of planning extensive counselling aimed at restructuring the personality, and the risk of thereby inculcating dependance on the counsellor in cases where termination cannot be easily structured (Kramer, 1990). Long contracts of psychodynamic or person-centred counselling are very ambitious in school, even if the counsellor has the necessary skills and training. To make an effective use of transference relationships and to challenge clients in a caring manner also require long contracts where trust and confidence have been established. For the counsellor to even begin to make a tentative interpretation of a client's defence mechanisms, a considerable period of finely tuned listening and reflecting will have been necessary. All in all, the resources for such extensive work are rarely available in school.

However, brief or focal psychodynamic work can be indicated for those pupils who have an increasing motivation for insight, those who are able to develop a rapport with the counsellor and those who are able to respond to interpretation. A current or recent crisis and an ability to identify a focus for working are also indications for brief psychodynamic and person-centred counselling (Dryden, 1984). Much of this applies to drawn-out counselling contracts with humanistic approaches.

The resource implications of family therapy will become obvious to any school counsellor who might wish to adopt the model in school. It is highly unlikely that a suitable room that offers space, furnishing and freedom from interruptions (let alone cameras, one-way mirrors and two-way linked telephones) can be found in most educational establishments. It is also unthinkable that the majority of school counsellors, least of all pastoral teachers, will have the necessary skills, personal resources or time to conduct this approach, even if they were willing. Finding the time and energy to draw in a whole family – with all the logistical difficulties and resistance – to work on a particular difficulty is an equally unrealistic objective in the light of other demands. The very idea of a co-worker in school counselling is unimaginable when so few schools have any formal therapeutic provision anyway.

Planning and sustaining counselling programmes

A limiting factor for in-depth therapy in school is the ego-strength of young people to facilitate the process of insight. Adolescents are essentially changeable and temperamental, and it is likely that only those students at the top end of school will be able to see the work through to completion. In psychodynamic counselling and extensive humanistic counselling some pupil-clients will drop out of counselling when the work is only partially complete, and others may keep returning with newly acquired symptoms. In practice, much in-depth work is terminated prematurely through clients failing to keep appointments consistently. Adolescents are in a developmental phase of emotional vulnerability, and to have to undergo the initial trauma of working through the resistance of well-fortified defences requires considerable commitment on their part. Denial is most potently expressed through avoided appointments. The early and middle stages of psychodynamic counselling can be painful and some adolescents have found difficulty in seeing the payback to warrant the enterprise. Challenging sensitive young people who have low ego-strength may need to be even more cautiously timed than when working with adults in other settings, for the telephone, the school bell for lesson changes and noisy pupils moving along corridors all represent distractions.

The relationship built up in any form of counselling that engages the trust and loyalty of two people, who virtually live inside each other's heads, will inevitably involve a sense of loss on the part of the client and counsellor at termination. Termination of counselling cannot be easy when both are engrossed in details of the most intimate kind over a considerable time. Premature termination in school can be harmful in the long term, which raises the serious question of whether the counselling context warrants taking on in-depth work.

Accommodating the pupil-client at the time at which the problem is at its peak makes appointment planning difficult, and an insistence that pupils keep up with the curriculum has implications for arranging counselling sessions with those undertaking examination courses or with those having poor attendance figures. In rational-emotive [behaviour] therapy (REBT), clients will fail if they are not prepared to work at their homework tasks (Ellis, 1983), since they are expected to be dedicated (both inside and outside counselling) to attending to the tasks that have been prescribed to bring about change. But getting pupils, boys particularly, committed in completing homework is a thorny issue for practitioners working in areas where pupils are disaffected or badly organized; and sometimes clients simply forget (or can't be bothered) to carry out homework tasks that involve recording information in personal journals. Counselling tasks which rely on clients writing self-analysis or appraisal documents outside counselling before the next session, such as are applied in cognitive-analytic therapy (Ryle, 1990) and narrative therapy (Payne, 2000; White and Epston, 1990), are likely to be thwarted because they are too similar to conventional homework assignments.

Effective counselling style

The psychodynamic counsellor style in its purest form is not conducive or attractive to adolescent forms of communicating. Too lengthy pauses (rule of abstinence), characteristic of psychodynamic counselling, can be off-putting for young people (who soon become bored and unfocused) and may have to be shortened.

Rogers's core conditions in counselling are viewed by some as an artificial stance that represents a role of acting and 'mere artifice' (Masson, 1992). There can be no doubt that a therapeutic alliance will not form readily for those clients with delinquent tendencies if they *believe* their counsellors can never make mistakes at all, however much they attempt to show unconditional positive regard. In spite of person-centred approaches producing low recidivist rates for those with aggressive tendencies in closed centres (Dryden, 1984), schools generally cannot establish a closed therapeutic communal environment. However, there is no doubting that the Rogerian core condition of warmth and empathy is effective for change for many pupils whose home circumstances result in poor self-esteem and a sense of low personal worth (McGuiness, 1998).

The cognitive-behavioural model that relies upon interventions and client motivation (rather than a quality relationship) for change fits well in school. Pupils on leaving primary school tend to be weaned off the idea that their educational attainment depends upon them liking and forming a good relationship with their teacher, for realistically not all pupils will like their teachers. Although it is not the case for the disaffected, it is evident that bright pupils see teachers as stepping-stones to academic success. In consequence, an approach that aims at meeting specific aims without thereby having a quality relationship with the person administering the therapy will not be out of the ordinary in educational settings.

When adopting a watered-down version of family therapy, the typical 'neutral' stance of therapists practising in school can result in tension if feminists attempt to change social constructs that devalue girls amidst their parents, since it is an open question whether political goals should be the province of family-group counselling in school (Walters, 1990). Similarly, the challenging of homophobic parents of gay and lesbian pupils may be risky if parties are not seeking this counsel from practitioners in school. With narrative therapy, which works on the basis of challenging western narratives, and social construction theory, it is a different question, for the re-authoring of the client's life is done collaboratively.

Suitable techniques in school

In days of integration and eclecticism generally, the application of a technique outside its mother approach is not considered to be invalid (Culley, 1992). It is hardly surprising, therefore, that counsellors have experimented to good effect with many of the techniques that have arisen from varied schools of psychotherapy – no less so for working in educational settings.

While many counsellors find the theoretical base of Gestalt therapy a little technical and obscure, there is no doubt that many Gestalt techniques have proved highly effective and have become part of the general armoury of integrative practitioners. Counsellors are freely using the empty chair technique, are commonly challenging dis-ownership of 'one' statements for 'I' statements, pointing out the hidden meaning of body language, using the medium of painting and clay modelling to evoke feelings – for these do not rely upon language skills and articulation. They are similarly conducting, to powerful effect, projection exercises through material objects with an aim of encouraging catharsis. With the integration of such techniques into the repertoire of counselling interventions, it is worth recognizing the potential that this approach has for those pupils who have grown up within a familial context that is formal and that has not cultivated a healthy expression of ambivalent feelings. Nevertheless, the counselling practitioner will need training in some of these powerful techniques for stirring the emotions, and must not use them lightly.

Family therapy and its related approach, group therapy, work under a therapist style of neutrality that can be used in school, particularly when adopting the 'no blame' approach to fall-outs and bullying. Further, systemic family therapy has a range of techniques and interventions that the eclectic practitioner can use to good effect under a different model and approach; techniques which include 'sculpting' and 'enactment' as developed from psychodrama, along with 'reflexive circular questioning', 'reframing' and 'perceptual redefinition' (Burnham, 1986).

One requirement for much school counselling, irrespective of which approach or intervention is used, is that it should be brief. Counselling contracts need to be short-term. Adolescence is an active period of development where regular change in affective states, interests, priorities and behaviour is the norm. Teenagers are in a state of becoming, and for many their problems are short-lived. Long-term counselling, therefore, is not the general pattern within educational settings, not only because of stretched resources but also because for the vast majority of pupils their counselling needs are immediate and transitory.

BRIEF THERAPY

There is a universal need for quicker therapeutic remedies, and there is a pressing drive in the United States for more precise accountability of counselling from insurance companies, government policy-makers, consumer groups and judicial authorities (Dryden and Norcross, 1990). A similar trend is apparent in Britain in GP surgeries, voluntary agencies and the NHS (Thorne, 1999) with the move towards briefer ways of working and evidence-based therapy. No longer can counselling be viewed as a luxury, long-term indulgence, and this is the case in school counselling as elsewhere.

Accountability has led also to the integration movement in psychotherapy and to the demand for cost-effective brief methods of counselling.

Some therapists regard themselves as eclectic (Egan, 1990; Lazarus, 1990), others see themselves as integrationist (Nelson-Jones, 1999a; Norcross and Grencavage, 1989; Ryle, 1990). In this book, I use the term integration to cover an informed combination of theoretical notions and practical interventions from different schools of psychotherapy. Whatever confusion persists in how practitioners describe their work, what is crystal clear is that a radical change is taking place through the changing requirements of the counselling profession and the pressing demands for brief methods that can be shown to work.

Brief therapy is not a specific approach or a model of distinctive theory and practice, but a description of time-limited counselling. It is foreshortened practice of mother models (Feltham, 1997; Talmon, 1990; Thorne, 1994). Freud practised brief therapy when 'curing' Maler with only one session while walking in the woods. Although Freud was proud of the analysis of the psyche, he was disappointed that the process of therapy was lengthy. Short-term counselling has developed more in the public service institutions because of the pressure to become cost-effective and to reduce waiting lists (Butler and Low, 1994). A comprehensive review of brief therapy can be found in the literature for practitioners and teachers (Davis and Osborn, 2000; O'Connell, 1998).

The last decade has seen a proliferation of research on the efficacy of brief therapy (Lambert and Bergin, 1994), particularly for less severe difficulties, such as job-related stress, anxiety disorders, mild depression and grief reactions, and for unusual stress situations, such as PTSD, earthquake experience and rape. Improvement in brief therapy for clients having poor interpersonal relations is also supported by research (Koss and Shiang, 1994).

Moshe Talmon studied 10, 000 patients over a period of five years and found that the most common number of appointments for any orientation was one (Talmon, 1990). He had discovered that the majority of clients dropped out of counselling because they felt sufficiently helped and had no need of further support. Of 200 clients, 78 per cent said that they had got what they wanted after one session. Of a sample of clients receiving planned single-treatment programmes, 88 per cent felt they had improved and that they had no need for further work, and 79 per cent said that one session was enough (O'Connell, 1998).

Single sessions are not to be seen as a failure, therefore, but as a success. Other research on short-term counselling indicates positive outcomes. Meta-analysis shows a 15 per cent improvement before the first session began, 50 per cent improvement after eight sessions, 75 per cent by session 26 and 83 per cent by session 52 (Howard et al., 1986). An early large percentage rise in improvement, therefore, is followed by a slower rate as the number of sessions increases.

In addressing the move towards brief therapy, Thorne recognizes a tension within himself between the person-centred virtue of establishing the time-essential counselling relationship as the process for change, and

Table 4.1   *Annual log of counselling sessions (143 clients)*

Category	Clients in single-session therapy	Clients in multi-session therapy
Counselling sessions	44 = 31%	99 = 69%
Boys	26 = 18%	65 = 45%
Girls	18 = 13%	34 = 24%
Contracts		46 = 32%
Two sessions		57 = 40%
Three sessions		25 = 17%
Over three sessions		17 = 12%

his feelings about the success of an experiment he carried out when offering early morning three-session focused work to university students (Thorne, 1999). The short-term counselling achieved, in addition, a bonding with clients and a genuine commitment on their part to attend, and attend on time.

Some have pressed counsellors to assume that short-term counselling should be suitable for everyone until there is strong evidence that brief therapy simply does not work (Wolberg, 1968). When a client is aware of a time-limited period of counselling she may better handle the disclosure of deeper feelings (Thorne, 1999). She may also cope with frequent and more intense sessions, knowing the time-limitations of the work and her right to decide what to disclose and what to withhold.

Brief therapy is the form to which most school counselling is committed, for any contract less than 25 sessions is brief therapy. As indicated in Table 4.1, 31 per cent of my clients in one year came for a single session and 40 per cent for two sessions (ranging from 20 to 45 minutes). Three-session mini-contracts were offered to 17 per cent of clients with only 12 per cent of clients receiving more than three sessions. The longest contract was seven sessions (twelve the previous year).

Short session work implies a compromise in theoretical perspective with those therapies that contend that timely in-depth work is essential for the approach to be effective, but brief therapy is indicated for clients setting themselves more limited goals than traditional approaches. It represents an opportunity to arrive at goals and solutions more quickly by the 'direct' not the 'scenic route' (Davis and Osborn, 2000: 2). Brief therapy is not a quick fix, but something designed to be narrowly focused, with a planned short-term intervention that aims not for a complete 'cure' but merely to set the client on their way (Davis and Osborn, 2000).

The adolescent client may enter and exit from brief therapy from time to time on an outpatient/drop-in type of commitment, being supported in day-to-day schooling. The approach is ideal for those who see counselling as an intermittent support as particular crises occur.

A common characteristic of brief therapy is that the counsellor adopts a more active role, which, in my experience, is what young people generally prefer. The counsellor functions by structuring the sessions, by putting more stress on teaching and on clarity, and by concentrating on the specific. The therapeutic alliance has to be formed very quickly, which means that those pupil-clients who are unable to develop relationships quickly will not benefit from time-limited work (Feltham, 1997). Power challenges must be avoided, and the seeking of the best interests of the youngster must be communicated clearly. The pupil's definition of 'the problem' has to be accepted unequivocally by the counsellor.

The number of sessions may be few but spread out, with periodic reviews and evaluations. Clear and limited goals have to be set. The client's motivation must be evident at the outset and reflected in the goals that are set. Past successes are validated, encouraged and built upon, being expanded to establish a pay-off for the pupil that makes for a positive outcome. By affirming an adolescent's confidence and competence in social relations, the counsellor learns from them what will help most. A number of models lend themselves to brief work in school, and these will be reviewed before my personal integrative methodology is articulated.

EFFECTIVE BRIEF COUNSELLING APPROACHES IN SCHOOL

Time-limited goal-centred counselling

One popular model with counsellors working with young people is Egan's three-stage model (Egan, 1990; Mabey and Sorensen, 1995). Egan's three-stage model is built upon the core counselling skills of congruence, unconditional positive regard and empathy. However, this approach gives more attention to directing clients in the creation of goals and tasks to bring about change. It is a practical, short-term method of working which is centred on problem-solving. At the centre of the model is an assessment of where clients are, where they want to get and how they may be helped to get there. This three-stage model makes use of a broad range of techniques from other established therapies (particularly behaviour therapy).

In the introductory session the client's current scenario (Stage 1) is explored. It is not very different from introductory sessions of many forms of counselling. The person's present predicament and those problems that are standing in the way of healthy functioning are explored, but the style is optimistic. The counsellor will help the pupil-client to see clearly that the presented problem need not be a permanent condition. The pupil will be asked to articulate his story while an assessment is made in an attempt to bring blind spots to the attention of the youngster and to see them as the cause of his malfunctioning. The emphasis is on achievement as problems are outlined in an order of importance so that only those that are solvable can be selected. The aim is to help the client *manage a current situation better*.

Stage 2, or an outline of the ideal situation in which the client would wish to be, involves the setting of goals and objectives, and this fits neatly within modern education and records of achievement. The pragmatic course of conduct-screening (arranging conduct difficulties in order of priority for change) and the setting of down-to-earth, specific and realizable goals which are right for *this person* – changes in lifestyle, associations with different friends, doing things differently, or changing routinely established behavioural patterns – helps clients to see where the counselling is going and what is its purpose from the outset. The approach recognizes that the more the pupil frames the situation, the more she owns the means of remedy and the more she is committed.

The practical nature of Stage 3 is equally attractive to young people in that it encourages a collaboration between counsellor and client in devising an action plan to attain the specified goals. It reaches outside the counselling arena in calling upon agents of support, which include people, places, things, organizations and the client's personal resources, in order to bring about change. This method has the attraction of being short-term, so that counselling closes with the accomplishment of the plan by the attainment of its goals. Evaluation is not left to the end, but takes place regularly – '*Is this helping*? *Is this making sense*?' It is in keeping with learning measures of continual assessment.

Motivational Interviewing (Miller and Rollnick, 1991) is a brief goal-centred style which helps people suffering from addictive or habit-forming behaviour to bring about change through a process of insight and active behaviour management. Motivational Interviewing (MI) has been applied to drug and alcohol abuse, offending behaviour, smoking, exercising, eating habits, patterns of relationships and sexual behaviours (Devere, 2000). The client is first encouraged to adress ambivalent views of continuing or ceasing the habit-formed behaviour, and then to enter the Cycle of Change (Prochaska and DiClemente, 1982) through free will and self-regulation. The brief introduction to the model (Devere, 2000) is initially offered to the client for understanding. The Cycle of Change (Figure 4.1) moves from 'contemplation' to 'determination' to 'action' to 'maintenance' to 'relapse', then back to 'contemplation' again. The client suffering from addictive behaviour may enter or exit the circle at any time. After relapse, for example, the client may return to the cyclic process with higher motivation to tackle the addiction again. Alternatively, the addicted client may internalize the model so as to serve as a future tool of recovery outside the counselling session, which holds out hope for long-term possibilities.

Refocusing on solutions

A number of brief therapies have evolved in recent years that are sensitive to the power of language in socially constructing people's lives. These include solution-focused therapy, narrative therapy and collaborative language systems.

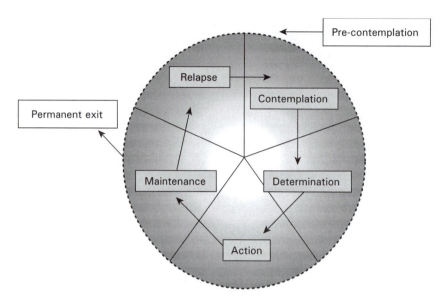

Figure 4.1   *Cycle of change*
Source: This diagram format was published in 'New models: the counselling of change' by Merav Devere, which appeared in the August 2000 issue of *Counselling* journal of the British Association for Counselling: This diagram is reproduced with the kind permission of the author and publisher.

The pragmatic, future-orientated style of solution-focused therapy (SFT) works step by step, encouraging clients to put into practice their self-selected goals, and has proved effective with as few as three sessions, the average being from four to six. It has been extensively used in education (Davis and Osborn, 2000; Durrant, 1993; Lethem, 1994; Rhodes and Ajmal, 1995) for empowering pupils to use their own resources in practical ways to solve conflicts in a non-blaming framework. The 'miracle question' (O'Connell, 1998) is enticing to the youngster's imagination: *Imagine you woke up one morning and a miracle had occurred and everything you had wanted to change had taken place. How would you know the miracle had taken place? What would be different? What would be happening that has not been happening before? What would you be doing that you're not doing at the moment? What else…?* The emphasis thereby moves from 'problem deliberation' towards a 'future pictorial' focus, towards viewing life without 'the problem'.

The co-constructed engagement with the therapist offers the client self-respect in the mutual entertainment of small changes of mental outlook to improve mood, communication or behaviour that is in line with his goal. Accurate assessment in *fixing only that which is broke*, in looking for *small change to bring about bigger change*, and the collaborative process of *keeping going that which is working* and *stopping that which is not working* highlight the empirical attraction of SFT (O'Connell, 1998).

The future orientation draws the pupil's attention from problem-saturated talk towards what might be: *When will you know when you're ready to leave counselling? What will have happened so that you no longer need my support?* The technique of scaling helps the pupil to maintain a true sense of objectivity and a means of measuring improvement that does not rely on inaccurate recall. The feedback to the client at the close of the session assimilates the client's deliberations and the counsellor's perceptions in shared discourse. This positive, non-critical and non-patronizing feedback motivates the youngster towards a successful outcome by praising his successes and validating his personal resources.

Collaborative ways of working

The validating of subjective experience in narrative therapy fits the philosophical climate of the postmodern world, and the highlighting of stories with which we make sense of personal experience is compelling for young people (Epston et al., 1992). Narrative therapy relies heavily upon social inter-relatedness and dialogue, which are two distinct tasks in adolescent development. Through collaborative dialogue, the client experiences the counsellor both as neutral and as an equal, with none of the disciplinary distancing that normally characterizes pupil–teacher relations.

The intervention of 'externalizing of the problem' (White, 1989) encourages the client to separate problems from the self, and to minimize unproductive conflict between people, particularly disputes over who is responsible. It undermines the sense of failure and paves the way for individuals to co-operate with each other. It opens up new possibilities for teenagers to take action to retrieve their lives, and it enables them to take a lighter, more effective approach to 'deadly serious' problems. Finally, it presents options for dialogue rather than monologue, about the problem.

Many young clients have a story to tell: a story of hurt, bewilderment, anger or disappointment; a story of an opportunity lost or of a relationship that has broken down. The therapist adopts a pose of 'interested inquiry' as she confronts a narrative that is persuasive and compelling. This stance of respectful curiosity communicates high esteem for troubled adolescents, since the therapist looks perpetually for areas of competence to combat the effects of the problem on the client.

The 'plot of the alternative story' invites the client to give explanations for those unique experiences which hint at more positive aspects of the client's personality, and this helps the emergence of their own resources to achieve pro-social outcomes. Through the counselling process, the counsellor helps the client see where the alternative story may have begun and where it may be developing. The closing techniques of what is termed 're-authored lives' in written narrative (Epston et al., 1992; White and Epston, 1990) may have limited effect in some cases, and the technique of enlisting an 'outside witness' group or 'audience' to consolidate the new narrative may not be practical. But documents of change (certificates, etc.) have undoubted merit in strengthening the significance of improvement for young people (Winslade and Monk, 1999).

The conversational metaphor of other forms of narrative therapy (Gergen and Kaye, 1992) encourages clients to explore their life meaning through many narratives. The open-ended nature of collaborative discourse for new meaning (Anderson and Goolishian, 1988) is useful for challenging older students who instinctively reject presented formulas of life-meanings. Postmodern consciousness favours a thoroughgoing relativism in expressions of identity, a multiplicity of accounts, and this approach has potential in brief spiritual counselling where youngsters wish to explore life meanings through presented signposts and templates.

Mind skills techniques

In addition to brief cognitive-behavioural counselling, another brief approach that has merit in school settings is Nelson-Jones's cognitive-humanistic counselling – a cognitive way of working that espouses the values of humanistic psychology and person-centred counselling (Nelson-Jones, 1999b). The emphasis on the primacy of mind underlying all affective states that are not autonomic responses, resonates with the way that many young people function. Young people can develop 'self-talk' to acknowledge the importance of listening to and understanding their feelings. They use their *minds* to manage unwanted feelings like anxiety, to question the reality of anxiety-evoking perceptions and to see how closely they match the facts (Nelson-Jones, 1999b).

'The Life Skills Counselling Approach' (Nelson-Jones, 1997) aims to encourage youngsters to take a pride in shared secular values through daily attendance to, say, altruism and compassion, rather than ignorance and selfishness. It sees the goal as empowering clients to develop their own humanity through appropriate owning and disowning of areas of responsibility, and so becomes a fitting model for adolescent development and autonomy. The 'mind skills' techniques of creating 'rules for governing', and the offering of perceptions, explanations and expectations, are powerful in regulating affective states and in shaping more productive lives. The teaching of partner skills in developmental education (Nelson-Jones, 1999a) builds 'the foundation for a more humane and compassionate family life', as well as sowing the 'seeds for future generations to possess better mind and communication skills' (Nelson-Jones, 1999b: 52–3). The particular skills of 'self-talk' and 'visual imaging' have applicability to young people in school in anger management and self-control at times when they have felt ridiculed and wound up and when they have felt their peers were laughing at them.

INTEGRATING PERSONAL STYLE

The issue of matching school counsellor with pupil-client has been discussed elsewhere (Lines, 2000), but appropriate therapy involves other considerations. For each case, practice issues exist for tailoring the approach and the technique to the presented problem. These call for early decisions and include:

- an assessment of whether there is a counselling task at all;
- the decision of who is the client – the pupil, the parent, or both;
- an assessment of the principal mode of client functioning (feelings, cognition, behaviour);
- the theoretical model to be selected for the presented problem: the choice of one model used exclusively, or an integration of models; whether to opt for individual or group therapy, or whether family members might be requested to come into school for counselling using a systemic style of therapy;
- the particular intervention/s to bring about a positive outcome.

All clients will have a dominant mode of functioning. Some function intuitively and others empirically. Some prefer to engage in a practical task, while others benefit from a cathartic expression of feelings. Cognitive therapy is suitable for those who function cerebrally, while Gestalt therapy has tended to appeal to those operating in an imaginative mode, such as pupils having an artistic and poetical bias.

The experienced practitioner will decide on his approach intuitively when listening to the referral data. He might revise such decisions as the work progresses, modifying contracts and programmes of work at significant stages as the focus is altered or through review and supervision. As the young client sits before me and describes the problem, it is not given as raw data without a context. The problem is presented within a narrative, a narrative that is supported by a range of stories, which collectively are the client's reality. Whether the problem is considered as residing within the person's head or located in her relational world, there will emerge a narrative that depicts a perspective, or range of perspectives, on how she sees the world or how she perceives the world as treating her.

But I learn as much from how something is said as from what is said; as much from how my client presents himself as from the words that make up the sentences; as much from the hesitancy and pausing, the holding back, the momentary reflection, the intensity of displayed emotion and the energy in delivery. Should I allocate time and sit back in psychodynamic opaque pose and allow for unconscious processes to emerge? Should I take up a person-centred stance and follow where my client will lead me? Alternatively, should I intervene at points for clearer understanding and attempt to structure each story in order to draw out what unconscious beliefs may underlie them?

When implementing a referral screening methodology during the introductory session, I ask 'What is going on in my head?' For while I cannot know what is in my client's mind, I know what is in mine. In my mind I rapidly run through a catalogue of styles and approaches that are filed away through learning, practice and experience.

Should I engage in spiritual counselling or existential therapy to explore her sense of being, her spirituality, her philosophical outlook? Should the counselling be directive and have a pedagogical emphasis? Is there a precise problem that can be addressed with solution-focused approaches, or is there a need to explore deeper and unclear levels of what to this point has not been articulated? Is the problem merely about solving a dispute between peers or between child and adult that might indicate a referral to a pastoral teacher or other agency, or is there a more comprehensive requirement to help my client with adaptive social skills because of more general communication difficulties? Is there a need to facilitate the expression of my client's sadness and validate her sense of loss through humanistic counselling, or is cognitive therapy indicated to help her rise above a depressive state, or, alternatively, to combine the best in each with cognitive-humanistic counselling? Should I engage in individual work or in couple counselling? Is there a need for in-depth work, or merely the passing on of information? These types of questions run through my mind as the client's material slowly unfolds and as the story becomes clear.

One research finding has particular relevance for young clients in educational settings. Discussing Lambert's research (1992), Davis and Osborn (2000: 25–8) highlight the importance of therapeutic factors outside the counselling room that contribute towards a successful outcome. Aspects of the client's life are termed extra-therapeutic, and are viewed as personal and environmental resources for change – for young people, they include friendships, family support and fortuitous events. These represent the largest contributory factor to successful outcome (40 per cent), followed by the counselling relationship (30 per cent), expectancy of positive change (15 per cent) and specific techniques (15 per cent).

In consequence, I become aware of extra-therapeutic details through finely tuned questioning and interested inquiry. But in the process, I must not lose my attachment to my client, for the counselling relationship (the second influencing factor for change) should not be forfeited for any unconscious wish to impress the young person by my expertise or sophisticated techniques. Whether timely interventions are made, or I sit in silent attention, my client is weighing me up, testing out the fantasy: can I be trusted, and does the direct experience of me today confirm or deny what has been heard within the home–school community? Whether I steer or facilitate my client's feelings, my counselling merit can only be evident for *this* person, and addressing *this* problem, within *this* particular context. Will the relationship itself be the catalyst for change, or will it serve as the conduit through which to deliver an intervention for progress? Is it the means of awareness-raising and empowerment, the process through which inner resources are discovered, or the means of instilling a degree of commitment to alter thinking and behaving to make things happen?

Outcome research suggests the need for careful screening in the introductory session and such data should inform counselling choice and preference. Miller et al. (1997) recommend that outcome research should enlighten practice rather than press for new models of counselling, but practitioner bias will nevertheless assert itself.

Most counsellors will have a bias even if they regard themselves as eclectic or integrationist. Although I am drawn towards the psychodynamic theoretical framework in understanding adolescent developmental needs and symptomology, in practice I am drawn towards the cognitive-behavioural approach and solution-focused styles within Egan's three-stage framework – yet always in the context of brief therapy. These leanings are largely influenced by how I function in my relational world and attempt to resolve personal difficulties. Given time, I confess to finding narrative therapy and spiritual counselling fascinating when the client's material suggests they may be of assistance.

Regarding practice bias, then, I suspect I look unconsciously to the merits of cognitive task-centred approaches in assisting my client to solve her problems. The client's evolving story will indicate, however, whether these suffice or whether I am rushing her unethically for a quick fix. So, although I am steered towards blends of Egan's three-stage model, cognitive and solution-focused brief approaches, the interchanges and cross flow of ideas, feelings and gestures are serving as checks and counterbalances to whether these styles are fitting.

Ideologically, I am drawn to the person-centred notion that my client knows best – even given the dependent status of young people and the fact that I am *in loco parentis* – since this insight strikes a chord with my belief system. Young people are 'experts' about their own experience. My aim, whatever approach I use as the means, is to help my clients resolve their own difficulties. I am committed to enabling them to find solutions from their personal resources. I have faith in human beings and the human spirit for healing and mediation, and will occasionally leave angry or upset youngsters together for self-recovery, without my presence (after laying ground rules ar d prejudging the potential risks with the characters involved).

I might, given a cue from one of those salient comments or emotional discharges that I call 'a gateway into the client's self', adopt a wholly person-centred or other traditional approach quite exclusively. I might modify the model or form a hybrid by introducing an intervention or technique from another approach. A request to alter a situation quickly might direct me to adopt a solution-focused approach in seeking a practical remedy. On the other hand, an unclear or ambiguous difficulty might indicate the need to travel with her on a life journey through the philosophical framework and tools of narrative therapy or spiritual counselling, as far as possible within a brief time-frame.

I have no overriding approach, then, or specific model for each and every client and her problem, but allow, through the dialogue, the appropriate model to emerge. A theoretical mould is not pre-selected for every presented dilemma in order to satisfy my ego or intellectual pride, but the client's material is the controlling feature of what to use. The information being disclosed becomes the dominating factor of where and how counselling should move, for the counsellor, not the client, must be adaptive. Counselling 'entails knowing who your clients are and adapting your counselling to fit or match their worldview, developmental level, values and ideals, communication style, and other distinctive aspects or idiosyncrasies' (Davis and Osborn, 2000: xiii). I do not wish to create a new approach or model, give it a catchy title, and demonstrate its efficacy, for this is constraining and falls foul of what has been said above about the potential dynamic of my client's narrative. No, the wheel no longer requires reinventing but needs to be used in different ways for particular clients in the setting in which therapy is conducted.

5

LOW SELF-ESTEEM, DEPRESSION AND SUICIDAL THOUGHTS

Depression may be viewed on a continuum where low self-esteem is at one end and suicidal thoughts are at the other. It is hoped that all forms of counselling raise self-esteem for clients. The very fact of arranging an appointment in school is an indication that whatever the presented problem the pupil-client's difficulties are being taken seriously and warrant attention. Whether the matter is advice over a predicament, an exploration of options to improve a situation, or the provision of a temporary holding arena to explore an issue for insight, the client is likely to have experienced a lowering of self-esteem. Traditional humanistic models have been effective in raising self-esteem and the client's sense of personal dignity, but these approaches may need adapting under the time-limited constraints of an educational setting.

'Clinical depression' in young people is likely to have been first diagnosed by a psychiatrist and addressed at off-site clinics through medication and cognitive-behavioural counselling. Many young people in school, however, can on occasion become 'depressed', or 'depressive' in their relational world, which indicates the need for brief, less intensive, cognitive-behavioural techniques without medication. It is essential that practitioners make use of these techniques in time-limited and integrated models of counselling, not merely to lift the spirits of young clients but to get them *on their way*.

It is recognized that some adolescents may experience suicidal thoughts. These nihilistic impulses are rarely thought out, but are articulated to friends or are written on scraps of paper for significant adults to 'discover'. They are cries for help. Nevertheless, they are real feelings that need addressing promptly. In general, youngsters who talk about suicide seldom take their lives, but it would be irresponsible not to take action merely from such an observation. The practitioner must consider how best to support young clients who on occasion entertain suicidal thoughts, and it is important to distinguish between planned attempts at suicide (where teenagers are clearly at risk) and suicidal thoughts.

All abused young people are likely to suffer low self-esteem in varying degrees, particularly through puberty. If the pupil-client is suffering from neglect, then peers who pressurize individuals to dress fashionably and to look 'attractive', to be clean and not to smell of body odour, will undoubtedly single them out for ridicule.

Those who have been physically abused may have poor social skills for relationship building as a result of fear, a lack of confidence or inadequate role models. Alternatively, their bullying behaviour may result in them being mistrusted by peers who will not have the capacity to understand why they are aggressive. Boys may devalue women staff through internalized family attitudes of male dominance, and girls may have developed a victim-identity.

If clients have suffered sexual abuse, the invisible emotional scars will run deep and may surface at the time of puberty and after, where sexual feelings and behaviours become overwhelmingly confusing and complicated in most young people. Counselling the sexually abused in brief therapy may be over-ambitious, but there are cases where therapeutic support has never before been offered, or has been thwarted due to lengthy legal proceedings, that require immediate therapy if only to 'hold' a youngster through a current crisis. The counselling practitioner must attend to this pressing need within the constraints of school and curriculum pressures.

RESEARCH ON STRESS AND DEPRESSION

Research on the continuum from low self-esteem to depressive and suicidal thoughts has revealed some helpful insights on the aetiology and management of stress. From an evolutionary point of view, response to stress has been an advantage to humans in coping with the demands of a primitive environment (Gregson and Looker, 1994). When under stress, three 'stress chemicals' come into play. As with a cornered animal under attack, human beings may fight using anger in order to survive, and this highly charged state causes increased levels of noradrenaline and adrenaline. Alternatively, with the emotion of fear, the instinctive response is to escape. Under such stress, increased levels of adrenaline, noradrenaline and cortisol come into play.

Adrenaline and noradrenaline put the body into a state of high alert: fighting or escaping requires much oxygen, so breathing becomes deeper and faster – under stress, we feel unduly exhausted. Cortisol, by contrast, induces depressive moods, in which a submissive stance of rolling over helplessly and handing over control to others occurs (McGuiness, 1998). Cortisol mobilizes our glucose and fat stores, sensitizes the immune system and reduces inflammatory reactions. All three chemicals decrease when human beings are relaxed. When youngsters experience being loved and supported and are in harmony with their social and natural environment they become less stressed.

Symptoms of high stress include increased heartbeat, palpitations, shallow breathing, a dry mouth, heartburn, queasy stomach, diarrhoea, constipation, muscular tension in the neck and shoulders, aches, pains, cramps, hyperactivity, finger-drumming, foot-tapping, nail-biting, trembling hands, fatigue, exhaustion, disturbed sleep patterns, feeling faint or dizzy, sweatiness, raised levels of smoking and alcohol intake, and decreased sexual activity. As McGuiness says, 'We are living highly stressed lives, and while the symptoms above can be the result of other life factors, they are identified by Gregson and Looker (1994) as indicators of stress' (1998: 113).

Clients can learn how to relax, however, through relaxation exercises, yoga, meditation, guided imagery and by use of Gestalt techniques to develop tranquillity and serenity (Oaklander, 1978). Often clients say that they 'can't relax', when what they mean is they are 'choosing not to relax'. Breathing exercises are invaluable through a range of breathing techniques (Kilty and Bond, 1991) in combination with regular exercise. Caffeine should be reduced under conditions of high stress. Techniques of relaxation and meditation exercises can help to bring clients down from states of high tension to lower mood states before integrative techniques of other approaches are used.

Psychological factors are known to produce low self-esteem and depression. High stress and depression result when an individual becomes overwhelmed by a loss of personal control. We all become stressed with change, particularly over major losses, but adolescents have the added ingredient of hormonal activity during puberty. Adams's (1976) patterns of high stress include *immobilization* (where clients shut-down in a self-protective way) and *depression* (where anger, despair, helplessness and hopelessness are the emotions which accompany behaviours such as lashing out, swearing, verbal aggression and a feeling that nothing is worth the candle). A depressed youngster may demonstrate extreme opposites in behaviour, ranging from social withdrawal to anti-social over-reactions, which makes the level of depression not easy to ascertain or quantify.

There is research to suggest that depressed people see the world more clearly, though more pessimistically, than those of us who are 'well' and who live behind a screen that obscures the stark realities of life (Alloy and Abramson, 1982).

Cognitive therapy is the classic approach for dealing with 'clinical depression' (Beck et al., 1979), but clients whose lowering in self-esteem borders closely on depression can also be lifted in spirit by utilizing features of Beck's work. Beck speaks of the damaging effects of 'automatic thoughts' and recommends that clients should, through therapy, 'refocus themselves from negative thoughts'. Cognitive therapy is an active, directive, time-limited and structured procedure based on the assumption that affect and behaviour are largely determined by the way we structure our world. The therapeutic method of change is through interview and cognitive-behavioural techniques. However, interviewing depressed people is not easy because of their inertia and indecisiveness, and in order to change learned patterns cognitive-behavioural techniques require a more controlled setting and more time than is always possible in school.

In spite of these drawbacks, 'the techniques of questioning, of identifying illogical thinking, of ascertaining the rules according to which the patient reorganizes reality' (Beck et al., 1979: 142) can be effectively applied in conjunction with Nelson-Jones's effective thinking skills (Nelson-Jones, 1996). Time-limited counselling which recognizes the relation of 'cognition' to 'anxiety' and which integrates this with goal-centred therapy is likely to prove effective in school for youngsters low in self-esteem.

COUNSELLING TO RAISE SELF-ESTEEM

Person-centred counselling puts emphasis upon the counselling relationship as the fundamental factor for change, and this sits comfortably with educational trends of pupil-centred learning. John McGuiness (1998) sketches the development in education of raising self-esteem through quality relationships. He finds comfort, he adds, in the vast corpus of psychological evidence that his ethical position has empirical support (Brammer and Shostrum, 1982; Carkhuff and Berenson, 1977; Norcross and Grencavage, 1989; Rogers, 1967; Truax and Carkhuff, 1967). He stresses the importance of seeing every individual pupil as unique and of intrinsic value and dignity, and speaks of a need for a school ethos where there are no losers but all are winners.

If a school counsellor is viewed positively by the school community – pupils, parents and staff – then a youngster's spirits will be uplifted by the very act of being offered one-to-one interaction with *this person* at *this time*. Self-esteem therefore rises almost before a word has been uttered. Conversely, if the counsellor is viewed negatively and the session results in the client feeling belittled for not being able to cope without speaking with the 'professional' (say, having to see the 'shrink'), then stigma results in a reinforcement of low self-esteem.

For brief counselling, the interpretative-explanatory dimension is not as important as *what can be done* about the problem. Two further techniques I find effective with overly sad young people are 'diversion' techniques, and a judicious use of humour and irony (Beck et al., 1979: 171–3). Diversions encourage the client to re-focus from the whirlpool of sadness through activities that require exercise and movement (particularly when accompanied by sensory experiencing), and humour discharges tension and heightens wellbeing. One bereaved client I see intermittently enjoys the sharing of jokes to lighten his depressed spirit. When he enters my room to protest about a minor hardship and wears a stern frown that says in effect 'You'd better take this seriously', I look at him in a certain way that makes him smile and this settles him from his angry state and enables him to cope with the matter more productively.

In raising a pupil's self-esteem, I have found it possible to integrate all that is beneficial in the person-centred approach with the fast-moving styles of cognitive therapy, particularly cognitive-humanistic counselling (Nelson-Jones, 1999b). The aim of the humanistic element is to help the client gain access to material in his person, material that is hurting, reducing effectiveness, and that is depressing or diminishing him. Sometimes painful material is within the defence system. The idea that we will accidentally set free some monster if material is aired, fails to take into account the powerful psychological mechanisms that the client has in place to suppress distressing material.

Phillip was referred for counselling by teaching staff for being withdrawn and socially isolated. Pastoral teachers commented on how supportive they had found his mother, who was devastated to discover that he had truanted from school for three weeks. Local residents had seen him sitting alone and looking glum in the park. Phillip was very unhappy. His mother was in a new relationship after splitting up with Phil's father, and was planning for the family (Phil and his younger brother) to move into her new partner's own property after marriage, much against Phillip's wishes. Being 16 and in his final school year, his social circle was restricted to the area where he had been brought up, and he was adamant that if his mother moved, then he was staying. He was confident that his friend's parents would put him up, and asserted that he would run away when the time came. This was not his greatest worry, however. His father was 'addicted' to drugs, and occasionally took heroin. He felt that he would get no sympathetic audience from his mother in voicing his fears to her, after all 'that's why I left him', she said, along with the 'drinking and getting knocked about'. Although he acknowledged this, he still worried about him and couldn't get him out of his mind, especially with Christmas coming up. He had visions of 'seeing him in an alleyway stoned' and 'out of his mind'.

Phillip recounted his last two visits to his father, both of which were weekend stay overs. He felt rejected by his father who showed no special pleasure in seeing him or taking him out, nor did he treat him as special. Instead Phillip was left with his paternal grandmother while his dad went out 'with his mates'. What hurt him most was seeing needle syringe marks on his father's lower arm. 'What's the use of going over? It does my head in. I can't hack it', he said, while breaking down in tears. Crying in front of a male counsellor doesn't come easy for boys, but he sobbed and sobbed in my presence. On his last visit, his dad had come home drunk, and when Phillip challenged him, he became violent and ordered him back to his mother's home, 'Get back to your mother!' From that moment he vowed never to see him again, and ceased seeing him on alternate weekends, but this didn't stop the worrying.

After a week, however, he regretted his decision, but his mother, in order to protect his feelings, this time put her foot down and stopped him from seeing his father for the time being. It was this adamant refusal that had caused Phillip to be sad, and in session he was visibly very low indeed.

Phillip's teachers had recognized his low self-esteem and lack of motivation and industry in schoolwork. His form tutor said that in form periods he had always been jocular and carefree, but had been downcast and dejected in recent weeks. Phillip's expression of his feelings of being rejected by his dad was facilitated by the core conditions and active listening skills. The brief integrative-cognitive elements of therapy are elaborated in further detail.

In addressing Phillip's problem, it appeared that there were two elements that had resulted in his sadness and low self-esteem. One was his thinking and the other his behaving.

Counselling stage I

Phillip identified two relationship difficulties: one was his relationship with his father and the other his relationship with himself. The latter was selected first.

The images of 'seeing his dad injecting' and 'seeing him huddled up in a doorway on a cold wintry night' were not pleasant images. First, we carried out *reality testing* dialogue (Nelson-Jones, 1996) by a series of questions aimed at establishing the likelihood of each scenario.

- How often does dad shoot heroin?
- Is there evidence of him *managing* heroin rather than being managed by heroin?
- Does dad have a supportive network of friends and family to suggest that it would not be likely that he would be left abandoned in a doorway?

Of particular benefit to youngsters who get stuck are the mind-skills techniques of creating 'self-talk' and 'visual imaging' (Nelson-Jones, 1996). These techniques address the thinking behind feelings. When Phillip pondered the answers to these questions his heavy spirit was lightened. The next stage addressed the negative image of the time he last saw his father. The destructive dismissal – 'Get back to your mother!' – burnt deep into his sensitive mind like a branding iron. It is very common for the last words spoken by an enraged parent to remain indelibly imprinted in the memory. The next stage, therefore, was to help Phillip to reconstruct a more positive mental image. 'What occasion has been the most pleasant time you have spent with your dad?' Phillip spoke of a time he had gone to Ireland fishing with his dad, when, on the last night, they had a barbecue and discussed future plans together. He was asked to practise a mental switch from the indelible words 'Get back to your mother!' to 'Well that's the end of our holiday, son. It's time to get back to your mother.' This was practised by rote till he felt able to make the switch unconsciously. I would look at him from a distance, nod my head, and he would rehearse the modified script.

While he recognized his limited responsibility in his parent's decisions and separation, he had *owned too much* responsibility for his feelings over his subsequent parting from dad. 'The life skills counselling approach' (Nelson-Jones, 1997) was adapted to empower Phil to develop his humanity through appropriate owning and disowning of areas of responsibility. Phillip was encouraged through counselling to explore where the responsibility lay in his father's condition and lifestyle, his mother's attitude over the divorce and his own part in the process (Beck et al., 1979).

Counselling stage 2

Change had begun with Phil's modified outlook. Bill O'Connell (1998) presents the SFT credo of *fixing only that which is broke*, and more particularly the notion that *small change brings about bigger change*, through a co-constructed engagement of client and therapist. Davis and Osborn (2000) similarly speak of the 'ripple' or the 'domino' effect, where a small change in the client's thinking or behaving can produce an exponential rate of improvement. The authors also illustrate the value of 'instead' talk, which I find particularly effective with young people.

In attempting to effect further change and avoid Phillip indulging in 'problem-saturated' talk, we agreed *not to fix that which was not broken*, which he identified as his relationship with his mother, but rather to set a goal for restoring his relationship with his dad. In setting practical goals, it was important to set a goal that was achievable. In education in Britain, pupils are encouraged to set SMART targets, which means they must be Specific, Measurable, Achievable, Relevant and Time-limited. Similarly, in solution-focused counselling, goals must be Specific, Concrete, and Measurable, for 'Goal formulation establishes and maintains a focus for counselling', and serves as 'A road trip with a specific destination in mind' (Davis and Osborn, 2000: 64–5).

A range of goals was brainstormed which included:

1 Do I ignore mum and after making contact go over to see dad over the weekend?
2 Should I write to dad or contact him by phone?
3 Should I forget about dad for the time being and wait for him to contact me?

Teenagers need support in goal-setting, which though collaboratively designed needs a little steering with pupils whose condition borders on depression (Beck et al., 1979). Adolescents may take uncalculated risks if the goals they have constructed are ambitious and not thought through. With goal 1, there was the delicate issue of 'ignoring mum' and, recalling the principle of *not fixing something that isn't broke*, Phillip evaluated the short- and long-term effects of this. Phillip was reminded of mum's dormant feelings over her ex-husband, which were stirred after his dad cruelly sent him home. Feelings and emotions, actions and behaviours are not difficult to change, but with attitudes it is another question. Occasionally with similar cases in which young clients wish to behave in a manner which challenges deeply ingrained attitudes and prejudices, I suggest that they try the 'drip test', which the Japanese mastered in the last war to get POWs to release secrets. Challenging head-on entrenched attitudes like a bull at a gate causes people to remain fixed behind an impregnable fortress of stubbornness, but letting parents know what is deeply felt over something a little at a time, regularly and consistently, like a drip, drip, drip, proves more effective in softening hardened attitudes.

The more Phil thought this through, the more he felt it would not work. He selected instead goal 2, which was to write to dad. The closing sessions of counselling were given over to helping Phil compose a letter to his dad. His first attempt was altered after collaborative work with the technique of 'Instead Talk' (Davis and Osborn, 2000).

Dear Dad,

I'm sorry we fell out last time but I was not to blame. You know it scares me when you get into drugs. Mum is angry and won't let me come. I was going to come last week; can I come this weekend?

Love Phil

xxx

Counsellor: Though it's your letter, Phil, and it's a good idea to write, I wonder if I could make some suggestions?

Phil was content for this to happen.

Counsellor: Instead of 'I was not to blame', could we think of a phrase that would not apportion blame?

He came up with the alternative: 'Perhaps we both lost our tempers.'

Counsellor: Is it wise to bring up past battles between mum and dad, I wonder? What can be put instead of mentioning mum? How about, 'Mum doesn't understand how much you mean to me.'

Phillip: Yea.
Counsellor: Could we soften the request by recalling the good time you had in
              Ireland, I wonder?

His final letter was sent and this closed our brief work with the satisfactory outcome of him regularly visiting his dad on alternate weekends:

Dear Dad,

I'm sorry we fell out last time, perhaps we both lost our tempers. You know it scares me when you don't look after yourself. I miss you so much. Mum doesn't understand how much you mean to me. I remember the great time we had together in Ireland, we got on so well, and I would love to come over as soon as you can spare the time to see me. I can be free any weekend.

Love Phil

xxx

COUNSELLING DEPRESSED YOUNG PEOPLE

Some levels of stress are actually enjoyable for adolescents whereby they seek this physiological state of pleasure through ploys of daring and through risk-taking activities. But there is an optimum amount of stress for each individual, and once that peak has passed the negative effects begin to kick in (Yerkes and Dodson, 1993). Thus we need to be alert to the danger signals and *take action*.

It is likely that external factors have brought about depressive states if the pupil has shown a rapid alteration in mood – factors such as major personal losses or communal trauma, being in trouble, or undergoing transition and change during vulnerable periods (McGuiness, 1998). Again, the work of Nelson-Jones on mind skills can prove useful for young people in temporary depressive states.

Ann-Marie entered secondary school under pressure because of having to manage severe eczema all over her body. So severe was her skin condition, which was clearly visible on her face, that she required the medical room at odd periods through the day to cream her skin to prevent irritation. She said that her condition was worse when she was tense. Through year seven she coped quite well, but part way through her next year peer pressure over her complexion and a little bit of name-calling began to have an effect on her self-esteem. By the Easter term, she had ceased attending school for reasons, claimed the educational social worker, 'of depression'.

Her mother paid a visit to speak about difficulties with her other child, and in passing I asked her about Ann-Marie. She became visibly distressed and said that she did not know where to turn. She said that Ann-Marie had refused to leave the house and was permanently depressed. I asked her what had happened during year seven that was successful but which did not appear to be happening now. Her mother was thrown by the solution-focussed form of question (O'Connell, 1998) and paused for a while before saying, 'I suppose school has become more difficult.' I requested her to ask Ann-Marie if she would try attending our School Restart Programme (a room set aside with one teacher dedicated to charting a course for nervous pupils by speaking with teachers and learning groups) to aid her cross the barrier of first entry. She was also offered counselling to help explore her self-image in the peer group, since, I continued, 'Many pupils find transition to senior school difficult at first, but Ann-Marie strode over the first difficult hurdle and fell at the third or fourth.' Her mother appeared very anxious and protective, but agreed to give it a go. I was wondering how much this mother–daughter bonding might have become a little too enmeshed within a circle of anxiety whereby the stress and worry of failure from one was ricocheting on to the other.

During the opening session, her mother sat close to Ann-Marie, but did not answer for her. Ann-Marie was keen to try again with school since she was fed up with staying at home, and said, 'I am sinking under depression.' She was dislocated from friends, imprisoned in the home and socially isolated. The aim was to use means of engaging her in a larger social world, to 'distract' her from her preoccupation with 'depression', and, in one sense, she had recognized it. She was extremely polite and subservient, and was very keen to work with me. There was optimism from Ann-Marie and myself about a positive outcome, but her mother remained unsure. Ann-Marie's mother was asked politely if she minded leaving Ann-Marie in school for the afternoon, at which Ann-Marie immediately intervened with, 'I'll be all right, mum. You do the shopping. I'll come home with Simon.' It has often proved more profitable in school to separate mother from child in cases of enmeshed relationships (Berkowitz, 1987), since collective anxiety tends to be more than the product of two anxious persons – both parties feed off each other, and the triggers are not always clear.

Ann-Marie was asked how she understood her condition. She explained that she got so depressed she didn't know what to do.

Counsellor:	How do you understand depression?
Ann-Marie:	I think it's feeling so fed up you don't want to go on, but want to give up.
Counsellor:	What do you mean by, 'You don't want to go on?'
Ann-Marie:	I don't mean committing suicide or anything like that. I mean giving up. It's all too much effort.
Counsellor:	How is your energy being taken up?
Ann-Marie:	By having to cream up ... putting up with the insults ... and ... going home angry.
Counsellor:	Do you get angry at home?
Ann-Marie:	Yes, quite often.

Counsellor:	Although anger and depression are similar, I wonder which of the two is setting you back at the moment?
Ann-Marie:	Depression, I would say.
Counsellor:	I wonder if we could consider seeing anger and depression a little differently. People often speak of anger as though it is part of their personality. They may say that 'something' has made them angry, or 'someone' has made them angry, but it is still 'them' that is angry. Depression is something similar. People speak of being 'depressed', or of 'getting depressed', as though depression is part of them. In the same way as people describe so and so as 'jolly' or 'outgoing', by which they see 'outgoing-ness' and 'jolly-ness' as what we call a character trait, which is another way of saying that they as a person are 'jolly' or 'outgoing'. Do you follow me so far?
Ann-Marie:	Yes, I think so.
Counsellor:	Shall we pay attention to 'depression' for the moment and see how we get on, since being angry is not always a bad thing?
Ann-Marie:	Yea.
Counsellor:	OK that's fine. Now, being 'jolly' and 'outgoing' are positive characteristics whereas 'being depressed' is considered a negative characteristic. I would like us to view 'depression' with a capital 'D', as a 'thing' that stands outside of you, like a bully in the swimming baths trying to pull you under [*the selected metaphor was drawn from the client's sentiment: 'I am sinking under depression'*]. You have floats tied to your arms, but Depression is tugging you down. I would like you to consider seeing how you might do battle against enemy Depression so that you can keep his grip from you and remain afloat. I would like you to try and re-find that part of yourself that worked in year seven but which has slipped away from you without you noticing and has left you unarmed to fight against Depression/boredom at home. Depression attacks you wearing different masks: 'Name-calling at school' comes to assist him by forcing you to stay at home where Depression has you all to himself. 'Hassle of creaming up each day' is another chum that Depression uses because he knows how to 'stress you out' and get your skin all enflamed to get you to take the easy way out and stay at home.

The counsellor elaborated the empowering effects of 'externalizing language' in greater detail. 'Externalizing the problem' has been developed as a linguistic tool to help clients to separate a problem from the personality (White, 1995; White and Epston, 1990). The intention is to enable the client to see 'the problem' as a depersonalized entity aside from the self in order to summon up inner resources for combat. Externalizing language avoids what White refers to as 'problem-saturated descriptions' and perspectives, and 'opens up new possibilities for persons to take action to retrieve their lives and relationships from the problem and its influence' (White and Epston, 1990: 39).

There are disadvantages in using externalizing language (Payne, 2000), particularly in school where the overriding cultural ethos is to make pupils responsible and accountable for their behaviour. But the counsellor is using metaphorical language for empowerment and improvement, and some authors have demonstrated the power of this tool for more troublesome behaviours than depression – behaviours such as stealing, class disruption, abusive behaviour and truancy (Winslade and Monk, 1999). When problems are identified as a product of the self, clients experience a sense of debilitating fatigue that leads them to give up. The counsellor needs to be imaginative in the use of externalizing language but must also use the metaphors which are owned by clients and which are therefore more meaningful to them.

We looked for sub-plots (Payne, 2000) in Ann-Marie's narrative of sinking under the weight of depression – events and experiences in her brief life which kept her from being weighed down and sinking further and further into the abyss. Ann-Marie, after a few moments of reflection, recounted two sub-plots where she had bravely stood up to a group of teasing boys and had come out best. She also remembered incidents with her brother and cousin where she had become assertive in challenging them when they poked fun at her complexion. I was gaining the impression that she was welling up with enthusiasm to get going, to be in school and to try again. This optimism was realized one week after the second session. Although her success was not plain sailing, the general trend was improvement, and when she found again the courage she had lost to keep her afloat from Depression's attempts to pull her down, her eczema improved remarkably. The point was to distract her from obsessive self-focusing and to redirect her energies for peer engagement, and increased socialization was taking place by being in school and out of the home.

After a few weeks of 85 per cent school attendance and positive friendship building on her part, I asked her mother to come into school to reinforce her gains and to serve as what White describes as an 'outsider witness' (Payne, 2000). Ideally, 'outsider witnesses' serve 'not to diminish or take from her account, but to reinforce it by resonances from their own lives' (Payne, 2000: 16). Her mother failed to keep to the appointment, in spite of her graphic accounts of success (which brought a tear to my eye). Nevertheless, Ann-Marie found therapy an exhilarating experience in enabling her to view herself not as a helpless victim to Depression, but as a leader for her mother to follow in escaping from her own anxiety.

COUNSELLING THOSE WITH SUICIDAL THOUGHTS

Suicidal states are as much to do with 'nihilistic life-meaning' constructs and the lack of future promise as with major loss events or psychological impotence. Spiritual counselling, psychodynamic counselling, Jungian analytical therapy and other transpersonal models are the traditional approaches for such conditions, but they are time-consuming in bringing about healing and require extensive counselling skills and resources. I have found time-limited spiritual counselling integrated with narrative therapy effective with young people in school for helping them begin the process of self-aided recovery.

Narrative therapy has been used recently with young people who are contemplating suicide, particularly two techniques that are termed 'taking it back' and 're-membering conversations' (Speedy, 2000). These dual techniques register how the client's material has affected the counsellor in re-viewing her own narrative, then sharing this with the client. The point is not to go for 'depth' (as in humanistic counselling) but for 'thicker' stories, that is, expanding the qualities of other people and exploring different ways of seeing things. 'They are contributions to conversations from counsellors who are aware of the two-way benefits of therapeutic conversations and who feel ethically accountable to their clients to take back the ways in which these exchanges have made a difference to their own lives' (2000: 629). Conversations from significant and influential relationships (with people who may be dead or alive) are described as 're-membered' conversations that have therapeutic import. Speedy (2000) uses her experience of personal bereavement to link in with her client's story of his uncle's suicide. The counsellor shares her own re-membered experience of a loss-event to thicken the narrative of her client's life, a technique which is illustrated in the case that follows.

Matthew in year ten had frequently drifted into the counselling room during breaks for little other reason than to avoid situations that might involve him having to mix with peers. He was not bullied but had elected to be mute every time peers spoke to him. Many pupils had attempted to befriend him, but he spurned them. On one occasion, pastoral teachers bought him a fashionable tee-shirt and persuaded him to go on a school trip and 'enjoy himself'. His routine duties, that he carried out assiduously, included picking up his younger brother after school. He would be seen walking home with his brother in tow, head down and looking miserable, even when no one was watching – his persona was dejection. Matthew had lost his mother when he was 7 and the family had never come to terms with the fact that she had taken her life and left her partner to bring up the family when in his sixties and unwell.

In year eight, he voluntarily engaged in group therapy work (Chapter 8) to help 'normalize' his loss and to articulate within a 'safe' group what the loss had meant for him, but he, unlike the other group members, benefited only marginally from the work (Lines, 1999b). He was referred for individual counselling after the educational social worker escorted him into school after discovering that he had spent two weeks locked away in his own bedroom. The previous day, he had written a note saying that he no longer wanted to live, and wanted to die. This was not the first time he had written such a note.

Counselling pupils and students who contemplate suicide or who want to die takes counsellor and client to the heart of their existential situations. Nelson-Jones (1996) speaks of a need for greater 'existential awareness' of our finite nature and mortality in a world that is preoccupied with youth-fulness and sexual attractiveness. Many of us view death as something that *cannot happen* to us and therefore we *postpone* the notion of non-being by failing to live life to the full (Nelson-Jones, 1996). Matthew had given up on life. He was clearly 'stuck' in his development, and as such was resisting his biological clock – he was physically small in build, looked drab in appearance, never smiled or spoke, and followed instructions like an automaton wholly out of touch with his feelings and wants. But as Nelson-Jones would say, Matthew was *choosing* to think and be this way. In fact all his socializing and growth energy were being taken up with grieving and longing.

While it is true that no one person can experience the experience of another – how do you empathize with a boy losing his mum when young? – it is also true that bridges can be built through experience-analogy. If the counsellor has experienced existential dread (fear of non-being), then she has the personal resources to help her clients. The great fear of non-being is the fear of being alone through the anticipation of non-being. As a counsellor who has a disability and who has once con-templated taking his own life (Lines, 1995a), I have a narrative to share with clients like Matthew. I began to share with Matthew my feelings after a spinal injury had left me paralysed and of my wish at one point to take my life – nothing during that dark night of my soul seemed worth fighting for. I began re-membering for myself the positive experiences of my deceased mother, the qualities and insights she had given me, and of her contribution to my life. I spoke to Matthew also of a boy who had helped me to walk and how he was tragically knocked over by a car and killed; of how I still imagine his presence alongside me as I walk, just in case I stumble. My aim in re-membering was not to compete with Matthew on the victimization scale, but rather to give him permission to begin visual-izing the contribution of other people to his life.

Reluctantly at first, Matthew began to speak positively of his mother's contribution to his life (in earlier work, he was angry that she had 'left him'), and once the words began to flow I couldn't hold him back. Beginning from the last holiday the family had spent together, event after event rolled from his lips, and his countenance and body posture came alive, which I was careful to point out to him. Matthew also brought up a long-distant friend who had taught him how to cook, an uncle who emi-grated to Canada who once showed him how to fix engines, and others too, to re-join the 'club of his life' (Payne, 2000). Then, as Matthew recounted, by contrast, the flip side of his life (when he felt powerless to resuscitate his mother from drowsiness after an overdose), I was moved to compassion for him and disdain for myself. The compassion was due to parental countertransference, but the disdain was for myself in revisiting the time I was paralysed and immobile and depressed. I had no hesitation in 'taking it back' to Matthew, which formed a therapeutic bond from which much of our future counselling benefited. Matthew began, albeit slowly, to rejoin the conveyor belt of life and is currently beginning to use his energy for more positive things than grieving.

COUNSELLING THE SEXUALLY ABUSED

The debate over false-memory syndrome (FMS) of sexual abuse in childhood has largely become frozen, with some taking up an affirmative position on the validity of 'recovered memories' of suppressed material (Sanderson, 1995) and others taking a critical position (Pendergrast, 1996). The prevalence of child sexual abuse is difficult to ascertain due to variations in classification of what constitutes unwanted sexual behaviour as 'abuse', variations in assessment methods, and inconsistent methodological sampling (Fergusson and Mullen, 1999). Meta-analysis gives figures for the prevalence of child sexual abuse as ranging from 3 per cent to 30 per cent for males and from 6 per cent to 62 per cent for females, which of course is meaningless (ibid.: 1999: 14). In those studies where the criterion is sexual penetration or intercourse, rather than indecent exposure by a male family member, 1.3 per cent to 28.7 per cent of females and 3 per cent to 29 per cent of males are classified as having been abused. Although there is at present no yardstick for measuring child sexual abuse, from 5 per cent to 10 per cent of children are exposed to serious sexual assault (ibid.: 1999: 32) not by family members so much as by other acquaintances known to the victim – and not always men (ibid.: 1999: 50–51). As Fergusson and Mullen (1999) note, this means that in every class of 30 pupils at least one pupil may have suffered serious sexual abuse and may never choose to disclose the incident.

There are two counselling models for children suffering sexual abuse. These are the preventative (Elliott, 1990) and the responsive (Courtois, 1988; Maher, 1990), the former being criticized (Adams, 1990) for assuming that victims have more control than they often have.

A central counselling task with abused victims is to help them explore the feeling that, though logically they know they are blameless, they still feel that they have contributed in some way to what has happened. The unconscious temptation in counselling is to rescue victims and to protect them from further harm. The client's self-analysis may be unclear. Knowing in her head that she was not to blame, there is nevertheless often a feeling deep inside that she was. It is inconceivable that a child could feel responsible for being raped, but it is known from adult therapy that victims sometimes say that despite all logic they have the terrifying experience of feeling partly to blame (Murgatroyd and Woolf, 1982). Abused children may misinterpret innocent gestures by protective adults, like the 'giving of money' or 'asking to keep secrets' as 'grooming' and 'complicity'

(McGuiness, 1998). The confusion of loving the perpetrator and hating the experience makes counselling work heavy, but must not be avoided if suppressed feelings are not to find expression in more destructive symptoms later on.

The counsellor will need to accompany the child as she confronts the ultimate betrayal, the total insult of being raped by the person who is charged with her protection and in whom she has faith. There is terror and rage in realizing that the centre of security in her universe is in reality a source of pain and hurt.

John McGuiness (1998) recognizes that counselling young victims of sexual abuse is 'deep work' which 'is powerful and scary' and which makes demands on the counsellor to connect with his own sexuality. Drawing on the theory of personality make-up of Brammer and Shoshtrum (McGuiness, 1998: 66–76), he suggests that effective therapy needs to reach the violated inner core of the person's being, for sexual abuse threatens the self-system. For this reason, the counselling must address in depth the sense of betrayal, terror, rage, and longing that has been affected by abuse. This is lengthy and involved work, however, which may not always be appropriate in a school setting where containment is problematic.

William O'Hanlon (1992) has presented a different and briefer model, which he calls collaborative solution-oriented therapy. The author recognizes the limitations of traditional approaches that work through memory recall and catharsis in that they fail to register how different each client is – 'everyone is an exception' – and recognizes how therapists cannot help but influence the life of the problem through attending to remembered details and sordid events. By encouraging clients to re-feel and express those feelings that have been repressed, there is a tendency to dwell too long on problem-saturated talk. In contrast, clients and therapists in collaborative solution-oriented therapy 'co-create the problem that is to be focussed on in therapy' (O'Hanlon and Wilk, 1987). Treating the after-effects of sexual abuse for a young person, the counselling needs to pay major attention to 'moving the client on' and focusing their attention on the *present* and the *future*. Through therapeutic conversation, the aim is to move away from pathology towards co-constructed goals which are solvable, and which utilize the client's resources, strengths and capabilities (O'Hanlon, 1992: 136).

Shane, a year seven pupil, 12 years of age, came for counselling after a telephone conversation with his father. His parents had split up and there was much rivalry between them. They couldn't speak with each other even by phone. A man named Ralph, who lived in the neighbourhood of his mother's home, had sexually abused Shane, and although his mother had brought him up the abuse caused Shane to be taken away from his mother to live with his father because of pending legal procedures and the need to protect him. For Shane's father, this incident became a further opportunity to gain an advantage in their quarrelsome history. On this occasion he argued that 'If she'd done her proper job this wouldn't have happened.' What made matters worse for Shane was that his mother didn't believe his story. She discounted the material in his written statement.

The accused man was known to Shane's mother and was regarded as her 'friend', and as a person of 'social conscience', a 'do-gooder'. For Shane, this made matters worse – not only had he been duped by a person whom he thought was a 'nice guy', but also his mother would never believe him. The abuser had lured Shane into a friendship, taken him back to his flat for coffee and become a father figure for him. He took him for driving practice in a local park, and invited him to sit on his lap. While he steered the vehicle slowly around the grounds, he took advantage of Shane's sitting position and began fondling his penis. This abuse took place over a period and led to much more serious abuse of sex play in the abuser's bedroom, to oral sex and to anal penetration. 'He did everything to me', he said; 'I had to do things to him.' Further details were not drawn from the client, but he appeared relieved to recount some of the details in counselling. Further, he was suffering flashbacks of particular sexual events that had occurred in the car and the abuser's bedroom, flashbacks which were occasionally triggered by sequences on films at home, material covered in class (sex lessons) and sitting in the front seat of his father's car – the smell of car mats triggered recall.

The introductory session was spent covering briefly his own narrative of abuse, the legal proceedings and the results of the abuse in respect of leaving mum to live with dad. During a collaborative assessment of Shane's thoughts and feelings, there emerged three goals. The first was that while he was happy living with dad, he had regrets that his father wanted him to have a temporary break from visiting his mother because 'she believed that Shane was lying about the abuse'. The feeling I had when listening to the details, particularly over the grooming subtleties, was that Shane would not have made up the story. This left me curious as to why she, unlike Shane's father, refused to believe him. The second goal was to reduce the flashbacks he was experiencing when travelling in his father's car each morning and when watching any form of sexual imagery on television. Some visual re-imaging work (Nelson-Jones, 1996) was carried out in session and rehearsed to reduce flashbacks, and after two weeks Shane reported that the flashbacks were less severe and less frequent. He re-viewed his father's car mats from being the 'floor of the abuser's car' to being 'the carpet in our first house when mum and dad were together and we played monopoly on the floor'.

The third goal became our primary focus of work. Shane felt confused by the series of events that led up to the final abuse. He spoke of being really fond of Ralph at first.

> *Shane:*   He was a good guy. He took interest in me. Took me places. Spent money on me. Then he … [the pain came visibly to his face when recollecting] I liked him at first. He was OK. He used to hug me and make me feel special, and then …

As he spoke further, he related ambivalent feelings. There was even a suggestion of pleasure over early light petting and fondling, which only became hurt, emotional and physical, when things went too far. He felt scarred and felt that he could never trust a man again.

> *Counsellor:* But you are speaking with me, a man, as your counsellor.
> *Shane:* You're all right. I feel safe with you.
> *Counsellor:* Are you sure? I can arrange for you to speak with a woman teacher who has counselling skills, if you'd prefer.
> *Shane:* No, I think I'd rather speak with you because it will help me get confidence in speaking with a man.
> *Counsellor:* So what is the goal we could work on?
> *Shane:* I'd like to understand why I was fooled by him, why he ...? Why he did it, and why ... It didn't feel too bad at first ... Why didn't I tell anyone, and why I went back. Why I ...?
> *Counsellor:* Why you enjoyed the early experience? [tentatively]
> *Shane:* Yea, I think so.

With Shane having found the courage to speak what he felt, the therapy now needed to 'move on' from this 'problem-saturated' material. After acknowledging his pain through brief person-centred listening skills, it was necessary for me to keep the possibilities for change open by using the *past* tense for his 'old self' as a person vulnerable to abuse, and the *present* and *future* tenses for the 'new self', as one more guarded and self-protecting (O'Hanlon, 1992).

In order to centre the counselling on Shane's resources and to stress the solution-focused nature of the treatment, I asked him, 'Shane, how will you know when you no longer need support in counselling?' He replied, 'When I have understood why he fooled me and did it.' Much of the counselling consisted in teaching Shane about 'grooming behaviour' by child sex abusers, to help him become more aware of 'supposed innocent friendliness', 'luring gestures' and 'sexually induced manipulation'. Through the conversations he was able to see himself as one cut off from a father figure and as one who innocently found in Ralph a person who regarded him as a very special person. Unlike in other forms of narrative therapy, it is the effect of the conversation that becomes the process of change. The purpose of giving a youngster the 'abuser' grand narrative was to help him locate alternative sub-plots to his 'being beguiled' narrative. He identified occasions where he could not be easily fooled, and we spent proportionally more time generalizing these self-skills than on his narrative of being abused.

Finally, we addressed the issue of his sexuality as being naturally confused by what had happened. He was taught that at his stage of sexual development many young people become confused, and that living in confusion was OK and quite normal. He found this enormously reassuring. Further frank and collaborative discourse over the nature of sexuality was helpful. Ambiguous narratives in western society, such as a preoccupation with sex on the one hand and a closeted inhibition on the other, were shared. Young people tend to see sex as exclusively the act of sexual intercourse, and the final session was spent in widening his understanding of sexuality.

> *Counsellor:* We are sexual beings *per se*, and we [*differently*] enjoy physical contact in many other ways than genital intimacy, from hugging to play wrestling, with adults and peers, and with both genders. When boundaries are crossed by adults, however, such as forced and unwanted sexual behaviour by use of power, or through seducing tactics for sexual gratification, then we need to see the red flag and say, 'something is not right here'.

CONCLUSION

Counselling pupils and students about a temporary lack of confidence and low self-esteem is likely to be focused on the setting of goals for change that will help them move on, since there is every likelihood that an event, or events, have knocked them off course only marginally in their developmental growth. Most counselling referrals are for quite practical and specific matters that can be addressed by methods that allow youngsters to explore their personal options. Offering counselling for any difficulty essentially raises self-esteem for the client as a by-product. Visualizing self-talk can be a useful intervention in bringing about altered thinking, and practical goal-setting has proved effective in altering behaviour.

For clients suffering more frequent depressive states, a more radical approach is indicated. Such pupils will not be 'clinically depressed' so much as severely down and in a state that they label as 'depression'. The classical counselling approach for depression is Beck's cognitive therapy, but there are limits in applying the model in school. Aspects of Beck's model can be integrated with problem-solution work and narrative therapy, however, and this chapter has demonstrated the effectiveness of 'externalizing language' in empowering clients to rise above their depressive states through 'distraction' and 'engagement'.

Clients at the heavy end of low self-esteem, who on occasion speak of ending their lives, face ultimate existential questions of life-meaning and mortality. This chapter has illustrated the benefits of the therapeutic techniques of 're-membering' and 'taking it back' in bridging the experience of client and counsellor. Through the process of conversation, the contributions of significant people in the lives of clients are amplified with positive effects.

Counselling pupils and students who have been the victims of severe sexual abuse is deep and taxing work. It calls for an understanding of how such abuse leaves clients with ambivalent feelings and confusion over relationships and their own sexuality. The work inevitably re-connects the counsellor with his or her own sexuality as well as with parenting experiences, which may or may not be helpful in countertransference. In child abuse cases, effective thinking skills which use visualizing self-talk and bringing about change through altered mental constructs can be helpful. Victims need a broader understanding of abusers' deviant forms of sexual arousal from child pornography and child sexuality, in order to help them interpret grooming tactics and take precautionary measures.

6

BULLYING IN SCHOOL

A gang leader knifes a boy on a run-down council estate for reporting bullying at school. A girl overdoses after repeated threats from girls in her year group and is found dead in her bedroom. Rarely does a week go by without a further calamity reported in the media. These tragedies leave a sense of perplexity about how to check the disturbing rise in school bullying. Such is the power of the peer group, that social difference and daring to stand apart from the crowd are met with more than indifference – they receive open hostility. Those who are different, or are perceived as being different, can have a hard time when adults are not around. Much bullying is covert and subtle. Parents feel powerless to support their children since school systems have altered so much since they were in education, and they are no longer sure what advice they can offer apart from a facile *'Try and ignore it dear!'* Some have become dissatisfied with schools' measures to curb repeated bullying and out of frustration are beginning to approach the European Court of Human Rights to seek redress for their children.

Headteachers have become a little nervous of these trends in spite of having anti-bullying policies in place and in spite of inset training for pastoral staff on how to confront bullying, but information is not enough. What is needed is not only vigilance in stamping out aggression, but imaginative strategies to cover the different forms of bullying. Much research exists on bullying patterns and the appropriate interventions to reduce it. The research shows that while bullying occasionally comes into school as a result of community unrest, schools themselves as institutions create a climate in which bullying can thrive. In this chapter, the particular role of the counselling practitioner, as distinct from the pastoral teacher exercising a disciplinary role, is examined indirectly through a range of brief counselling techniques and interventions that have been found to work in practice.

RESEARCH ON BULLYING

From the early research of Olweus (1978, 1991, 1992, 1993) in Scandinavia, school bullying has gained an international focus (Lines, 1996, 1999a). A number of studies reveal an almost universal picture. They illustrate that on average one in five pupils is being bullied in school, that one in ten admits in anonymous questionnaires to have bullied others, and that bullying can be reduced in school (by 50 per cent) with a range of imaginative interventions that keep the profile of bullying high.

Whole-school anti-bullying policies that are drawn up and collectively owned by members of the whole school populace are considered to be essential to bullying reduction (Cowie and Sharp, 1996; Olweus, 1993; Smith and Sharp, 1994). Unmonitored periods of the school day, such as breaks and lunchtimes, are recognized to be occasions of anxiety for bullied victims (Patterson, 1982), where unsupervised adolescents find opportunity for anti-social behaviour – a situation that is soon rectified with more rigorous surveillance (Patterson and Stouthamer-Loeber, 1984).

Attention has been drawn to the group effect ('mobbing') of bullying behaviour (Pikas, 1975), and to the level of empathy that can be experienced by 'bystanders', or by gang participants, who are not the primary instigators. Strategies for bullying reduction can draw on natural feelings of pity for the victim (Salmivalli et al., 1996). In addition, studies in criminology support the findings of Davies (1986) and Elliott (1986) in illustrating that trauma is experienced by those who witness attacks on the defenceless.

The Sheffield project was launched in 1990 (Whitney and Smith, 1993) through Gulbenkian Foundation funding. This surveyed the largest sample in the UK (over 6,000 pupils). It applied a methodology that isolated such factors as year differences, gender differences, types and locations of bullying behaviour, and reporting patterns. This work expanded previous research to investigate a number of strategies, such as, for example, self-assertion, that were designed to empower pupils in responding to victimization in ways that were different from those they instinctively deployed, so as to produce a more favourable long-term outcome (Smith and Sharp, 1994). Playground environments were redesigned to stimulate bored pupils who might otherwise revert to bullying. Bully Help Lines and Bully Courts were set up, peer support was tried, and approaches such as the 'No Blame Approach' and 'Circle Time' were tested, to good effect. Of these, peer support in particular is being researched as a proactive means of reducing bullying (Carr, 1994; Cowie, 1998; Cowie and Sharp, 1996; Naylor and Cowie, 1999).

Although the research into verbal bullying is limited, sufficient work has now been done to raise a number of concerns. It is known that victims lack confidence and have low self-esteem, even in later life (Cowen et al., 1973). It is known that passive spectators as well as victims are affected by bullying (Davies, 1986; Elliott, 1986).

Several authors have pointed to the psychological effects of name-calling which leaves the youngster open to public ridicule, and to the common terms of abuse which are targeted at those vulnerable individuals who are outside the cultural 'norm' (Lines, 1999a). Practitioners in the field are all too aware that particular children become subjected to name-calling, that name-calling results in stereotypical racial classifications (Lines, 1999a), that many older adolescents find physical abuse easier to deal with than racial taunting (Cohn, 1987), and that name-calling is more difficult to spot and check than physical bullying (Besag, 1989). But these extreme cases do little to dissuade large groups of pupils who are daily engaged in what they would regard as trivial teasing, and who see name-calling largely as play and 'just messing about!' Reporting patterns of name-calling are influenced by previous experience of reporting outcomes in primary school, parental advice and the perceived motives of the main instigators (Lines, 1999a).

A number of theoretical interpretations of name-calling exist in the literature (Lines, 1996). Terms of verbal abuse that infuriate young people include, among racial and idiosyncratic terms, names which denigrate the family, such as 'your mum is a ...', (often abbreviated to just 'your mum!') particularly in neighbourhoods that have high single-parent (normally mother) figures, together with those that ridicule achievement, such as 'boffin!' (Lines, 1999a). It is the emotional reaction to a given label by the targeted person that is the predominant factor in whether or not the label will stick, a process of social reaction and interaction (Besag, 1989). The cognitive changes occurring in children who have been subjected to continual bullying may cause a belief that they deserve the derogatory names they have been called – they must indeed be 'ugly', 'a pervert', 'a wimp' or 'an idiot', for otherwise they would have been able to cope. Their inability to cope proves for them that they are inferior, resulting in a gradual but pervasive erosion of self-esteem (Seligman and Peterson, 1986).

The literature would indicate that victims often show a submissive posture to a perpetrator just prior to attack (Besag, 1989; Schafer, 1977). Thus, a stage exists in secondary school for power-seeking individuals to exhibit their prowess and control over those who are unable to withstand.

DECISIONS ON WHOM TO COUNSEL

Overall research shows that those having developed strategies of self-assertion and temper control have far fewer difficulties in dealing with physical and verbal abuse. School pupils often believe that by ignoring the tormentors the problem will go away. It is a forlorn hope that appears to be little affected by personal experience, and suggests that a victim becomes frustrated by not knowing what to do other than repeat defensive behaviour (like ignoring the bully, or calling names back) that has in any case been found not to work.

Victims of name-calling, particularly, have low status among the peer group, but this can change through natural maturation. The tendency for bullies to wind up volatile youngsters and humiliate them publicly lessens in the closing period of secondary education (Arora and Thompson, 1987), but in the early years the environment can be very hostile, competitive and non-accepting of social difference.

When reviewing the referral data the counsellor must first make a choice of whether to work with the bully, the victim, the friends of either, parents of either, supervising teachers or the 'observing group' – either with the victim or in their absence. The counsellor will apply different models when working with the bully from those used with her victim. Some pupils receive continual verbal taunting from different groups and within different contexts, which suggests that their responses (consciously or otherwise) provoke attacks against them. It is as though they carry the label of victim as part of their self-identity. These pupils are termed 'provocative victims' and are often the most difficult pupils to support. Effective treatment programmes are those centred on the victim changing his behaviour rather than the many who inflict verbal intimidation and low-level physical abuse.

COUNSELLING BULLIES

Teachers are aware of the dilemma of trying to penalize the perpetrators of fights, since the punished tend to be those who are actually caught exchanging blows – those who stir up trouble usually walk away scot-free. Some youngsters fight and incite violence as a result of emulating the behaviour of aggressive adults – habitually 'lusting for blood' – and appear amoral. But research shows that violent bullying can have as damaging an effect upon bullies as upon their victims (Forero et al., 1999). Such research indicates that some bullies suffer depression through their uncontrollable aggression, which indicates that they, along with their victims, deserve counselling support.

Counselling approaches based upon the notion that 'insight produces change' (brief psychodynamic and humanistic) prove particularly useful with those pupils unaware of how their aggressive behaviour is perceived by the peer group generally. This is to use peer-group influence positively, for although younger adolescents look up to tough characters, if only for self-protection, admiration for those who are 'hard' certainly fades away in the closing school years. Trading on what does or does not make a person popular can be effective in the developmental process of identity formation and individuation (Erikson, 1968). I have found it possible to modify behaviour with only one or two brief counselling sessions that draw for the pupil the connection between modelling influences of the home with aggressive behaviour in school.

Boys and girls will be asked where they think their aggressive tendencies come from, and often they will reply that a family member says they follow their father or mother, or an older sibling. Other cases reveal that the client has not dealt with bereavement issues or parental desertion issues, which have left the person living as though a cauldron of fury is about to boil over. With these pupils, the aggressive tendencies are merely managed with cognitive-behavioural techniques that draw the person's anger arousal to his attention, say by wearing a rubber band around the wrist, while counselling addresses those primary factors.

> Geoffrey found the rubber band helpful in reminding him of his volatility in situations where the counsellor could not be. Pulling and releasing the band signalled to him that he was being aroused, and the subtlety was not evident to those around. The band was not the source of his self-control, which was the mental connection with his counsellor and the relaxation sessions in which we had become engaged to desensitize his anger. The technique is a form of containment at a distance.

Other pupils who are prone to become impulsively aggressive require, in order to avoid showdowns, an escape route that has been planned and communicated to teaching staff.

> This was the case with Larry who had never come to terms with his father running off with another woman and leaving him. He would explode with extreme violence on every occasion that teachers corrected him for playing up, or when friends teased him. I needed to organize an escape route for him to withdraw from the situation by coming to the counselling room as a place of refuge to help desensitize his anger.

We engaged in mind-control therapy and brief loss therapy through cognitive-humanistic counselling (Nelson-Jones, 1997, 1999a), and once the work was completed the incidence rate of Larry's outbursts declined to a point where he had more self-control and took more personal responsibility. When pupils and teachers get locked into heated altercations, both parties are the losers and ultimatums and enforced apologies rarely suffice in making reparation. Given the high exclusion rates of very violent pupils, these remedial therapies are important.

There are pupils in school who appear to revel in aggression and in the experience of themselves fighting, or in seeing others fight at their instigation. The counsellor may elect to work exclusively with the bully, using narrative techniques that call into question the obsolete nature of the 'domination-macho' narrative (Payne, 2000). With other cases that are less malicious albeit more tormenting, where aggression is shown merely to see a fellow upset, narrative techniques which draw on the power of the written document may prove effective (Epston et al., 1992; White and Epston, 1990).

Bob came for counselling in tears during the lunch break saying that two of his peers in science kept name-calling, picking on him and digging him in the back before the lesson began while they queued outside the room. Bob said that he did not want the boys to get 'into trouble' and felt that the 'no-blame' approach might better resolve the conflict than reporting the matter to his Head of Year. An introductory session was held to offer Carl and Scott support and to enlist their commitment to work on their aggressive inclinations. Awareness-raising over how they were viewed by peers other than those of the neighbourhood was by use of a counsellor-composed narrative. The following written assessment of Bob's statements and those of witnesses was given to Carl and Scott to read:

> Carl and Scott were whispering names about me in the queue. Carl said, 'Bobby, come here you twat!' I knew what would happen so I moved away. They followed me and began name-calling again and digging me in my back. Scott grabbed me by my coat and called me 'bean pole' because I'm tall and thin. Carl tried to trip me up, but I was hanging on to the door handle to stop from being dragged into the sixth form room.

> Carl and Scott keep doing this to *humiliate* Bobby and to *torment* him. They *get pleasure* from *putting him down*. Scott isn't as bad as Carl, who *shows off in front of the girls whenever they're around*. Scott's trying to get Bobby wound up because *he knows he's on his last chance*. Carl hates Bobby because *he thinks his brother grassed Carl's brother for nicking cars*.

Carl read this narrative and was invited to comment and modify the text, especially the italicized words that express opinions and suppositions rather than facts. Scott did the same exercise separately. This was a powerful means of getting both boys to reflect on their identities as perceived not by moralizing pastoral staff but by observing peers. Within a no-blame counsellor stance, both boys began to analyse their respective aggressive self-identities, and think about where their reflexive behaviours may have originated and where their behaviour was leading. They were invited to modify the narrative, which was honestly done and which became the means of altering their humiliating tomfoolery that was beginning to spread to other social contexts.

COUNSELLING THE GROUP

One effective strategy to consider is to speak with the group of tormentors, or significant leaders, in the absence of the victim, with the aim of describing how the individual has been left feeling, thus enlisting their empathy and good will (Pikas, 1975; Salmivalli et al., 1996). Circle time is a therapeutic exercise of sitting a group of pupils in a circle and encouraging each person to voice their feelings, but the running and management of circle time is not easy with adolescents in the later years of school, unless pupils have consistently practised it and have valued it since primary school. This is largely because of the increasingly self-conscious nature of youngsters going through middle adolescence and the powerful dynamics of peer-group affiliations. Handled sensitively with smaller and 'safer' groups, circle time can resolve many misunderstandings and over-reactions arising from poor communications and ignorance of how intolerant and spiteful behaviour can hurt other people. Protagonists largely act in ignorance of the effects of their verbal abuse. Handled well, individuals of the group are able to gain insight into the sensitivities of those who are singled out. Such a strategy has limits, however, within the changing learning environments of large schools where consistent control and regulation are difficult to ensure. It also runs the risk of an over-dependence of the victim upon the teacher.

It is considered to be an ineffective strategy for a pastoral teacher merely to admonish, humiliate or exclude a perpetrator of name-calling or physical bullying without any sensitivity to its later consequences for the victim. When threats are made for 'grassing', the belief is reinforced that telling teachers about bullies inevitably makes matters worse – in some cases of lax management it actually does. Creating a win–win culture in solving group feuds and in conflict resolution is a more effective treatment than admonishing the 'supposed' guilty parties, for the cause of feuds that go back for months, particularly if they have originated in the community, are often difficult to trace. In practice, therefore, partisan alliances, or miscalculated judgements will lead to grievances about injustice and to future revolt.

Bringing selected individuals together in group therapy has many advantages, particularly where hostile feelings are still fermenting. The counsellor's aim in group therapy is to create a fair and neutral stance in the hope of achieving a win–win solution (Smith and Sharp, 1994). The technique of 'reflexive circular questioning' (Tomm, 1985), where the aggressors are invited to voice a victim's feelings from the victim's frame of reference rather than from their own, can be a very powerful way of gaining shared insight. Each involved front player is asked to voice what they feel 'as though they were the victim', by adopting the personality and name of the victim as they speak (Lines, 2000).

Karen was asked to voice how she thought Jackie had felt when the gang had turned on her after Darren had asked her out. 'I suppose she thought that she was two-timing Steve, her ex-boyfriend', she replied.

Counsellor: No, Karen, speak as though *you are Jackie* and say what you think you would feel in her situation as you see everyone turn on you for something somebody else has done when asking *you* out.

After some fresh attempts, what she came up with was the cause of insight not only for her, but also for the group:

> *Karen:*   I feel that you're all being unfair and unreasonable. Darren asked me
>   out. I didn't ask him. And Steve dumped me last week. What am I
>   supposed to do? I thought we were all mates!

COUNSELLING VICTIMS OF PHYSICAL ABUSE

Strategies that have been tried in school to support victims of physical abuse include self-assertion exercises to engender confidence (Smith and Sharp, 1994) and the teaching of self-defence. In my experience, such strategies can go wrong in situations where adults are not present, and can in certain circumstances be misused when, for example, a victim becomes a bully from newly found confidence. Other strategies centre upon general social skills training (Lindsay, 1987), the reasoning being that when an adolescent becomes self-confident and adept in social relations, then taunting will have less effect.

Self-assertive role-play is effective for those victims of bullying who regularly have their dinner and bus fare extorted from them by power-abusing peers. They are challenged at the school gates or in secluded places to turn out their pockets and pass over their money under threat of being beaten up. When they comply, it is often in the hope that the intimidation is a one-off experience, but alas they tend to become a tagged person by offering no resistance, and so the pattern is repeated.

Occasionally, some feel that by yielding they gain popularity among tough peers, perhaps even protection, but these are pseudo, highly-manipulative friendships. Because of fear of reprisal such victims rarely report the theft to those responsible for discipline, and so their self-esteem is lowered and the extortion continues unabated. Self-assertion training is often the only means of dealing with such bullying, and through role-play the victim is taught to look the bully in the eye, non-provocatively, and say, 'Sorry, but I don't give my money away!' Although trying this out requires a measure of confidence from those who have little of it, I have found that victims will eventually pluck up the courage and give it a try, to positive effect.

COUNSELLING 'PROVOCATIVE VICTIMS' OF VERBAL ABUSE

Payne (2000) has recently argued that the practice of giving victims strategies for social survival fails in recognizing the true culprits of bullying behaviour. He believes that the work should be focused upon the bullies rather than their victims (who merely need support) and that school systems ought continually to confront bullying head on, since the common practice of school bullying is a reflection of unchallenged societal attitudes of abusive power and exploitation. While not fully denying this, it can be counter-argued that 'provocative victims' often elicit hostile and fun-poking responses from their tormentors by their reactions. Blame is not the point here, neither is it to prescribe a pragmatic course that has no regard to what is just. The following strategy is aimed to make the victim aware of the patterns and effects of their inter-relating with others, and to reduce tormenting by sharing the responsibility for change so as to make school life less arduous for all.

I have found less submissive strategies that make use of humour to be highly effective with those pupils referred to as 'provocative victims' who suffer repeated verbal abuse. These victims, who are volatile yet who have heightened imaginative capabilities, become susceptible to being called names and to other covert bullying behaviour because of the emotional effect that derogatory images have on them. Younger, more immature adolescents may imagine an audience that scrutinizes their appearance and actions, and that assumes huge and irrational proportions when they are under pressure of ridicule. When called names, an anxious pupil will stand out in a group more in imagination than in fact. The following strategy aims at minimizing the effect of this. The chapter closes by outlining this strategy as a proactive means of challenging tormentors.

A novel way of dealing with victims suffering from repeated name-calling, then, is through a particular form of self-assertive response combined with a reframing, or re-storying technique (Epston et al., 1992; White and Epston, 1990), that I call image replacement and narrative adoption. 'Reframing' is a cognitive restructuring technique derived from family therapy, which uses those very same imaginative abilities that are attacking the self (Burnham, 1986; Watzlawick et al., 1974). The approach involves a co-constructed modification of a victim's narrative (McNamee and Gergen, 1992), combined with a non-aggressive challenge. Through altering images and thinking in an atmosphere of humour, the incidence of name-calling is reduced and the victim is left feeling more under control and less at risk of intimidation (Lines, 2001).

Reframing

The pupil is encouraged first to reframe her situation. In place of believing that she is *hated* because she is called names, she is encouraged to view herself as the object of play and sport, which is perhaps just as harrowing but far less debasing. Teasing occurs not because of what *she is*, but because of *what she is allowing to happen to her*.

The self-assertive response involves displaying confidence and acting in a way that is least expected. For instance, those who come from a different part of the country are encouraged to try an experiment. Rather than attempting to disguise their accent and feel ashamed of their dialect because of the jibes that ensue when they speak, they might try to exaggerate it and see what happens.

> Terry, a Welsh boy, struggled in vain to hide his accent, but when he exaggerated it and spoke in a broad Welsh accent not only did he laugh but his peers laughed too, and this proactive response caused the taunting to cease.

Other victims may be targeted for reasons of their looks, their body form or their mannerisms, such as the way they walk that fits a stereotyped caricature of stigmatized groups, particularly homosexuals.

> Chris was given a counselling appointment after exclusion, and in the introduction he related frequent episodes of losing his temper through rising to the bait of name-calling. He was taunted by being called 'queer', 'gay' and 'bent', which is a dilemma that many boys find difficult to counteract and ward off. In a letter to Chris's parents excluding him for reasons of 'abusive behaviour towards a member of staff', an accompanying report stated:
>
> > Chris was asked to leave the room for swearing. I allowed him back into the room when he promised to get on with his work. However, an argument ensued between Chris and Gemma with repeated name-calling. I again asked Chris to leave the room but he refused saying I should ask Gemma to leave...

This report illustrates a common occurrence in class where order breaks down through anger that is fuelled by unchecked name-calling. It is not that teachers turn a blind eye to such taunting, but that with some unruly groups the name-calling, though low-key, can be almost uncontrollable.

I explored what lay behind his anger and what his beliefs and feelings were about people who were not ashamed of their homosexual orientation. His reply was that he had no strong feelings against gays, but since he was not gay himself (he asserted), he found the name-calling offensive. It would be tempting to apply the principles outlined above and encourage this client to exaggerate what he imagined to be homosexual mannerisms so as to show the group that he was unaffected by their goading. But there is a problem with this particular name-calling that does not apply so much to other sexual labelling – it reinforces stereotypical attitudes of homophobia in school. Instead, I asked him to look at those who taunted him and wink at them in a self-assured manner when they called out gay terms of abuse. We practised this in front of the mirror until I felt that he was comfortable with winking expressively. Then he could try the proactive response for real. After two weeks of trials, he reported a distinct decline in the teasing, which was confirmed by his newly confident demeanour.

Underlying these strategies is the notion that bullying is often not over-malicious or power-abusive, but designed to arouse the subject to over-react in such a manner as to amuse an audience of fun-seeking peers, which in fact comprises the majority of name-calling incidents (Lines, 1996, 1999a).

Image replacement

By replacing an image, or images, in the mind of the youngster (and his fun-seeking peers), the victim begins to take control of the game by regulating his own affective state. I have a string puppet hanging in the counselling room, and this is often shown to victims to indicate how powerful characters within contained group settings are able to pull strings that control the actions of puppet-like characters. I explain to my clients that the strategies I wish them to use are designed so that they may metaphorically take hold of the strings from their (perceived) adversaries and begin to control the show.

> One pupil became increasingly agitated when his friends taunted him by calling out 'granddad', to the point of explosive outburst (his granddad had died three years earlier and it was for him a great loss.) He remonstrated with the teacher for not challenging the tormentors, and stormed out of the classroom, occasionally attacking them as he left and disregarding classroom protocol and order. He became aggressive when he was aroused. He was depressed at having been manipulated by his peers, some of whom were his 'best friends'. They had not known why he would over-react, but they could predict that he would. 'Granddad' meant much more to him than they could imagine.

The problem was resolved through the technique of image replacement. Being asked what 'granddad' media figure made him laugh most, he chose the character in *Only Fools and Horses*. He recalled a scene that he had found particularly amusing, and tried with success the strategy of mentally focusing upon that person wherever he heard the taunts of 'granddad'. It worked: he smiled when they taunted him, they were surprised and confused, and when pulling the strings no longer got the predicted responses they ceased to torment him.

Narrative adoption

The idea of reframing situations is one of adopting a slightly modified narrative that has been co-constructed by the counsellor and the client from the material of which the person makes sense of her personal experience (Anderson and Goolishian, 1988).

> A year eight pupil reacted negatively to the suggestion that her mother was a prostitute by looking down and by pretending not to have heard the ridicule. The more she continued her 'hard-of-hearing' pretence, the more the players intensified their mockery.

She found that the scoffing ceased when she humiliated her opponent amidst group laughter with the assertive rejoinder: 'Well, me mum went off with your dad last night but he wasn't very good.' Here, from feeling miserable in the belief that her mother was debased, she turned the image around to put down her tormentor's father in quick-fired wit – all in harmless fun.

Being called a 'midget' tormented Trevor, a year seven boy, and caused him to lose his temper. I asked him what came to mind when he thought of something small and deadly (I was thinking of a virus). He said, 'a bullet'. We rehearsed a saying that he used to positive effect in reducing the name-calling and in monitoring his anger: 'Midgets are small, but so are bullets!'

An extended case example of this dual technique has been written up (Lines, 2001).

A note of caution

The school counsellor has to be cautious about 'experimenting' with these techniques for those 'provocative victims' who are devoid of all social skills and imagination, and those suffering from borderline Asperger's syndrome. Jack was referred for counselling after a fight, which was untypical of his behaviour. He had been repeatedly bullied through the early years until he could stand it no longer, and so lashed out and got into a fight. What is more, he was congratulated by his mother and by some teachers surreptitiously for standing up for himself. If the intimidation had ceased, it could be argued that all was well – he had become assertive and the tormentors had got the message! This was not the case, however, and in fact the taunting grew worse.

I asked Jack to log the teasing and tormenting over the week, and his record was pitiful, illustrating that he had suffered low-level physical assault and intimidation three to four times a day. Ideas about the motives for teasing (above) were discussed, but I felt that he was not grasping the point but showing only a blind willingness to try out a suggested narrative adoption. I kept the trial period to only one day and his log the next day confirmed my suspicions. When wished 'Good morning' by a peer, he wrote: 'I didn't reply because he always treats me badly.' When James asked to work with him in science, he wrote: 'My reply was, "Go away".' In French, when the teacher left the room, the class started to bully him and call him 'sheep-shagger', and he wrote: 'Laura said I should take it easy, but I don't take any notice of her because she's a slacker who does not want to get on in life.' These responses indicated that Jack was unable to be less intense, unable to differentiate between friendliness and spitefulness, and found it difficult to display any comradeship and warmth.

When we covered past events in session with a view to learning how he might have responded differently, he looked blank and promptly insisted on writing everything down to retain the idea. I felt uneasy, in that he was not genuinely *seeing* what was going on, not *grasping* what needed to change, but was prepared to act by rote rather than by intuition.

I was not surprised to find that he had had a sheltered upbringing, that he never mixed with peers socially, and that all through early schooling he had spent break and lunch periods with teachers rather than peers – this was a safer option, which avoided mixing with peers. Jack was wholly unskilled in adolescent conversing, and was not in tune with youthful thinking and play. The counselling role was altered to encourage Jack to engage in greater socialization with protective groups – school clubs and societies, Church groups, small local youth clubs – and this was the recommendation to his parents. Jack needed regular opportunities of speaking and socializing with peers away from adults, as befits adolescent individuation.

CONCLUSION

No school can afford to be relaxed or dismissive about the prevalence of bullying among the most vulnerable. A range of strategies for the counsellor has been presented for use with both bullies and victims where conventional disciplinary measures fail to check the practice. The significant factor emerging from research on victims of bullying is the relationship between a lack of confidence in challenging perpetrators and high recidivist rates.

I contend that the more name-calling is effectively challenged the less will be the incidence of severe physical bullying, since I believe that verbal taunting is the precursor to much violence and community unrest. The high self-esteem that enables a pupil to ward off a barrage of insults by *genuinely* ignoring the tormenting and ceasing to react also reduces the rate of taunting.

Bullied victims need to understand the social rules of fun-centred name-calling and to see the connection of over-reaction with repeated teasing, for much name-calling is not intended to be malicious. Incidents involving the management of 'provocative victims' are demanding on time and patience, since they appear to bring about the victim's own downfall, but the bullied are acting largely from a dysfunctional repertoire of reactions. The strategy that I have found the most effective has three processes that can be applied briefly, far more briefly, in fact, than the time taken up with managing the aftermath of classroom disruption resulting from verbal abuse.

During the awareness-raising phase, the client needs to recognize the game and its performers, to understand the roles of all involved – including the passive features that maintain the tormenting. The second phase is a combination of narrative adoption and image replacement. Narrative adoption involves an imaginative co-construction of the victim's narrative that becomes the new property of the client. The modified narrative is a revised frame of self-understanding through which victims may re-interpret the motivations of and maltreatment by those around them, a new cognition by which to interpret reality. The new narrative is not forced upon the client but is merely offered for trial.

Image replacement is designed to alter the affective state of the victim. In the final phase, the aim is to diminish verbal taunting by encouraging the victim to try out something that is instinctively unnatural. They must, for the sake of the exercise, accept the ridicule and go along with what is said (not because it is true). They must try the new narrative as a means of gaining power, confusing the perpetrators by responding in a manner that is least expected. This will help them to learn to change their affective state from anxiety to relief (perhaps even elation), which in turn will reduce the potency of the image in their self-debasing thinking.

This intervention has been tried out with many pupils suffering social isolation through verbal taunting, with those who are beginning to accept negative labels of themselves and who are beginning to believe that they may be what they have been called. The individual strategies have in common the use of humour by which the victim joins in the game rather than becoming psychologically isolated, and in consequence achieves better social relations.

7

PARENTAL SEPARATION AND STEP-PARENT CONFLICT

Many youngsters experiencing parental separation come forward for counselling, for this can be a very anxious time. For reasons of 'political correctness', I use the term 'parental separation' instead of 'divorce' in order to be inclusive. I view young persons' adult monitors and providers as their 'parents', rather than 'guardians', for this is how youngsters generally see them even if they don't address them as 'mum' or 'dad'. I thereby imply no detriment to guardians who in many instances may parent the child better than the biological parent does.

So common is the single-mother family in some areas of the UK that I wonder what concept of 'normal' lies in the minds of many youngsters as a template for future familial relationships. In fact, as my clients come forward for counselling appointments in school, I find I am surprised when a youngster tells me that he or she is living at home with both biological parents.

After outlining the statistics and research on family make-up and current trends in western society, I consider in this chapter brief integrative approaches that can be applied to three groups of young people: those experiencing trauma at the beginning of parental separation; those suffering a loss in self-esteem after parental separation; and those experiencing conflict with a step-parent. The first group needs support in facing the inevitable consequences of the tensions beginning to be apparent in the home, and the other two experience readjustment difficulties when a parent leaves and may begin a new family with another partner.

RESEARCH ON PARENTAL SEPARATION

Statistics on parental breakdown in the UK

The Marriage Guidance Council was established in 1938 in response to the meteoric rise in divorce rates. It was renamed Relate and operated as a mediation counselling agency in London. Relate served over 8,000 couples from 1983–1988, but in the Jubilee Year of the organization, numbers increased to nearly a quarter of a million a year in the UK (Litvinoff, 1991).

Nearly one in five of all children in the UK live with one parent (1996 figures) and of this number, with the exception of about 14 per cent who live with their fathers, most are raised by their mothers. Marriages and partnerships are entered into today in the belief that they can be ended easily. Consequently, the 'nuclear family' is no longer the norm in some areas (Pechereck, 1996), with as many as 900,000 stepfamilies living in the UK (Webb, 1994) and 200,000 children living with only one of their biological parents (Holland, 2000). This change in family structure results largely from the liberalization of public attitude over parental separation and divorce. The increase in cohabitation as a preferred 'family' model also results in instability – sadly, in some deprived communities children experience repeated parental changes with a diminishing network of support.

Although those under 5 are often thought to be especially vulnerable (Dominian et al., 1991; Elliot and Richards, 1991), adolescents are similarly a high-risk group, particularly those experiencing a second separation of parents and step-parents. Adolescence is considered by some to be the worst time, especially for girls (Smith, 1999).

Effects of separation

Young children may respond to parental separation by 'freezing emotionally' and may regress, but adolescents are likely to become depressed and lose enthusiasm for living (Smith, 1999).

Research has been carried out to examine the common features for youngsters in school who have been bereaved and those whose parents have separated. Lewis (1992) found that many children find in school a safe haven from parental conflict and separation, with teachers generally being more able to support them over this than over bereavement. Raphael (1984) suggested that bereaved pupils and those suffering parental separation were able, as Holland (2000) says, to 'mark time' until the teacher was free to attend to their distress.

Loss is only problematic 'when it overwhelms the individual', says Holland (2000). Some theorists view grief as a series of fixed stages, which are predictable emotional reactions to severe loss – from initial shock, disbelief, anger and depression to resolution and an acceptance of loss (Kübler-Ross, 1982) – but others see such stages as reciprocating from state to state (Parkes, 1986). Loss necessitates the completion of a range of tasks from experiencing grief to reinvesting energy into former or different activities (Worden, 1984). Elmore (1986) felt that the fixed stage model of loss applied as much to the experience of parental separation as to bereavement, where children clearly react negatively (Longfellow, 1979).

Loss is known to create a range of physiological disorders, emotional vulnerability and behavioural disturbance. Research has related loss experience to delinquency and anti-social behaviour, to 'clinging' behaviour, neurotic behaviour, childhood depression and psychiatric disturbance in adult life (Holland, 2000). Refusal to go to school, disruptive behaviour and learning problems have also been associated with marital or cohabitee separation (Holland, 2000).

Societal factors of parental separation

It is not uncommon for unions to break down while the woman is pregnant, or during the early months of the infant's life, for these periods test relationships to a considerable degree (Smith, 1999). Increased teenage pregnancy is a cause for concern in the UK, not least because unprepared young parents are commonly living in inadequate conditions for child rearing.

Feminism, resulting in the changing role identity of women, has been one reason for partnership breakdown. Many women are seeking more in their lives than motherhood. Seventy per cent of women in the UK are working mothers, which is a rise of 20 per cent from 40 years ago (ONS, 2000). Women are increasingly attaining high professional qualifications, and in many modern households the male is taking over the child-rearing duties quite ably. In the modern labour market, the shift from manual work has left many men confused over their masculinity, and fathers may experience a dilemma when dealing with family conflict in ways that are largely out of step with modern societal attitudes. Women are no longer staying in relationships with abusive partners, and when couples 'fall out of love' or become 'sexually incompatible' there is no longer a social stigma in putting their own wants and life fulfilment above the ethic of 'staying together for the sake of the children' (Litvinoff, 1991). There can be little doubt also of the subtle erosion of religious principles that underpin marriage vows, thus lessening feelings of guilt when couples choose to part against the wishes of their children. There is no question that the self-centred trend of short-term partnerships has had a serious effect on children's wellbeing and stability.

The prevalence of domestic violence is a cause of parental separation. It is alleged that those who grow up in violent families may become violent adults or victims of violence through life, and may go on to abuse their own children. Since the research for this finding is based upon what adults remember of their childhood, it cannot be wholly reliable (Smith, 1999). In the UK, the Department of Health annually receives around 120 notifications of child deaths caused by physical assaults by parents or step-parents. A large proportion of these are fathers or stepfathers having an earlier history of violence towards female partners as well as towards children (Smith, 1999).

One in seven of the children who called Child Line in 1998 over family relationship problems said that the main problem was physical assault and one in 30 spoke of sexual assaults. Violence can exist within families both before parental separation, and during post-separation contact. A review of research suggests that 40–60 per cent of children are physically abused in families where there has been violence against women partners, and Child Line confirms these figures (Smith, 1999). Nearly all children in one North American study could give details of violence from one parent (Chase et al., 1990, cited in Smith, 1999). Since children are adept at 'crying silently', the level of abuse is not always detected.

The research is not conclusive in correlating violent upbringing and parental separation with violent behaviour in adulthood. Canadian research found that about a quarter of children raised in an atmosphere of domestic violence were unaffected, and further that two-thirds of the boys and four-fifths of the girls functioned within 'normal' limits (Wolfe et al., 1985). Researchers found that the recovery rates for all children were high if the violence ceased and if support was promptly available. Hence, the importance of counselling in school.

Is parental separation always traumatic?

One study, which listened to young people themselves, concluded that, in spite of initial trauma, children can feel secure and settled in time if separation is managed well (Smith, 1999). Society expects divorce and separation to have terrible consequences for the children, but this is an assumption that is rarely tested.

It is an open question whether boys suffer more significantly from parental separation than girls, since the research is contradictory (Smith, 1999). According to Child Line boys who live with depressed fathers who drink a lot have greater difficulty in coping with the situation than boys living with their mothers.

In answering the question of what makes for a good parental separation, Smith (1999), writing from a mother-centred perspective, outlines three factors.

- Children need to see their father and have his support, approval and loving care – to be very special for him. This means not just seeing him, but experiencing genuine interest and encouragement in place of unsympathetic discipline.
- Children want their mother to get back to some form of normality after separation, to be warm towards them and respecting of their feelings for their father.
- Children want to be told things, and have information honestly shared with them. They do not like having to keep secrets and want to cease being the go-betweens in parental battles. Parents need to be honest

and open, and know that children can handle deep feelings. Perhaps information about infidelity should be kept from children, but in other respects lying to children is not good, and continual lying by both parents is even worse.

There is some evidence, concludes Smith (1999), that children involved in parental conflict may not do as well as they could at school. Concentration is affected by anxiety and feelings of low self-worth, by living in a hostile atmosphere of anger, and by being exposed to adults who continually lie to one another. Parental modelling of dishonesty undermines a child's sense of truth. At the time of separation all children, without exception, want hostility to end. There does not appear to be any direct relationship between parental separation *per se* and the child's subsequent wellbeing (Rodgers and Pryor, 1998). Entering new family compositions where step-parents become involved is another matter.

COUNSELLING YOUNGSTERS AT THE BEGINNING OF PARENTAL SEPARATION

Angela came for counselling initially over theft of school property from a stockroom. Her Head of Year referred her because he wondered whether or not she was caught up with the criminal fraternity. An early analysis, however, established that this was not the case and that the theft was a one-off event from which she had learned her lesson. Later, Angela approached me over another matter since she had found the earlier experience of counselling helpful. She was worried that her parents were not getting on and that a split was imminent. There were frequent arguments each evening, and one fight in which her dad had hit her mum with a kitchen pan had resulted in him leaving the family home to live with his parents. The last occasion her father stayed away was for over a month. Finances were regarded as the source of conflict rather than extra-marital relationships, but they no longer loved each other and slept in separate beds.

Angela was very close to her mother who had confided in her that she had not really loved him for over a year. Angela's father had his own business, which meant that the parental split would have grave consequences for the family's standard of living. Unable to continue mortgage payments, Angela's mother felt that she would have to sell the house even though her husband had agreed that she should stay with the children in the family home.

Counselling for Angela consisted of supporting her for a future that looked uncertain, and over altered family conditions that would bring hardship. Her request for counselling followed a discussion in the home the previous night in which both parents called the children together to share with them that they were about to separate. Each of the children could choose whom they would like to live with. Both parents were keen to maintain frequent contact.

Nelson-Jones (1996) speaks of clients being able to *predict and create their own futures* with effective thinking skills and a sense of optimism: 'You have no facts about the future since it has not happened' (1996: 113). One way of looking at the future, he says, is to view it as a 'mental construction based on your subjective as contrasted with objective reality. It is the words and pictures in your head about what is to come' (ibid.).

After a short session of facilitating her feelings of loss and disappointment over imagining a bleak and unpromising future, she found the means of contemplating an altered world more optimistically with effective thinking skills. Pupils in school facing the prospect of their parents' separation often have a pessimistic view of the outcome, and this has to be handled tenderly. But predictions of the future often contain perceptual distortions. Clients who have experienced parental separation, although suffering trauma at the time, often view the separation as a positive and more beneficial outcome in the longer term, but for those at the beginning of this process and without the benefit of hindsight this can be a very troublesome period – not too dissimilar to bereavement, as the research above has shown. Clients will often underestimate the good consequences and overestimate the bad consequences of their parents ceasing to live together.

Obviously the fear of change is unsettling and young clients need to feel supported during this delicate phase. The fear of failure also weighs heavily and often has an effect on peer relationships. Clients often *catastrophize* their situations and make absolutist demands on themselves (Ellis, 1980). Pupils also *misattribute* (Nelson-Jones, 1996) the cause of the split to their behaviour, and they increase thereby the tendency for self-fulfilled prophecies. Since they cannot change their behaviour overnight, they must be responsible for their parents continuing to fight, and such reasoning shifts blame and makes splitting up 'legitimised'.

Scaling can be a useful method of helping such clients weigh up the advantages and disadvantages of their parents parting, and this technique was used to help Angela see that all was not lost with her parents choosing to separate. 'Can you scale from 1–10 (high number to represent gains) the advantages in terms of a reduction in hostility, shouting, mistrust and violence that would result when your parents part? Can you similarly scale the disadvantages?' Her scores and reflections are illustrated in Figure 7.1.

From her imagined predictions, Angela was encouraged to conduct *reality testing* on whether the future would be a catastrophe once her parents had parted. Nelson-Jones (1996) suggests four stages in setting personal goals for reality testing:

- authorship of your life
- clarity of focus
- increased meaning
- increased motivation

advantages	disadvantages
8 ~ no shouting, no fighting, no mistrust	not much money coming in ~ 7
6 ~ I can concentrate on school	mum or dad may get lonely ~ 5
4 ~ I can bring friends back to an argument-free household	friends ask embarrassing ~ 4 questions

Figure 7.1   *Scale chart*

Claiming 'authorship of your life' meant for Angela that her future prospects were not wholly dependent on her parents' happiness, and that energy spent in fruitless longing was distracting her from personal goals. Increased motivation derives from increased meaning and clear goals, and this became the focal point of therapy. Angela, through the Miracle Question (Davis and Osborn, 2000), was encouraged to imagine awaking one morning with the world being very different (Lines, 2000). Her parents were no longer together; she lived with her mother and visited her father at weekends. What would the world look like? As she began to speculate more positively, she began to realize that her social world as an adolescent of 14 would not alter very much. Yes, there would be an initial sense of lost-ness, and less money for designer-label clothes and for going out. But then, her visits to her father over the weekends might present other social opportunities and, possibly, pocket money to continue her pursuits with friends.

We needed in the final stages of therapy to set a goal to help her think positively and to operate in a *doing* rather than *being* mode. Adolescents speak the language of activity, and this can give an impetus and optimistic outlook in reality testing. Through brainstorming, we explored a range of goals within the process of the Egan framework of her preferred scenario. The goals were as follows:

1   to spend more time out of the house with friends;
2   to remain neutral over her parents' decision and be mature in accepting that this was their choice;
3   to voice her disgust and protest, and to let both parents know in no uncertain terms how their future plans had left her feeling terribly disheartened.

Goal 1 was selected, with goal 2 being a secondary and subsidiary goal to work upon. This gave her not only a more settled feeling about her parents splitting up, but also a clearer understanding of adult responsible decision-making and a more realistic perspective that her life, with two parents apart, would not be for her the end of her world.

COUNSELLING AFTER SEPARATION

Children in individual counselling for parental separation are not to be seen as patients in need of in-depth therapy, but as clients in need of considerable short-term support.

> Luke was referred to counselling over his difficult behaviour. He was very rest-less in lessons, attention-seeking and easily aroused when peers provoked him. The teacher was particularly skilled in observing disruptive behaviour that was not simply caused by wilful nonconformity. While Mitchell, Luke's older brother, had left the family home to live with his grandmother, Luke and his young sister (known as 'Princess') had been left to cope in an unsettled home with two parents with severe alcohol problems. This continued for a year until an aunt took over their care and allowed access for both children to their parents (who by now were separated) on a weekly basis.
>
> During the introductory counselling session, Luke said that although Mitchell had a close relationship with his grandmother and Princess was dad's favourite, he felt close to no one. Luke was very keen to receive coun-selling, for there were unresolved issues over his relationship with his father. He knew he could never compete with Princess, but, nevertheless, his father was still special. A recent event, however, had been a cause of concern. He had gone along with his brother to a premier league football match, where his father sold football programmes. He considered himself fortunate to receive a free ticket from one of his father's friends, since Mitchell regularly attended the match. After the game, the family met at a nearby pub. While drinking lemonade, his sister slipped from a stool and accused Luke of messing about. By this time, Luke's father was 'merry' with drink, and though he was not drunk he began to take it out on Luke after Princess had accused him of push-ing her off the stool. Dad shouted aggressively, using foul language, and when Luke protested and stormed off to the toilet his father followed him. Fortunately, the men in the group, being fully aware of the situation and of the volatility of Luke's father, followed him into the toilet. Luke's father had set about Luke, punching him in the ribs and kicking him while on the floor. It took three men to pull Luke's father off him. Apart from suffering many bruises, Luke was very traumatized by this experience and vowed never to see his father again. Luke's grandfather admonished his son and social services were called to monitor the situation temporarily under Child Protection regulations.

For children who are still traumatized by family violence, person-centred counselling is often indicated; and where children have been separated from parents and are undergoing a deep sense of loss, humanistic counselling and psychodynamic counselling have often proven beneficial (Lines, 2000). These approaches can be time consuming, however. The advantage of Nelson-Jones's cognitive-humanistic therapy is that there is within the single approach the useful integration of brief humanistic counselling, aimed primarily at validating clients' feelings of loss and sense of being let down, with cognitive styles that combine thinking skills with time-limited problem solution. Nelson-Jones speaks a lot about 'mind skills', and about the ability to think about problem solutions and the choices which are open to clients in resolving their own dilemmas (Nelson-Jones, 1996).

The humanistic element of counselling was centred upon Luke's ambivalent feelings for his father, combined with the practical considera-tion of how he might deal with visits to stay with him over future week-ends. This was particularly important after Luke's father had apologized and was beginning to speak to him again by phone.

After person-centred counselling, Luke was asked how he saw the future. In the counselling session, he had brought up three issues. One was whether he could ever trust his father again after the pub incident. Luke said that he was not afraid of his father being drunk, that he had learnt to cope with that many times before, but that the assault had left him very upset. It added to his sense of loss that his mother, who was in a new relationship was, according to rumour, currently pregnant. The third issue was that, unlike Mitchell and Princess, Luke had no parent with whom to form a strong attachment and model himself for adult-hood. These three issues were written down thus:

1   How could I deal with the possible risks of dad's drunken aggression on future weekend stays?
2   What does it mean to me that my mother is pregnant by another man, that she wants a 'replacement child' to myself?
3   What does it mean to me that I no longer live with either my mum or dad?

In the next session, I asked Luke what he could remember and what stood out for him from our discussion in the previous session. It was a combi-nation of the second and third issues. Luke clearly had a good relation-ship with his auntie, but he could not resolve his sense of loss of both parents through alcohol misuse, a loss that was reinforced by the fact that his mother had a replacement child.

The underlying issue in counselling was to ascertain to what degree these experiences of loss were being generalized and were affecting his behaviour with peers. There was the question of the emotional, social and behavioural consequences that could result from 'thinking' that 'neither mum or dad live with me and consider me of unique worth' (McGuiness, 1998).

Through mind-skills work, we looked at what he might be telling himself from very real feelings of rejection. The counselling relationship was fundamental in raising his self-esteem, yet the counselling needed to move on from validating his sense of loss to giving him a real sense of importance. The very act of selecting *him* and giving *him* time and an arena for *special attention* was in itself the beginning of a process, but counselling needed to address termination issues and to enable Luke, even as a minor, to function self-sufficiently.

Nelson-Jones reminds us that 'One way of viewing personal problems is that they are difficulties that challenge you to find solutions' (1996: 3). But how can a child persuade a parent that he or she is worthy of love? In the majority of cases, children do not have to. Parents have a biological predisposition to love their children, just as children are predisposed to be loved and nurtured by adults, and unconsciously send out dependency messages to that effect. In Luke's case, the goal had no practical task but was one of positive thinking, in spite of received messages to the contrary, messages that shouted out, 'You're of no importance to me!'

How did Luke think of himself, among peers who, at the very least, lived with one biological parent while he was living with his auntie because his parents had proved inadequate to care for him? Nelson-Jones (1996) suggests that we cannot cease but to think, and when we think we *choose* what we think, and, by self-control, choose *what not to think*. He also speaks of an existential awareness for each of us of my finite existence and the need to take responsibility for *my life* in *this period* in which I occupy *my place* on the earth. People who have suffered accidents (Lines, 1995a), or who have come close to death with cancer (Eva in Yalom, 1990), or who have survived national tragedies like the Holocaust (Frankl, 1959), often feel as though they are living a second life on borrowed time. There is an outlook, a philosophical stance, so to speak, that does not harp on past losses and bitter regrets, on wishing life had been other than it is, but rather re-focuses on that which is, on taking responsibility for one's own existence with regard to those opportunities for growth that come along.

It may appear ridiculous to suggest that a 12-year-old such as Luke should re-view his situation, of loss of both parents to drink, in a more favourable light, but this is what Luke needed to do to move on and get the most from life. Apportioning blame rarely helps parties move on. Luke's parents had so many problems that they could barely look after themselves, let alone their children. Luke was beginning the process of individuation, and engaging in a peer group would be the direction in which to steer him. Effective thinking skills for Luke meant reframing his situation of loss. Against those approaches which encourage catharsis to temper strong feelings, Nelson-Jones says, 'Feelings tend to be the parents of choices. You can decide whether to develop them, to regulate them or to treat them as unimportant' (1996: 36). Choosing what to think involves listening to your body, and assuming responsibility for what you think involves listening to your inner valuing processes.

Luke was fully aware that he had been poorly parented, that his mum and dad, in different ways, had not come up to scratch, and that their selfishness was wrong and had had effects on his wellbeing – the early work covered this material. But this effect did not need to be permanent, nor his situation irretrievable. In the carefully phrased questions, I persistently asked Luke whether he thought these early life experiences would always hold him back. Assertively, he said not, and this assertion was beginning to give birth to a more determined spirit that said in effect, 'I won't let this beat me, but will rise above it.' Empowerment for Luke was in him taking advantage in his thinking of the opportunities which living with his auntie was offering him. I asked Luke to spell out the social advantages of living with his aunt. 'I've formed a friendship with Jason and Michael, and I hang around with them. We go bowling on Wednesdays, swimming with my auntie and her kids on Sunday mornings, and rollerblading down the park most nights.' His social world, once he was *freed* from the responsibility and daily worry of parenting parents, was beginning to blossom.

Countertransference issues of unconsciously 'wishing to parent' clients can get in the way of client empowerment, particularly for those clients in homes where alcohol is misused. The counsellor must find ways of helping clients move on through the individuation process, *because of*, not in spite of, early familial impoverishment. Effective thinking skills offer the integrationist counselling practitioner a means of bringing about this end. Pupils will be reminded occasionally of their losses through material delivered in the curriculum. Through peer boasting of good times had in wholesome families, they will feel deprived and sad, and may have memories of violent and social unrest by contrast. In order to counteract these disabling images cognitively, the client needs a perspective that is enabling and not destructive. Luke was able to progress from an environment of little hope and promise to another that was nurturing. From a negative self-frame, he formed through counselling a new mental construct that said: *This is my life. I will make the most of it. I don't have to let my unfortunate start hold me back. I can move forward through positive thinking.*

COUNSELLING ON LIVING WITH STEP-PARENTS

Karl's parents had split up three years before he came for counselling. His form teacher had asked him, months earlier, to attend counselling to seek support over his temper and to receive anger-management training. In spite of three exclusions for very aggressive fighting and two visits by his mother to his Head of Year to relate his abuse of her and his explosive temper in the family, he failed to heed the advice to come for counselling until the family moved in with Jack, who became his stepfather. When his mother had begun this new relationship with Jack, Karl had bitterly and vocally protested. He said that his mother was 'building a new life for herself in preparation for when us kids leave home'. When they were to move into Jack's house, there was a violent scene that prompted Karl to run away and live for a week at his girlfriend's home. Karl eventually gave in and moved into the new house.

The tension rose almost daily, as his feelings for Jack turned from dislike to loathing. Karl was to reach his sixteenth birthday in two months' time, after which he was off! His request for counselling was to help him cope and see time through. A further reason was to explore whether to stay and make his mum see 'how much she was being hoodwinked by him' and get her to leave. The night before approaching me, Jack had chased Karl from the house after a heated verbal exchange. Jack raced after him in his car, slammed on the brakes and squared up to him. They were braced face to face, but neither would throw the first punch.

Selecting a short-term goal for Karl was through collaborative counselling during a mini-crisis period. Managing aggression was important for Karl because it was being manifested in other contexts that would affect future socializing with peers. Clearly his behaviour was an unconscious manoeuvre to get Jack out, behaviour which might prove counterproductive and which would involve him in investing too much energy to too little effect, and at the expense of his individuation. Although there were issues of his feelings for his father who was 'down' after the separation, the dominant issue was how he could live for a short while with a stepparent that his younger brother and sister had apparently accepted.

Person-centred counselling facilitated his growing sense of loss at seeing his mother besotted by a man other than his father, but Nelson-Jones's effective thinking skills of 'coping self-talk', 'coaching self-talk' and 'doing as well as I can' helped Karl maintain his self-control (1996: 46–56).

Coping self-talking (Meichenbaum, 1977, 1983, 1985, 1986) is used for managing stress, anger and impulsiveness. Negative self-talk focuses on the possible *outcomes*, which for Karl meant wishing to be rid of Jack, but positive self-talk focuses on the *processes* of survival, which for Karl meant 'coaching himself through' his final stage of adolescence before 'moving on', given the possibility that his mother might remain with Jack. Negative self-talk for Karl involved him catastrophizing (Ellis, 1987) a life for his mother living with Jack as being unbearable, and, for him, impossible to imagine.

Self-talking skills should be used alongside other skills such as relaxation techniques. I felt it would be helpful to teach Karl how to relax, since much of his agitation was thought-induced while he sat in his bedroom, rather than incident-induced. Relaxation exercises were conducted in session following the customary method of 'progressive muscular relaxation' (Jacobson, 1938) and breathing exercises from deep to shallow inhaling, together with visualization to help calm his situational stress. Clients usually choose the visualizing scene, in which they recall a situation of their younger childhood where they have felt really at ease with themselves and at peace with their relational world. Failing that, I find the most evocative visualizing location is a beach scene, though I check out that clients have not had a bitter experience at the seaside. The scene is imaginatively described as though by the young-ster (donkeys, ice-cream, ball games, sandcastles etc.). I then lead them on to view themselves running towards the shoreline and taking off in flight, lifting up to the sky like a seagull, higher and higher and way above the clouds till they imagine themselves floating over the land below them. After this dreamy phase of detachment has continued for a spell in silence, I talk them down again, step by step, towards the cold reality of banal existence.

Elements of Nelson-Jones's structured approach were made use of as a framework for counselling:

- Get yourself relaxed.
- Emphasize coping rather than mastery.
- Strive for a clear image. Verbalize the contents of the image.
- Take a step-by-step approach. Visualize the less anxiety-evoking scenes before moving on to the more anxiety-evoking scenes.
- Use coping self-talk, with its coaching and calming dimensions. (Nelson-Jones, 1996: 136)

When Karl visualized the worst possibility, or worst-case scenario, of his mother being happy 'in the arms of Jack', he became angry in session, since he felt powerless to alter his mother's feelings for Jack. He was even angrier when he recalled the street incident with Jack. However, once Karl had begun to focus on his mother 'being happy' as opposed to 'being depressed' as she had been before meeting Jack, his expression was more of regret than of anger. Redirected visualizing was a start. 'Calming self-talk' and 'coping self-talk' serve to reduce hostile feelings in situations that cannot be changed, but change is necessary. Karl had no power or responsibility to change his mother's feelings for her new partner, and it would have been unproductive to think otherwise. But Karl could alter *his* feelings through effective thinking skills about how he allowed his mother's preferences to affect him. The point was to help Karl to divert his thinking skills from 'self-oppression' to 'self-support'. This was the major focus of the next few sessions.

It required little work to enable him to see philosophically that this must happen, that his negativity was affecting his peer relationships adversely, and that his resentment was worsening his relationship with his mother. 'Calming self-talk' was rehearsed in session with Karl saying to himself: 'I can remain calm and relaxed. I wish things could have been happier with dad and mum together, but it's not the end of the world; she's obviously in love with Jack and I can't alter that. I'm glad she's no longer depressed.' 'Coping self-talk' was also rehearsed: 'We have to move on. I have my girlfriend and we're happy, and I'll be out of here when I'm 16 to live with her. I won't let this get to me. I can put up with it for a few more months till after my exams.'

In addition to 'self-talking' thinking skills and positive visualizing of 'mum being happy' rather than 'mum being depressed', other coping management skills to defuse enflamed anger were offered to Karl in case of a further heated exchange with Jack. Youngsters often resent being corrected by step-parents, and although most couples recognize this it occasionally results in arguments where strong adolescents exploit power relations. In Karl's case, this had already happened. Karl was encouraged to create positive images of himself being powerful, not over Jack but over his affective state, and the techniques of thought-stopping and vacuuming the negative thoughts and images from his mind were taught as an emergency aid at moments of crisis (Nelson-Jones, 1996). The counselling contract closed after 'coaching self-talking' skill work had been completed in anticipation of a probable confrontation with Jack. Karl described what led up to a typical altercation – usually Jack correcting Karl for speaking down to his mother after she had repeatedly ordered him to come in on time. 'When Jack steps in to protect mum, I must see where this may lead and back off for mum's sake. I have to look away, take a sharp intake of breath and relax my shoulders.' We rehearsed what he might say in 'coaching self-talk': 'I will say, "Sorry", even if I don't mean it. I will let Jack have the last word even though he has no right to butt in, again for mum's sake. I will then seek to escape from being near him, and slide away upstairs to my room, where I will carry out relaxation exercises.' This self-talking coaching was learned by rote and was practised in session a few times to help generalize the principles that could be applied in other possible scenarios.

CONCLUSION

There is no doubting the demographic change that has occurred in the 'nuclear' family in western society in modern times. Different notions of family composition include cohabitation and homosexual unions, and these changes illustrate the broad diversity in nurturing and bringing up children. Sadly, these liberal changes have led to a less committed approach to parenting relationships, large-scale abandonment of marriage, rising rates of parental separation and divorce, and ongoing family upheaval. Some children experience more than one step-parent within their childhood years.

Parental separation and divorce need not be traumatic, however, and enlightened parents who arrive at a long-thought-out decision that they can no longer live together 'even for the sake of the children', and who can manage their parting well, may not cause irreparable damage to their children. Although research suggests that in the long run teenagers come to terms with their parents breaking up, in the immediate situation the news can be devastating. Counselling pupils in school involves supporting three groups. First, many clients become troubled when their parents argue to the point of deciding to have trial periods apart, and particularly when there is a formal separation. A second category is those youngsters whose parents have separated and where the resultant conditions have become hard to bear, such as post-separation parental contact and being expected to keep secrets. Finally, there are youngsters who find living with step-parents heightens their sense of loss and results in fractious relations. Teenagers are particularly reluctant to receive correction from a non-biological parent.

The experience of parental separation has been likened to the experience of bereavement. Brief cognitive-humanistic counselling offers scope with three groups of clients – those undergoing the onset, the process or the outcomes of parental separation.

For those facing the prospect of parental separation, reality testing through the construction of goals designed to offset the often distorted prediction of a bleak future helps clients to move on in their development in spite of their parents' decision to part. Restructuring thought processes helps teenage clients to re-view their reactions to situations in which they have little control. With those clients whose parents have parted, effective thinking skills involve them in choosing how they construct their parents' splitting-up and reframing their affective states to self-protect rather than self-oppress. The final category recognizes that living reluctantly with a step-parent can be troublesome. 'Coping self-talk' and 'coaching self-talk' skills can help youngsters not only to manage their own stress, but also to live in potentially explosive situations without rising to baiting.

8

LOSS AND BEREAVEMENT

Traditional approaches have proved effective in supporting bereaved clients in school (Lines, 2000), but the limitations of time and lack of a suitable counselling arena of containment may not allow the processes of transference and healing to take place completely. Even brief models of psychodynamic, person-centred or existential therapy may not realize their potential in a setting where non-interruption cannot be guaranteed. This chapter examines both individual and group therapeutic means of helping pupils and students deal with their losses through brief integrative models. Therapy needs to be geared to the setting and to the developmental transfer of adolescents from parental dependency to peer-group allegiances.

In this chapter, loss and bereavement as they affect pre-pubescent and adolescent pupils within western society are first examined, particularly as they impact within school. The theoretical insights of how bereavement affects young people through their transitional stage are then reviewed, with a particular emphasis upon stages of acceptance.

There are counselling agencies (such as 'Cruse' in the UK) that are dedicated to bereavement work with adults and youngsters. Short-term counselling may be offered also from hospice resources to particular family members who cannot cope either before or in the aftermath of the death of someone they have loved and nursed. Counselling in school is not intended to replace such provision but to supplement it, since many pupils feel a greater need to be strong in the family home than in school. The curriculum will provide occasional stimuli on death and dying that may trigger flashbacks and suppressed grief, catching youngsters off their guard and causing them to break down in class. On-hand counselling provision can be invaluable in such cases.

Schools are large cross-cultural communities in themselves and on occasion have had to face tragedies that affect the whole community. Education authorities have begun to provide guidance and strategies for major disasters, and there is also a demand for proactive curriculum input on death and dying to be given as a matter of course, particularly in Australia and North America. Unpredictable events, along with stimuli in lessons, may trigger latent unresolved bereavement issues. This is more likely to be the case in a society that pushes death under the carpet (Nelson-Jones, 1996).

THE CONTEXT OF BEREAVEMENT FOR WESTERN YOUNG PEOPLE IN SCHOOL

There is denial of death and dying in modern times. Western society has equipped young people poorly to face the prospect of dying, compared with those in eastern cultures. An eastern Buddhist story teaches the universality of dying and the futility of looking for a cure for death (cited by Farrell, 1999). A mother who is bereaved of her daughter is given the impossible task of entering a village to collect mustard seeds, but only from those houses where no one has died – none could be found! In every home death had left its mark. By contrast, many of us in the west live our lives cherishing our bodies for perpetual existence as though immune to future extinction. We live within a transitional phase, where ideas of going to heaven still hold influence with many, in spite of the erosion of traditional religious belief.

The clinical administration of modern-day funeral rites, and the continual viewing of facile images of killing that bombard us from the television screen, tend to sanitize the cold reality of death and dying. Young people can suffer in three respects:

- They are not encouraged to take their spiritual development seriously.
- They are 'protected' from visible grief that is customarily expressed at funeral ceremonies.
- They have much spare time in which to watch television.

All this leaves pre-pubescent children and adolescents wholly unprepared to face the loss of a loved one upon whom they had been dependent for emotional support.

There is evidence of a great deal of hesitancy in talking about death with young people in school, in spite of the vast evidence of its debilitating effects (Rowling, 1996). The reasons given vary from it being a reflection of teachers' own fears of death and uncertainty, to a wish to maintain the 'innocence' of young people, and to beliefs that the issue is either too deep and complex or too personal for public airing. The high numbers of pupils in many schools will mean that bereavement will be a frequent issue for teachers, not only in the management of their pupils' losses but also in their loss of colleagues. More particularly, teachers have to deal with tragedies of their pupils dying or being killed, with all the heartache that accompanies such loss, and this can have traumatic consequences for a school.

Managing bereavement in school

For most schools, the task of supporting youngsters who become visibly upset or withdrawn in lessons falls to individual teachers who might just happen to rise to the need if they have the time, good will or personal resources with which to help. In my own school, two of the most dedicated teachers died of cancer within a year, and left a profound void for the school community. Bereavement counselling is demanding, and requires practitioners who can handle deep feelings and who have resolved their own loss and bereavement issues (McGuiness, 1998).

In addition, some schools have had to manage the aftermath of major disasters in recent times (school trip tragedies and minibus accidents in England, the massacre at Dunblane, Scotland, and shootings in the USA) which have left the school community devastated (McGuiness, 1998). Materials have been produced in Britain to help teachers to handle grief and manage critical incidents (Yule and Gold, 1993). There is in the United States and Australia a growing recognition of the need, in the aftermath of school shootings, bus crashes and natural disasters such as hurricanes and bush fires, to deal more directly with loss issues in the curriculum. Rowling (1996) summarizes the materials that are currently available.

Rowling (1996) presents a study carried out with year eleven pupils in two schools (having mixed cultural and rural/urban catchments) in Sydney, Australia, to emphasize the value of teaching about loss in school. The study showed what could be achieved by teachers 'being human' and by sharing in a frank manner their own experiences of loss and grieving – some personal accounts left pupils stunned and silent (the 'not-talking' phenomenon was felt to be a powerful indicator of engagement). The lessons helped in 'normalizing' their deeply felt sense of loss. Pupils reported in their evaluation responses some understandable ambivalence over the value of lessons in bereavement and loss. While not necessarily liking such lessons, they felt that confronting bereavement issues was necessary and helpful for their current and future life experiences; pupils rated their importance far higher than their teachers believed was necessary. The study also highlighted the valuable strategy of a 'buddy' system approach where pupils talked with peers over their loss experiences (Rowling, 1996). School is the place where youngsters look to adults for models of behaving, and a school counsellor with a rich experience to share is a great asset. I wish to show, however, that carefully selected 'buddy' figures also have a therapeutic role in group work for bereavement.

Loss for children and adolescents is not just about bereavement of relatives and friends, but about the death of pets, and the separation of parents or guardians. It is a mistake to focus on death as the only loss experience. Other loss situations include the following:

- change of schools or neighbourhood
- migration to a new country
- loss of health through illness or accident
- loss of expectation, such as failing to make a team
- loss of self-esteem through a rejection by a friend or a failure in school
- break up of the adolescent's first girlfriend or boyfriend
- passage from one life-stage to another. (Rowling, 1996)

The varied curriculum will present numerous images of death and dying that could prompt flashbacks and memory tracings quite unpredictably, which suggests that such issues are rarely thought about in curriculum planning or dealt with properly in life. Children are essentially power-less but through adolescence they are striving to rise above this depen-dent status and become autonomous. But how will bereavement affect this process?

THE EFFECT OF BEREAVEMENT ON DEVELOPMENT

There can never be a right time to lose a close loved one, either by sepa-ration or bereavement, and adolescence is certainly not the best time to experience such events. Adolescence is a particularly trying phase of development, marked by some theorists as itself a period of mourning for an irretrievably lost childhood (Noonan, 1983).

Some adult carers loathe this period and describe their offspring with derogatory words, such as obnoxious, rebellious, cantankerous, morose, diffident and so on *ad infinitum*. But the phase is necessary in growth towards 'ego-identity' (Erikson, 1956), where the need to understand oneself as a separate differentiated being has to supersede an identity that is defined by particular subjective roles (Erikson, 1963, 1980). Without a degree of rebellion and reaction to authority the individual cannot become born, and the family dynamics of over-control and letting go are not irrelevant to meeting the adolescent task of autonomy (Berkowitz, 1987).

Emotional effects

Unexpected bereavement of a parent or an emotionally dependable figure will inevitably affect the developmental process. Adolescent tensions were described in Chapter 3. The Oedipus myth in the psychoanalytical tradition is an account of the process of individuation (Jacobs, 1993). While not beyond criticism (Howard, 2000), the story explains the ado-lescent experience of needing metaphorically to 'kill off' both parents in order to find the true self. Thus, through much pain and heartache, the developing adolescent pushes the boundaries of control and containment in order to reach the status of adulthood. If, however, the process is thwarted by an untimely parental death, there is no authority against which the adolescent may revolt for self-differentiation. The adolescent is not only robbed of his agent of support and nurture, but of the very mechanism of personal self-development.

The transition from child to adult is an oscillating experience where the self identity of each is set upon a stage of strong contending forces of wanting to be cared for, nurtured and loved on the one hand, and of wanting to be free on the other. Autonomy is both exciting and scary, therefore, and opposition and resistance to authority mark the switchover from dependence on the parent or guardian to dependence on the peer group.

The 'highs' and 'lows' of hormonal activity at puberty intensify the emotional responses of adolescents, and the developmental, cognitive and psycho-social changes 'put young people particularly at risk of the multiple impacts of loss experiences' (Rowling, 1996). The loss of a parent through bereavement or separation has a two-fold effect: security is disturbed because the concept of 'the family' is shattered, and the adolescent's world is less predictable.

Cognitive effects

In challenging and dispensing with parental authority, adolescents unconsciously look around for substitute authorities, either in alternative parental figures or friends, or moralistic ideologies, such as are found in religion, politics, humanitarian concerns or environmental issues (Lines, 1999b). Young people in their cognitive development acquire the faculties to challenge the received world-views of their upbringing (Jacobs, 1993), a process of moving from literal views of the universe to ones more figurative.

Literal views, such as 'God provides for all those who love him', may be retained if supported by authorities, such as the 'inspired holy text' (Lines, 1995b), the religious leader or the sacred community, but by and large the general trend is towards symbolic accounts of experience, in metaphor and paradox. This 'formal operational' thought occurs between 12 and 16, and is the capability to think abstractly and to form hypotheses to deduce meaning (Inhelder and Piaget, 1958).

Cognitive development is highly significant in the mourning process and in coming to terms with loss by forming a convincing rationale to account for what is felt. Religious belief, or lack of religious belief, becomes paramount, with no guaranteed outcomes that all will be well: some gain greater faith, some lose faith and some begin to face up to radical doubts they have fostered secretly and which have lain dormant for some time. Although the nature and content of religious belief is culturally determined, it is nevertheless for many a time of spiritual growth or decline towards nihilism. Spiritual questions rise to the surface after bereavement (Lines, 1999b), and paranormal accounts may also become credible.

Social effects

Bereavement is a time when one's mortality is brought very much into question. It is a time for radical re-evaluation and reorganization of the self, but adolescents who are already going through a transitional phase will be knocked off course and left temporarily disorientated. The adolescent may become depressed, detached and unreachable, even by those familial fellow-sufferers who have the capacity and will to offer emotional support. They need strong supportive adults around them to carry them through. In some cases this support is not available, hence they turn to their friends and peers – if they have such a network of support – even though the latter seldom have the capacity for empathy.

In cases where individuals have weak social skills and little friendship-building appeal, they may withdraw into themselves and become social isolates. Irritability and unprovoked anger displayed by grieving youngsters make them unattractive to peers who often feel they make all the moves to be sympathetic, to little account.

Children generally have very little awareness of how other people think and feel, and, as with cognitive development, their innate empathic capabilities have to be nurtured (Rowe, 1996). Socialization helps in the process, but there is the need to facilitate personal sharing of experience through communication in aiding adolescents to develop a higher sense of human 'connectedness' with other people (Lines, 2000, 2002).

Materially, all human beings are made of the same substance, our Darwinian roots point to our commonality, and we each breathe the same breath (spirit) of God according to the Genesis story. Any means of drawing attention to our interconnections with each other – comradeship, collective ritual, team spirit, friendship-bonding and the counselling relationship, etc. – will help to foster empathy (Rowe, 1996). The counsellor's personal resources and empathy are a prerequisite in helping the bereaved to cope. Ultimately, for most, there occurs a healthy acceptance of the loss and an adjustment to the altered circumstances that death brings about.

BEREAVEMENT COUNSELLING

Bereavement counselling attends to the grief experience and the maladaptive behaviour that results from the client's loss. Theoretically, it is directed towards the recognition of patterns or stages through which bereft individuals pass following a death. It helps the clients in coming to terms with grief, or helps to encourage adaptive responses (Parkes, 1986; Worden, 1984).

Theoretical perspectives on bereavement counselling

Some researchers contend that bereavement and mourning have a necessary survival value, but Farrell points to the limitations of biological behavioural mechanisms of survival according to attachment theory. He argues that grief and occasional flashbacks should become eased the more they occur, but this is not normally the case.

As Farrell (1999) recognizes, the working through of grief does imply some sort of end or completion of the grief process through 'a gradual decline of grief', the consigning of it to a hidden place in the unconscious or subconscious. What is occurring at a spiritual level of consciousness is a *denial of intrinsic human impermanence*. Death represents a challenge to this deep denial: 'intrinsic permanence is a quality we bestow on life to help us maintain our continuity, our sense of reality, that thus enables us to continue our existence with some degree of happiness' (Farrell, 1999: 145). The inability to accept one's mortality is recognized by many counselling theorists (Ellis, 1987; Jacobs, 1993; Nelson-Jones, 1996).

The counsellor might address the consequences of the death of a loved one, but the stark reality of life's impermanence (drawn into focus through bereavement) will be dealt with more fittingly through counselling that has a more philosophical, existential, religious or spiritual orientation, since such approaches draw attention to the powerlessness of those left behind:

> We have no power to interfere in the process of disintegration.... We are helpless: we cannot help them on whatever journey they may be about to undertake, we cannot guide them or give them words of love or encouragement; we cannot tell them they are safe; we cannot hold them or comfort them; we can no longer protect them. (Farrell, 1999: 145)

Perhaps, the commonly felt guilt is in part due to the fact that we have allowed ourselves to become totally immersed in the search for happiness based on an erroneous sense of permanence.

Kübler-Ross (1982) has argued convincingly that physicians, practitioners and counsellors must avoid dealing with bereavement and loss by denial if they wish to prevent their patients and clients from doing the same. There is a fundamental need to confront the issue, to discuss the fears and to share with others any sense of preparedness or otherwise. Kübler-Ross (1982) has identified seven significant stages of people suffering terminal conditions:

1 a sense of 'numbness'
2 denial and isolation
3 anger
4 bargaining
5 depression

6 acceptance
7 a sense of hope

These stages are common but are not watertight or predictable states occurring in a natural sequence. There is much overlap and some stages will hardly be discernible in some people. The timing and period of each stage is equally variable and, as mentioned in Chapter 7, it is possible that clients may experience a reciprocal change from state to state rather than a progressive movement (Parkes, 1986).

After suffering a spinal injury in 1986 I can personally vouch for many of Kübler-Ross's findings (Lines, 1995a). Anger and depression, particularly, characterize adolescents suffering bereavement – 'How dare they leave me in this way!' People facing loss and bereavement find it difficult to speak meaningfully of the love of God, and some have a 'death-wish', a morbid desire to commit suicide whereby the patient feels compelled to become isolated from loved ones, who wrongly interpret this as rejection and ingratitude (Lines, 1995a). Elements of Kübler-Ross's stages were evident in each of the cases outlined below.

BRIEF INDIVIDUAL BEREAVEMENT COUNSELLING

Judging when a young person may require bereavement counselling is not easy, and boys particularly are not 'permitted' to show grief publicly in western society.

> This was the case with Dennis, a year seven boy, whose father had been killed in a motor accident. His behaviour indicated to all his managers that he was not coping but he spurned every offer to address his loss, until a fight with his best friend brought him under escort to me for counselling. This being an involuntary referral, Dennis sat with a downcast look and refused to talk.

I used a diversionary tactic (Beck et al., 1979), and asked him to make a cup of tea and to water the flowers in order to withdraw him from a 'counselling-seated' pose where he was 'expected' to articulate his feelings. He was at the numbness stage (Kübler-Ross, 1982), but, in carrying out the menial task, he loosened up and began chatting about his father's interests in classic cars (a mutual interest sparked off by pictures on my wall), which began to sow the seeds of a workable relationship. I have on occasion taken pupils out into a different environment to ease the tension of therapeutic-talk expectations of sitting in the counselling room. This was not necessary for Dennis, however, who began to speak through the 'scribble' technique.

The 'continuous line' or 'scribble' technique has been used to positive effect with bereaved young people whose behaviour has become troublesome and who have communication difficulties (Le Count, 2000). The technique involves the client drawing freehand with his non-dominant hand, with eyes closed, for 30 seconds, after which he is asked to identify with a little added detail two animals or human shapes within the line. It is hoped that images are thereby released from the unconscious to act as a prompt for counselling. Feelings of anger are articulated through drawing and verbalizing of what is seen and interpreted. From his scribble, Dennis drew a monster on wheels that had killed his 'daddy' and from this lead he began to articulate ambivalent feelings of love and hate for cars.

> Kirsty was excluded for continual abuse and bad language to teachers. During her reintegration interview, her mother disclosed that Kirsty had nursed anger after the death of her grandmother. On an earlier occasion, Kirsty was offered bereavement counselling but she declined this, saying, 'It upsets me so much, I can't hack it.' The loss of her grandmother took a heavy toll, not only of herself, but also of her mother. Kirsty had lived for a while with her grandmother, and before her death had frequently visited her after school, since she lived only two doors away. At times now when she visited her grandfather he was low and weepy, and Kirsty would fetch her mother to his aid. The family routinely visited the grave where flowers were placed every Sunday morning. Since this was three years after the death, the family appeared 'stuck' and unable to move on.

Again, the client was 'sent to the counsellor to be fixed', and initially she declined to speak, being at the bargaining stage – 'Give me my nan and I'll behave for you!' (Kübler-Ross, 1982). An initial diversionary tactic from the loss-event enabled us to begin to talk, however. Kirsty's grandmother had loved the music of Bryan Adams and kept a scrapbook of photos and magazine articles on him. I asked if she'd mind bringing it in to the second session. She not only brought it in but brought also her gran's favourite tape, which she played in session. The music, and particularly the lyrics, 'Everything I do, I do it for you', reduced her to tears, and I also felt a depth of sadness that made me cry. As I pondered the sentiments and imagined her sitting at her grandmother's bedside in her dying days, in tears, and looking into her eyes, I again was touched deeply:

> Look into my eyes
>   You will see, what you mean to me
> ... it's not worth dying for
>   ... everything I do, I do it for you
> ... I'd die for you.

This was the beginning of a therapeutic bonding that had healing potential, in that the song became the key to unlock her feelings of loss. Time and again she visited me during the six months after our four-session brief therapy to thank me for 'being with her during that difficult time'. The song became the link between us and we explored through phrase after phrase the wants and wishes of her grandmother for Kirsty to have a fulfilled life in the strength of their relationship – without her in body but with her in spirit. Five years after working with Kirsty, I still am unable to hear that song without becoming 'connected' to the memory of Kirsty's sadness.

> Carina was a year nine girl, who again was 'stuck' in therapy. In her case a different integrative approach was used to get therapy moving towards goal-centred work. She had lost her brother Darren to cancer, and at her insistence his bedroom and belongings had not been touched since the day of his death. She said that sleep was a particular problem, and that she often cried herself to sleep just thinking about her brother. Friends were almost abandoned when she refused to go out, and for school assignments there was no motivation since the future held no promise. With more precise questioning, it appeared that her depressive state was also caused by seeing her mother and grandmother broken in spirit and tearful. The counselling, therefore, apart from validating her sense of loss through a person-centred approach, was primarily focused upon setting goals to help move her on, to shape a future, to improve her sleeping pattern, and then, secondarily, to consider how she might deal with mum's and gran's feelings.
>
> She was keen to bring to my attention two paranormal events, which, although not frightening, were intriguing to her. She said that on many occasions her bedroom radio came on by itself, and that the CD, which rarely worked, had come on a couple of times. She was convinced that Darren had done this, and her mother claimed that she had seen Darren on a few occasions. Carina said that she had never seen him herself, but would have dearly loved to.

I rarely rate paranormal experiences high on the therapeutic agenda, since these experiences right themselves and become integrated into the person's belief system once emotional and social healing has taken place. I have spoken elsewhere (Lines, 1999b) of the need for young people undergoing bereavement therapy to hold on to belief systems. It is important not to crush these beliefs no matter how tentatively they may be held, since they serve as cognitive supportive systems to help deal with loss. Consequently, I use these beliefs in paranormal activities. I asked Carina what she thought Darren wanted of her, and this gave authority and 'permission' for her to develop a future-centred perspective and a sense of hope (Kübler-Ross, 1982).

We became solution-focused for three sessions. On electing not to remain 'stuck', we moved on towards an imagined future scenario. Her 'stuckness' was the *decision* to hold the hands of the clock still, as though frozen, at the point at which Darren had died. It seemed painful for her to live without Darren, and an approach that registered *that pain* within a goal-centred programme was required. Such an approach has recently been constructed by Christine Dunkley (2001), and represents the pain barrier diagrammatically in order to assess the state of 'being stuck' within movement towards a preferred scenario. The model in Figure 8.1

1 How things were	2 Now	3 Pain barrier	4 Future

No zeal for future
No energy for
  friends
School
  unimportant
Being lonely
Depressed
Not sleeping well
  and always tired
Carrying   **A** •——→ *progress*
  mum & nan   **B Stuck** •———
	Begun talking
	Determined to
	  change
	Want to let
	  Darren go
	More encouraged
		Guilt about altering
		  Darren's room
		Feeling selfish
		Taking responsibility
			* Have a future
			* Have friends
			* Get on track
			  in school
			* Improve
			  sleep pattern

C ←——————•
            •
           •——→ **D**
	Options •	→ **E**

		beginning | middle | end	☺

Figure 8.1   *Pain barrier diagram*
Source: This diagram format was first published in 'The pain barrier diagram' by Christine Dunkley which appeared in the February 2001 issue of the Counselling and Psychotherapy Journal, published by the British Association for Counselling and Psychotherapy. The diagram is reproduced with the kind permission of the author and publisher.

has four columns and brings together motivational interviewing (Chapter 4), the cycle of change (Chapter 10) and bereavement coping within the Egan three-stage framework (1990). The diagram is self-explanatory, and in Carina's situation it served to move her on more rapidly by 'seeing' in print the painful obstacles that needed to be over-come in order to reach the desired goal. Like most goal-centred models, options are collaboratively constructed with no prescription, and the emphasis is on future-orientation.

At A, Carina had registered progress and renewed optimism after the second session; she felt better after seeing her situation diagrammatically and after sharing her feelings in counselling. She reflected on the oscillat-ing stage at B, the frustration of an intolerable past and a future that could only be enjoyed through passing the pain barrier, and she recognized her current scenario as 'stuck'. The option to go back (C) was unimaginable; to remain in pain zone (B), but to push through the pain barrier (E) was felt by her to be the only viable course for a future of friendships, inde-pendence and autonomy. The line at B helps to replicate the meandering experience of actions driven by feelings, and the division of the pain bar-rier into 'beginning, middle and end' (D) creates the real experience of the process of overcoming resistance for long-term benefit, a process that is different for everyone. The diagram is not therapy, but, as Dunkley (2001) says, serves as a therapeutic tool. I have found the model beneficial with young people.

Although meeting the goal in full was not achieved in the four pre-planned sessions, she had begun the process by moving some of Darren's belongings out. To find energy for social integration, she needed to attend to her insomnia. I asked her how often and for how long she lay awake before falling asleep. She said, 'most nights', and for up to 'three hours'. I asked her if she had pictures of Darren in her bedroom. She replied that she had, and that she had often looked at him before falling asleep. I said that I thought this was a positive thing to do, but that when looking at the picture she should recall the good times they had spent together rather than thinking about what was lost, to celebrate his life in place of over-mourning his decease. I asked her further to consider a sleep strategy different from the one she had been using.

> *Counsellor:*   Rather than lying for hours trying to *will yourself* to sleep, try getting
> up and doing a different activity: remove your quilt, sit on the edge of
> your bed and read a page of a magazine, or listen to music on your
> CD player. Alternatively, you might find it helpful to go downstairs
> and make a drink. This often helps by taking your mind off negative
> thinking, and somehow helps your exhausted body to overcome
> your active mind and allow you to slip into sleep.

She found this helpful in giving her energy to complete her remaining tasks, which later follow-up sessions confirmed were completed, including ceasing to take undue responsibility for family grief.

BRIEF GROUP BEREAVEMENT COUNSELLING

Four boys had received from two to five sessions of individual coun-selling before I decided to bring them together in three group sessions, the last being recorded, for later review, without my presence. The group ses-sions were not the culmination but the mid-point of each client's pro-gramme. The aim was to 'normalize' the varied experiences of four bereaved boys through joint communication in the hope that the more experienced members might help the others through their loss traumas (Rowling, 1996). Group bereavement counselling provides the opportu-nity for adolescents to confront their losses together with those who can experience the same, and to explore in a spirit of inquiry what might result from shared dialogue (Gergen and Kaye, 1992).

> James had received two sessions of person-centred counselling before group therapy, Phil five sessions and Matthew three. Clint had received three sessions of person-centred counselling with two sessions of cognitive-behavioural work.

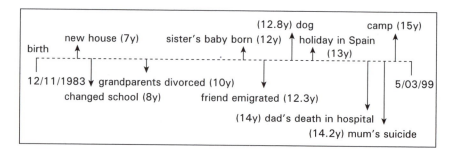

Figure 8.2 *James's loss diagram*

James was in year nine, aged 14 and, although he had self-referred for relationship difficulties, he had much to offer as a 'buddy figure'. Phil, Matthew and Clint were in year seven, aged 11–12, and were referred by pastoral teachers for behavioural reasons.

Phil was difficult to manage: he refused to come to school, threw tantrums in the corridors, was found sitting and crying on stairwells, and had often spurned teachers inappropriately with comments such as 'You don't care!' when they were trying to settle him.

Matthew refused bluntly to do PE, claiming that he should not be made to carry out physical exercise after having lost his mother. He wrote a note to his PE teacher during a non-activity lesson: 'My mum was a PE teacher and she's the only one to teach me PE.' He also wrote on his progress statement that he hated life and wished he were dead.

Clint was the most articulate and intelligent pupil of the group. He was confrontational towards teachers at times, challenging when corrected, but was normally reduced to tears after the crisis was over. It was claimed that he was sometimes difficult to satisfy.

All the boys clearly carried the wounds of their bereavement – the development of each was held in check by their loss experiences.

The sessions prior to the group session had involved the sharing of narratives, beliefs and measures of loss through the completion of loss diagrams. James's Loss Diagram shown in Figure 8.2 is presented as an example.

Loss diagrams are a powerful means of helping the bereaved to place their loss in a broader context of life-experience. Naturally, this is not easy for adolescents and young children. Clients are asked to draw a line representing their life-span from birth to the present. Each of the clients has to draw, bisecting this line at time intervals, another line upward or downward to represent a life-event which they would regard as a gain or loss – bereavement, separation of parents, move of house, birth of a sibling, etc. The length of the bisections represents (say, from 1–10 mm) the degrees of gain or loss. In this way bereaved clients are encouraged to develop a perspective of relative gain and loss. In some instances, losses can be re-viewed as gains in the sense of growing independence.

Narratives of bereavement

The discourse begins with accounts of each participant's bereavement, and then moves on to present fascinating records of how each individual was making sense of his loss in accordance with his current belief system and cognitive ability. Finally, and curiously, the discourse closes on a spiritual theme of a speculative post-death existence, a theme I have discussed elsewhere (Lines, 1999b).

It was evident how James took up the leading role in the interview throughout. He assumed this for himself, possibly because he was senior. James lost both parents quite recently, while Matthew's mother had died seven years ago. The group was content for James to lead the discussion and to take responsibility for the interview. He became the expert, though at times he found it difficult.

James: Well, I lost my parents last year, er, I lost my dad first after he went into hospital with stomach ulcers and it caused a disease that destroyed his liver and kidneys. Several weeks later my mum died of an accidental overdose on paracetamol. Er, so, she, er, they both died around the same time. My dad died in the February. My mum died in April. Er, you never learn to get over it but you learn to carry on – Phil.

Phil: I lost my brother about two years ago. He died of a heart problem, 'cause I was in junior school, and my mum's friends came and told me that my brother died in the afternoon. I started crying and I went home and saw my family crying. And I didn't want to sleep upstairs at bedtime. We didn't want to sleep upstairs 'cause we were scared just in case we saw a ghost of him. [*pause*]

Clint: Well, I lost my dad not so long ago when we broke up for two weeks off. It was on the day that we broke up when he died. He was actually in hospital at the time when he died, and he died of a blood clot on his lung. Even though on the day he died he was diagnosed as having cancer, he died of a different thing. Erm, we had, sort of had [*pause*] good times when he was alive. [*Voice breaks up, chokingly, then a pause.*] And seems as, it seems a bit boring [*breaks down, then a pause*] now that he's dead. I sometimes come to see Mr Lines. [*pause*] And, sometimes I talk to my mum and stuff.

Mat: I lost my mother in [*pause*] 1992... [*pause*] ~ She died of a heart problem.... ~ Well, every time I try and talk to my dad about it he starts being upset as well.

Each participant gave a much fuller account when the second opportunity presented itself, in spite of competitive interjections and interruptions. Each appeared very keen to hold the floor and amplify his narrative on loss. It seemed to be cathartic to tell the story, and tell it fully. I present the discourse of the two respondents who illustrate the two extremes of coping.

James's introduction is comprehensive and has 80 words. His first expansion has only 107 words (a 27-word increase) and is a poignant development that bears more than a hint of guilt, while his second contribution, which has an amusing anecdote, extends to 252 words:

> James: That's a lot like my mum, 'cause my mum – But the way my mum was positioned. [*pause*] Was, er [*pause*], like, she was trying to crawl to the phone. [*pause*] And in a way I still blame myself because she called out to me at six o'clock in the morning but I was groggy and I didn't know what she was, what was wrong with her – didn't know what she was on about. So [*pause*] I didn't know what was wrong with her, and I couldn't understand 'cause I was half-asleep. So I went back to sleep, like. I woke up in the morning. (*pause*) Her bedroom door was closed. [*pause*] So [*pause*]…
>
> James: ~ I think it is better when you. (*pause*) My dad died on the night I left the hospital. I'd been at the hospital for about two days and mum knew he was going to die and mum said, 'I want to be with your dad when he dies.' Er, we all knew because at first the doctor said part of the next twelve hours was crucial, then he, er, said, 'Oh, your dad's got two days to live.' [*pause*] Then they said, 'He's got, got about twelve hours to live.' He had to be awkward – he lasted eighteen. That was my dad; he was always awkward [*group laugh*]. [*pause*] So, with my mum I was the one who got my sister. The spooky thing is my sister was having a dream about someone ringing her up to tell her mum had died, which she didn't know who it was on the phone. She found out in the end it was me. [*long pause*] Well, I think it's better to, [*pause*] erm. [*pause*] I think Clint was right, it's better for them and for you if you're, like, with your family rather than be pulled out of school, 'cause if you're pulled out of school it's a lot harder because you're just with your friends. You're not with any family. [*pause*] And at that time you need family as well as friends. And to actually find my mum was probably the worst day of my life. [*pause*] No matter how much bullying I've gone through; no matter how much pain I've gone through.

Matthew's early account has only 32 words, but his later development has 91 words:

> Mat: No. I wasn't in school. I was at home. [*pause*] Well I found out when my sister came crying downstairs 'cause I was watching something and she came crying downstairs and she picked up the phone and dialled 999. So I said, 'What's wrong?' But she didn't answer. So I went upstairs to say 'good morning' to my mum and when I opened the door of the bedroom and I saw everyone crying. [*pause*] So I walked over to my mum's side and I saw her lying face down on the floor. [*pause*]

Respondents were asked to prepare questions to ask of group members prior to the recorded session, and though I had not seen them, it was not difficult to guess what they were after studying the transcript. The questions were significant and marked new themes in the discourse. James repeatedly asked in the beginning, 'How do you think you're coping?' Matthew asked, 'What things do you have in common with your parents?' Phil asked James, 'Where do you reckon heaven is?' – the question that prompted the spiritual theme at the close of the session (Lines, 1999b). But Clint's question was more tentative. As a means of coming to terms with the shock announcement *at school* that his father had died, he asked Matthew, 'Do you think it was, like, better… to find out when you were at home with all your family…?'

The session allowed each participant in turn to explore the answers of the group to their most pressing questions, which was in itself a window into what stage they had each reached in their bereavement (Kübler-Ross, 1982). From pre-planned questions, therefore, the group elected the topics of central concern: Phil wanted to recount his brother's decease to open up the way to speculating where his brother might be 'now'; James to come out as an authority on coping; Matthew to press for identity with his mother, since this was the only thing he had left; and Clint to assess whether school was the best place in which to hear of his father's tragic death.

Although these issues were as yet unresolved, the opportunity was provided to voice them in the group setting as part of the acceptance process. There was evidence, then, that such an approach facilitated a confrontation of each pupil's loss at a significant point in healing, but can such novices in experience handle the deeper feelings that bereavement inevitably brings out?

Empathy and handling deep feelings

There was evidence of varying degrees of acceptance of what had happened, particularly the use of stark terminology, such as the term 'dead' to replace the introduced term 'lost'. James took the lead and gave the group the clause 'I lost my…', which each respondent borrowed. The term 'lost' was first replaced by the term 'died' by James ('My mum died'), then was repeated by each respondent in turn: Phil, 'He died'; Clint, 'He died', 'He's dead'; Matthew, 'She died'. Death and dying did not imply nonexistence, however (Lines, 1999b).

There was clear (and understandable) evidence of James carrying guilt over his mother's call for help and his lack of response – 'And in a way I still blame myself because she called out to me…' – which he later contradicted when recounting how he had been taunted:

James: One boy sang, 'Now where's your dada gone?' And it was only a
           couple of days to the funeral. [*pause*] I lost my rag. That's one thing
           you should never do [*with emphasis*]. You should never lose your
           temper with someone 'cause it's not their fault. You should never
           blame someone, especially yourself, 'cause it's no one's fault. [*pause*]

This was entirely consistent with his philosophy of 'You never get over it', but you 'learn to carry on'. James felt that he should provide all the answers. Like a mini-philosopher (Parkes, 1986) he found patterns in each of their experiences:

> James: So, there is a connection between you two, as in, his mother died with a heart problem and your – was it your brother? – died with a heart problem, and you both got a heart problem. So in a way, yous two should, like, you know, the similarities are quite close and the comparison is quite close. [*pause*] Erm, what happened to your dad again? ~ I think that, the thing we all have in common, we all carried on, we don't loaf around. And I think you get some people who just loaf around, you know, after death [*mimicking, altered voice*] 'Oh that's so unfair. Why did they have to take him?' But that's it. Crying isn't going to do any help.

Although this was an assumption made by James, prompted by a need to find commonality in their varied experiences, it no doubt was of much assistance to Matthew and Clint in restructuring their thinking and behaviour to face loss and to get on with the business of living. James offered a pragmatic explanation for death:

> James: Well, I was just thinking [*pause*] OK, my dad always said to me 'When it's time to die it's time to die.' You can't, like, stop it. So I just think, well, that's it, they're gone, can't do anything to change it. And they wouldn't want me moping around for the rest of my life. So I try and do the best I can, not just for me but for them as well.

He had an answer for everything, offering sound practical advice: 'I work hard, enjoy life. Enjoy life while you can. Any chances you get grab them 'cause you won't get a second one.' He felt that he should take bullying on the chin and not blame others for insensitivity and mockery, since 'The good times will always run over the bad.' One should be content with few material possessions – he only wanted a bag for Christmas.

There was little evidence of any respondent feeling for the pain of the others, then, but the emphasis, as dictated by James, was not upon 'feeling' but upon 'saving' group members by giving advice on how to cope – 'It's no good grieving'; 'Moping around is not going to help'; 'Work hard...', etc.

Phil was quite egocentric (as they all were at their transitional stage). He showed more than a passing interest in astronomy, not for its own sake but in a forlorn hope that he might see his brother in some distant star or something – he did not specify. He described the effects of his loss, as first being scared at night in case he saw his brother's ghost and, second, a sense of numbness: 'I felt I was dreaming.' His primary interest, however, was in seeing his brother again – 'Er, James, where do you reckon heaven is?'

No one (James included) was able to contain Clint's brief upset – 'It's [life's] a bit boring now that he's dead' – though clearly James had registered it. Clint was assertive in character, a trait that prompted the pastoral teacher's decision to refer him, and one that became evident at various stages of the interview – 'But I think it [crying] does… It's not like that for me though…'

Most of the coping strategies were philosophical in directing thoughts towards attitudes and beliefs that were accepting and getting on with the business of living. There were some practical coping strategies offered by Clint, however. These involved:

- voluntary counselling – 'I sometimes come to see Mr Lines…'
- talking – 'I talk to my mum…'
- looking at photos to remember the good times – 'I look at photos I think that helps…'
- crying

> James: Crying forever, moping around is not going to help, it's not going to do anything ~
>
> Clint: It's not like that for me though. It's, like, sometimes I can be fine. One day I can be fine, but then and the next day something could happen, someone ~

Matthew was the most reserved and offered little in terms of support for the others, yet it was interesting to see how concise and direct his deliberations were, once prompted. When presenting his question from a powerful need to press for a son/deceased-mother identity, he felt assured and said:

> Mat: To my mum, I've got the same colour eyes, the same colour hair, the same hearing problem [*James and others laugh*] and the same heart problem.

His voice pattern was fluid, economical and rapid after initial delay. Seven years had separated the interview from the bereavement event, but for Matthew it was as if it was yesterday.

It was evident how current conditions were more influential in fuelling his nihilistic attitude towards life and his resistance to PE. This was evident in the interview when he indicated that his father was not coping and was unable to talk about his mother's death – 'Every time I try and talk to my dad about it he starts being upset.' Matthew was thereby having to parent his father (and younger siblings – picking them up after school, cooking their teas, etc.) when what he perhaps yearned for, psychologically, was to be cuddled and nurtured by a mother who had been snatched away unexpectedly.

Although the boys had not the resources to handle each other's bereavement feelings in depth, their coping strategies and basic pragmatism appeared mutually effective for the giver and the given. In spite of little empathy on the part of each of the boys, there was evidence in follow-up individual counselling that the process of narrative sharing and the phenomenological sense of group 'connectedness' had fostered a deeper level of 'feeling for others outside of the self' than was evident before (Rowling, 1996).

Outcome of the group session

The four boys illustrated different degrees of numbness, denial, anger and depression as they struggled to accept and cope with their losses (Kübler-Ross, 1982). Clint carried the most overt anger (targeted against his mother and teachers) and depression (moving towards acceptance), while Matthew appeared to direct his anger inwardly and towards his PE teacher. With Phil, there was marginal evidence of numbness and denial. He oscillated between these and anger, but was a long way from acceptance, and still dreaming (Parkes, 1986). James on the surface was accepting but was also angry (though not depressed); at one brief moment there was catharsis as he vented his anger over divine injustice, but generally he maintained a controlled and stoic demeanour that appeared to be detached from true feeling. Their hope lay in literal conceptions of an after-death continuance (Lines, 1999b).

Three of the boys continued in brief individual counselling after this session and focused on many of the themes on the tape. James worked on issues of guilt. His older sister parented him and his peer relations improved. He accepted an invitation to go on a camp that had been organized by an outside agency, a voluntary care group.

Matthew was bitter over his loss and had suffered long-overdue effects, as demonstrated through his anger and resistance to doing PE. In this respect, James's stoic advice proved helpful – in fact, he took up PE voluntarily after this interview.

Clint had a few brushes with peers, but became more conciliatory towards teachers managing him. He left for a grammar school at the close of year eight, but not before coming to the counselling room to shake my hand in gratitude for all the support he felt he had received.

Phil attempted to break free of his mother's constraints by wandering from home to play. His mother had another baby. The family accepted family therapy with the aim of establishing some emotional space in the mother–son enmeshed relationship, and to help his mother see the tenuous connection of loss and risk of further loss through Phil dying in the same manner as his brother had done, a neurosis hindering Phil from growing up. Having built stronger friendships with peers, Phil became more content in himself and better able to accept his loss and face the future.

Each of the boys was asked to speak on the benefits of the group session and to say whether it had helped. Matthew smiled and said, 'Yea, it was good.' 'But how did it help?' I asked. 'You've got to get on with life', he replied. I asked him where that idea had come from, but he could not recall that it was from James.

Matthew was much more outspoken in the next session of individual work and revealed information not previously disclosed, including that his mother had taken her own life (a heart problem was his earlier account, perhaps influenced by Phil), and that the family had (deliberately) never been away – his mother died just after a family holiday. Matthew came again for counselling (Chapter 5) to help build better peer relations and to learn 'to be happy' (Nelson-Jones, 1996) but, sadly, ceased attending school before work was complete.

James said, 'I felt less isolated, as though I was not the only person who had gone through losing my parents.'

Phil said, 'It was OK. I wasn't the only one going through it.' He also shared more sensitive material in individual work, including that his father had taken his own life when Phil was only a baby. He described how his baby brother had taken Phil's brother's place, and how he thought he had become, for the family, his dead brother's replacement.

CONCLUSION

Individual in-depth bereavement counselling is not common in school because of the unavailability of suitable counsellors. This chapter has illustrated a range of techniques and approaches in brief counselling for bereaved youngsters, and has focused primarily on stages of acceptance (Kübler-Ross, 1982) and the benefits of using 'buddy figures' to help 'normalize' the experience of loss (Rowling, 1996). Boys are not forward in asking for bereavement counselling, even though they have sensitive non-communicable reactions to loss. It is not easy to ascertain whether (or when) a youngster who has been bereaved *needs* counselling, but the use of peers to help 'normalize' teenage experience has unquestionable merit. The practitioner may choose to use diversionary tactics with resistant youngsters when attempting to engage them in therapy.

An intermediate group session within a counselling programme facilitates the need for young people to confront their loss and to communicate their pain through their life stories in a therapeutically safe setting; collectively to explore the meanings of their experiences through dialogue (Gergen and Kaye, 1992). The purpose of such a venture is primarily to validate each individual's views by giving an opportunity for expression, to pool varied experiences in the secure trust that they will be respected, and, hopefully, to enlist from the group a level of support through practical coping strategies in the healing process. Therapy is designed to help 'normalize' their experience.

Clearly, the practice of placing such a group as the four boys together would not have been appropriate if a workable group of bereaved pupils that could be judged to be mutually facilitative had not emerged. My decision to bring the four together for the group session was not planned in advance but appeared right at the emotional point they each had reached in individual work. The approach would be risky if clients had not been prepared before group work in order to see where each was in adjusting to his loss.

The attraction for myself of group sessions with the bereaved is that it is in keeping with adolescent development of moving from adults to peers for psychological and social support. Three of the clients were able to share their narratives frankly with surprising clarity and confidence, and the process appeared more cathartic on hearing the tape than in reading the transcript.[*] The approach gives each respondent an assurance that his own feeling and experience are not entirely unique. What better way of affirming their feelings of loss than through an approach that elicits the views of 'buddy' figures and peers who speak with such authentic voices?

[*]A full transcript is available from the author.

9

SEXUAL INCLINATION
AND CONDUCT

There are two anomalies in sexual inclination and conduct that leave educationalists unsure of how to support youngsters in school. The first is the fact that the UK has the highest number of school-age pregnancies in Europe at the time of writing, in spite of lessons on sex education in most schools. Secondly, at a time when young people have become more open and expressive over their sexuality, there is evidence that extreme homophobia still prevails in some quarters.

The professional, legal and ethical position of school counselling was examined in Chapter 2 with reference to the level of confidentiality that can be afforded to pupils in school where professionals operate *in loco parentis*. In this chapter, the implications of those boundaries with respect to teenage heterosexual and homosexual inclination and conduct are explored. Because of the pressures in school arising from homophobia, homosexuality will be covered in greater detail than heterosexuality.

Counselling agencies currently receive more referrals from counselling teachers worried about their professional position when speaking with homosexual pupils than over any other category (Carmel Hartley, personal communication), which suggests that schools are beginning to respond to a need but are unsure of their legal position. Ian Rivers (1996) urges teachers to combat homophobia within the classroom, and asks, 'In an educational environment where lesbian, gay and bisexual issues are all too often swept under the carpet, how can we challenge homophobia effectively?' The question divides the domains of the curriculum and counselling, with the former being responsible for challenging prejudice and the latter for picking up the pieces. The pastoral teacher's role is to challenge discrimination and victimization under an ethic of mutual respect and equality of opportunity, but the counselling role will be to challenge homophobia more indirectly by role-modelling attitudes of acceptance within a spirit of celebrating sexual difference.

HETEROSEXUAL INCLINATION AND CONDUCT

First sexual experience

In Chapter 3, I spoke of Erica who lost her virginity in an unpleasant and unplanned manner, and I think her case is not untypical. Of those teenagers brave enough to bring up the topic, the loss of virginity has not generally been a wholesome experience. Geldard and Geldard (1999) correctly view sexual behaviour as one of the many hazards adolescents have to face but without properly considering the social, psychological and physical consequences. In some cases, younger girls, quite inexperienced and carried away with the appeal of dating older boys, find themselves trapped in compromising situations, such as in rear seats of cars, and lose their virginity before they know what is happening. In others, girls or groups of girls have their first experience of sexual intercourse at parties where parents have naïvely relaxed control and allowed too much alcohol, or been unaware of the misuse of cannabis in getting girls stoned and out of their minds. In most cases, first intercourse among younger adolescents takes place without protection.

A few couples decide to engage in intimate sex after reasoning through the consequences and after having dated for some months and found kissing and hugging boring and not satisfying their sensual needs. In my experience, these are in a minority. Most sexually active teenagers regret they did not put off the day of losing their virginity till they were older and wiser, and unplanned pupil parenthood is commonly regretted. Once sexual intercourse has been experienced and natural inhibition overcome, it seems that adolescents tend to engage in sex frequently rather than sporadically (Tubman et al., 1996).

Dating older and more sexually experienced boys brings risks of sexually transmitted diseases and unwanted pregnancy, which, not surprisingly, is taken more seriously by females than males (Geldard and Geldard, 1999). Girls tend to view sexual urges as being more controllable than do boys. They are more likely to discuss sexual issues with their parents and view sexual activity as being detrimental to their future goal attainment (DeGaston et al., 1996). Geldard and Geldard caution counsellors to, 'Remember that sexuality is a major and positive dimension of human development. It is important that adolescents come to terms with their sexuality in ways which are positive' (1999: 40). Both teaching on responsible decision-taking, and non-judgemental counselling styles have important roles in addressing the casual attitude towards early sex, and the rise in teenage pregnancy.

Peer influences on sexual behaviour

Dusek (1996) discusses the broad diversity in cultural attitudes towards early sexual behaviour and the anomaly of parental influences being minimal, whether promoting strict abstinence or premarital sex. Conversely, there is some evidence to suggest that when mothers monitor their daughters rigorously then this will tend to reduce unprotected sex. My own experience confirms the finding of Geldard and Geldard (1999), that peer relations are the major influencing factor in opting for early sexual intimacy and loss of virginity. Teenagers who have sexually active friends, or friends they *believe* to be sexually active, are more likely to be drawn to early first intercourse through pressures of 'normalcy' and of not being left out, particularly female adolescents.

Mid- to late adolescence is a bewildering period of new urges and rapid mood swings, where the emotions are stirred by internal hormonal and external social factors. These sensory and psychological drives coincide with the transfer from parental to friendship bonding. Fierce competition takes place during courtship, and many feel awkward and out of step with the perceived norms:

> At 18, Leanne felt pressured by her friends to go out with a man she hardly knew. She wanted sex and to lose her virginity, so as to appear 'with it' to her friends and not 'frigid', but her first, unplanned, sexual encounter was a tragedy – she was raped in a field. She suffered repetitive nightmares in which she saw herself tangled up in long grass before the brutal taking of her virginity. This left her with no confidence for further intimate relationships. She saw her youth passing away as she witnessed her friends entering longer-term engagements. Counselling for her consisted in restoring her confidence, providing a strategy to reduce the potency of her nightmare, helping her to decide what she wanted from male relationships, and giving her self-protective strategies for risky situations.

BRIEF COUNSELLING FOR HETEROSEXUAL YOUNG PEOPLE

Authors highlight the dominant discourses that underlie abusive behaviour (Payne, 2000; Winslade and Monk, 1999). Payne (2000) contends that over-concerning oneself with counselling victims of abuse fails to challenge the patriarchal narratives that authorize such behaviour. Winslade and Monk (1999) illustrate narrative questioning interventions that aim at combating abusive behaviour through the work of Alan Jenkins (1990). The problem I find with such approaches is that in my experience abusive people are rarely available or accessible for therapy. It is the victim who arrives at the counsellor's door. In the following case example, counselling boundaries are highlighted with regard to under-age consenting heterosexual behaviour. The case illustrates how the practitioner may choose to support the young client in school by supporting her parents or guardians in the home. An integrative method with a solution-focused perspective is illustrated through a goal of opening dialogue between a mother and her daughter (Davis and Osborn, 2000).

Caroline was approaching 12 and had been going out with a boy aged 13 for two months. She came voluntarily for two separate counselling sessions over sexual matters. On the first occasion, she approached me feeling very anxious that her mother and stepfather might discover something through her cousin 'grassing her up'. She talked around the issue for some time, and the counselling was going nowhere. She said that something had happened the night before with her boyfriend, and I guessed that it had something to do with sex. Her stepfather was strict and it was fear of what he might say that was crucial. As Caroline sat beside me, she made fixed eye contact, and I felt she wanted me to know but was embarrassed to outline what had happened. I decided to challenge her and asked 'Have you had sex with your boyfriend?' She immediately looked relieved and said that she had. 'Did you take precautions and use a condom?' I asked. She replied that they hadn't.

I arranged for her to speak with the school nurse, who organized a pregnancy test at a nearby clinic. She also engaged her in sexual health counselling and offered her personal contraceptive advice. School counsellors in the UK are not allowed by law to give individual contraceptive advice, as discussed in Chapter 2, but the school nurse – having a medical responsibility for her patient – has no such restriction. Since this was dual support involving myself as school counsellor and the school nurse, we discussed the case at length and I further took the case to counselling supervision. After sharing Caroline's reflection that this was a one-off event for which she did not feel ready, we felt there were no immediate risks facing my client. Nevertheless, my supervisor's counsel was that I should offer a follow-up session to monitor her progress in dealing with the issue. Over the first incident, then, the school nurse and I decided not to inform Caroline's parents, though this was no easy decision.

Having experienced a non-judgemental reception, Caroline approached me a second time, arm in arm with a friend, to announce that she had had sex again, but this time not with a peer but with a young man of 17. I judged this to be more serious. Her first sexual experience might be put down to experimentation, but this time I could not rule out exploitation and the need to consider child protection procedures. We discussed this fully in session, and I felt it was necessary to explain to her that I considered her welfare was at risk and that we should seriously consider sharing this information with her mother. I was acutely aware of the issue of 'client confidentiality', here in tension with 'respect for autonomy', but, as is my normal practice in giving my client the opportunity to take the initiative, I asked her if she would speak to her mother that night. Although she said she could 'if the right opportunity presented itself', I was doubtful. After putting off the ordeal of facing her mother, I spoke to Caroline's mother on her behalf, which, again, brought her relief.

Her mother was naturally devastated and said that her partner had not been surprised to discover she might be sexually active. 'The signs were there', he said, which made her feel doubly foolish for not picking it up. She saw me regularly to discuss an appropriate course of action. Apart from my concern over Caroline's welfare, I was also worried about the 'normalizing'

Dominant Narrative	Applied Narrative	Modified Narrative
Adolescents go their own way.	My daughter is lost to male sexual predators.	We are still close—Caroline needs me now, and *we* decide on whether our relationship is lost.
With premarital sex, girls are sluts, boys are studs.	Promiscuous girls vaunt their sexuality to vulnerable boys and lose their virginity early and justifiably.	My daughter has been exploited by someone who is responsible for a criminal offence of sex with a minor.
Emancipated women neglect their children.	I've been too busy working to notice my daughter's needs.	The income I generate improves my children's lives and models an example of industry.
Females are responsible for sexual protection.	A 17-year-old man would not care if my daughter were pregnant; she must safeguard her own welfare.	My daughter needs my experience to better prepare her for such events that border on rape and exploitation.

Figure 9.1   *Mary's narrative chart*

influence among her girlfriends of losing her virginity at such a young age, and of giving a subtle endorsement of this by receiving counselling that was neutral in most respects. Counselling was offered, therefore, to Caroline and her friends in order to place 'normalizing' perceptions in a broader context. The counselling work focused primarily on work with Caroline's mother, whom I refer to as Mary.

Mary and I agreed that she and her daughter needed to find the opportunity to speak openly, and this became our goal in therapy. I reiterated the importance of this by saying that there was no time Caroline needed her more than at this moment. Mary kept punishing herself with guilt and cried bitterly over the realization that her 'innocent daughter' was no longer a virgin. Her grief was accommodated in person-centred counselling and an exploration of the dominant narratives which were operating unconsciously on her thinking was undertaken. Cultural narratives came to the fore, were applied to Mary's situation, and were modified (as shown in Figure 9.1) to help Mary support herself and to see her natural feelings of guilt and sadness in the broader social context.

In spite of feeling a little better about the destructive thought of 'if only' (I'd have spent more time with Caroline…, spoken to her more…, given her appropriate sexual information, etc.), Mary was acknowledging that wishing to speak with Caroline was not going to be easy. It is important to recognize how difficult it is to confront those we love and to get it right. An enormous pressure builds up, and well-rehearsed scripts work better in the mind than in practice. Nelson-Jones's (1996) effective thinking skills of 'thinking positively' were used to good effect. I often find transferred thought helpful when I am faced with a difficult challenge – for example, when I go to the dentist, I do not dwell on the needle and the drill, but on imagined situations and on having left the unpleasantness behind me. I asked Mary, in preparation, to focus mentally on an enriched relationship of closeness and adulthood from sharing information on the most delicate area of relationships, sexuality. While Mary felt confident to describe in counselling the occasion of her first sexual experience and loss of virginity, she was not sure she could share this with Caroline. I was not prescriptive about this, but asked her to remain solution-focused, and to believe that the powerful feelings of love that caused her to bewail her daughter's loss of virginity would clearly shine through in creating an opportunity for bridge-building, so long as she insisted on calmness. Finally, we planned what Mary would say and the tone in which she might say it. Although no follow-up session was planned, Mary thanked me on the phone and Caroline confirmed that my support had brought her and her mother much closer together.

HOMOSEXUAL INCLINATION AND CONDUCT

Theories on homosexual inclination

For some young adolescents, feelings about sexual preference can become confused with a common need for same-gender friendships. Same-gender siblings may become engaged in sex play when sharing bedrooms/beds, largely through curiosity:

> Erotic play between children of the same sex is very common round about the age of twelve or so. Actually, I don't really like using the word 'homosexual' here because it doesn't mean they're likely to become gay later on – they're just practising on someone like themselves, as a first step to approaching the opposite sex later. (Skynner and Cleese, 1989: 271)

This experimental phase seldom lasts long and could hardly be described as homosexual, since brothers and sisters may also experiment with each other's bodies – even practising imitative sexual intercourse – secretly within the home (Skynner and Cleese, 1989). For others, their same-sex sexual urges are an early indicator of leanings towards same-gender partnerships, which if known can result in excessive taunting from homophobic peers (Rivers, 1996).

> Two 13-year-old boys, Damian and Clive, camped out in a tent in the back garden, and among acts of petty devilry they engaged in homosexual play and oral sex. They enjoyed the experience and planned to repeat the activity the following week. The next day, however, Damian – through fear that he might earn a pejorative label in the eyes of 'the lads' – began to spread rumours that Clive was gay (a 'dick-sucker') and that he was attacked in the night by Clive trying to force his 'dick' into his mouth while asleep.

Damian's fear was not so much about his reputation as about the fact that he enjoyed the experience and felt unhappy for doing so. He was anxious about the implications of enjoying a homosexual act in respect of his own sexual identity. Clive, needless to say, was very angry and felt let down by such disloyalty and dishonesty. As a result, both boys came separately for person-centred counselling, but for very different reasons.

Same-gender sexual experiences in early adolescence are not in themselves evidence that either party is gay, but are examples of youngsters experimenting with their sexual urges in situations that are mistakenly thought to be safe in a society that is largely homophobic.

At middle adolescence, such boys and girls may not be wishing for sexual intimacy so much as wanting to come to terms with feelings of having 'fallen in love' with friends of the same gender, and to understand a sensual wish to hug and fondle each other. Fond embracing is not uncommon with adolescents in secondary school and is not in itself an indicator of sexual designs, though boys are less likely than girls to be seen hugging each other publicly.

One theory of homosexuality from the male perspective treats it as a condition brought about by gender bonding and identity. According to this view, homosexuality is a failure of the boy (at 6–13 years) to completely cross the psychological bridge towards the same-gender parent. There is the subliminal urge for the male adolescent to move away from his mother to the position of his father, and to mate with his mother in competition with his father – the Oedipal triad. If he fails in this transfer to maleness, the adolescent will seek substitute figures in an endless and unsatisfied attraction to the penis, as a symbolic longing for the father-figure who was never reached:

> Male homosexuals have rather powerful, possessive mothers.... He remains on the bridge, facing towards the father, or rather the father-he-wanted-and-needed-but-never-got. So his attachment stays on males instead of returning in a sexual form to his mother and hence to females generally ... [He misses the romping, cuddling, non-genital horseplay activities of his father.] The gay male hasn't usually got over his hurdle about authority and spends his life going through the motions of doing so by perpetually seeking the symbol of the father's authority and strength, in the form of other men's penises, rather than the real thing.... The penis stands for the father's love and warmth ... symbols of that – other men's penises – are collected instead ... the person is never satisfied, never has enough, and often goes from one partner to another. (Skynner and Cleese, 1989: 254–5)

Another theory is that homosexuality is a learned condition that affects (it is claimed) an estimated 10 per cent of the population (McLeod, 1993). In looking at the research, the point at issue is whether social conditions have any influence upon a person's sexual orientation. Freud (1933) believed that homosexuals had failed to accomplish a stage in some part of normal sexual development, though critics contend that some of Freud's confessed homosexual patients were never really homosexuals at all, but were merely playacting (Masson, 1992). Perls et al. acknowledge the 'impossibility of "changing" homosexuals who have once gotten important sexual satisfaction, especially since they have creatively overcome many social obstacles in order to get it' (1972: 424). Ellis (1977), an early sex therapist, describes homosexuality in pejorative terms and sees it as a 'neurotic problem', an 'emotional disturbance', and as 'perverted behaviour'. His claim is that 40 per cent of males and a significant proportion of females have had some homosexual experience at some period of their lives without them becoming 'fixed' homosexuals. Ellis refuted the belief in 'fixed' homosexuality, as a condition of birth, but sees it as a learned response capable of 'cure'. However, Ellis's research subjects were already clients, that is, people who were in therapy not for sexual difference but for a range of personality disorders. His subjects were not representative, therefore, which leaves open the question of whether homosexual inclination is a learned condition that is capable of cure.

Harrison (1987) counters Ellis's view that homosexuality is a 'neurotic problem' of learned behaviour, arguing that there is no essential difference between homosexual and heterosexual persons in the distribution of psychological health and pathology. He showed there to be no single profile of the gay person, that sexual orientation was established early on in life and that it was not subject to change (Hooker, 1985).

Other evidence contradicting the idea that homosexuality is a learned condition is found in studies of anthropology and sociology (Harrison, 1987) and from observations on sexual arousal from visual images. A further study similarly pointed to the futility of seeking cause or 'cure' for homosexuality, on the grounds that 'most men [sic] have some amount of both homosexual and heterosexual fantasies, feelings, or behaviours' (Hall and Fradkin, 1992: 372).

The later evidence suggests that sexual orientation is unlikely to be experienced 'as a choice'. This is particularly relevant for bisexuals. Bisexuals feel an inclination to satisfy both their heterosexual and homosexual drives, and are largely to be found in heterosexual marriages (Scher et al., 1987). It is recognized that most bisexuals marry into heterosexual relationships long before they discover their gay inclinations. The rush to enter into heterosexual marriage is in itself a denial of a sexual orientation that would bring with it a measure of social and intra-familial conflict (Matteson, 1987).

More recent research into genetics similarly questions whether homosexuality is a transitional failure in development or a learned condition. Geneticists have identified a gene in the homosexual different from those in the heterosexual. Earlier theories that suggested that as many as 10 per cent of people were homosexual have now been discounted in favour of figures as low as 3 per cent of men and a smaller percentage for women (Bragg, 1999). Dean Hammer has identified a genetic marker on the

X chromosome that is associated with homosexual men. This indicates that homosexuals, though a minority, have inclinations caused by a different genetic make-up (Bragg, 1999).

Some outspoken antagonists claim that homosexual activity is 'unnatural', but zoologists and social anthropologists have observed that homosexual practice is not uncommon in the animal kingdom. This, together with liberal views that sex is not exclusively for procreative purposes, tends to contradict the belief that it is only male–female sexuality that should be deemed 'natural'. This issue is one of semantics, for contraception can be viewed as an obstruction to the 'natural' process of procreation if definitions of 'what is natural' are pushed to their limits.

On balance, the contention that homosexuality is 'perverted behaviour' that is capable of being 'cured' is wanting in the light of later research into genetics. The findings of such research is that gay people do not 'choose' their sexual orientation. They are given it by genetics (for the secularist), or by God (for the theist). This combined evidence suggests that the counsellor must now move from a pathological model towards a gay/lesbian affirmative model of psychotherapy (Hitchings, 1994).

Cultural influences making up homosexual narratives

Grand narratives on homosexuality influence youngsters' feelings in school. The late Cardinal Basil Hume of Westminster, in response to the Pope's hard-line condemnation of homosexuality as an 'aberrant deviation', called for a much more moderate response: 'Love between two persons, whether of the same sex or of a different sex, is to be treasured and respected' (as reported on the BBC News in 1999). Hume, however, was not advocating free licence for homosexuality. The Catholic theological stance is that gay and lesbian people are stigmatized no less than those who practise sexual relations outside marriage are, a stance that thus upholds the figure of Christ being wedded to the Church. The traditional heterosexual marriage is therefore endorsed, and the functions of the sex act are first to procreate, and second to unite two people. It is obvious, then, that gay and lesbian relationships, along with premarital sexual relations, fall outside the pale (Catholic Trust Society, undated).

The official Anglican stance is no less condemning of homosexuality. Anglican bishop, Derek Rawcliffe, after public confession of his homosexuality, said on the BBC News in 1999: 'It is cruel to expect homosexual priests to remain celibate, to expect homosexual priests to "respect" their sexuality without also being able to practise it.'

Religion has undoubtedly encouraged homophobic narratives and many of the most outspoken critics of the current 'gay scene' are those belonging to conservative and fundamentalist religious groups. Christian fundamentalist sects and denominations whose beliefs are based upon the authority of the Bible condemn it outright. They quote the biblical text condemning homosexuality that appears in the Old Testament: 'If a man also shall lie with mankind, as he lieth with a woman, both of them have committed an abomination: they shall surely be put to death' (Leviticus 20:13). Biblical scholars point out, however, that the Hebrew word for 'abomination' is the same as is used to condemn the wearing of men's clothes by women (Deut. 22:5), the eating of non-ritually prescribed foods (Lev. 11:10–42) and the incorrect carrying out of Israelite worship (Lev. 7:18). There is a considerable moral contradiction here, since clothes, ritualized foods and worship are cultural determinants that have no absolute value in the modern secular world – even for many fundamentalist groups. Why, then, should sexual orientation be singled out and given such religious significance, and would not such biblical moral imperatives be more fittingly interpreted from the perspective of the biblical writers themselves (Lines, 1995b: 7–31)? This pejorative stance has been reapplied in the New Testament, where the writers take over the ethic of the Old Testament in some respects and reflect the cultural milieu in others (I Cor. 6:9).

Besides the Church, the armed services and nursing are two professions in the UK which are currently struggling to come to terms with homosexuality. In today's society, the media has much more influence in forming narratives of social attitudes and tolerance than religion and the legacies of tradition. British television has in the last few years raised the issue of gay couples through soap dramas, such as *Brookside*, *Eastenders*, *Coronation Street* and even the children's programme, *Byker Grove*, with the result that programme-makers have become more radical and topical. There is a paradox here, though, for there are still strong homophobic views prevalent in society in spite of liberal media portrayal of gay and lesbian sex (for example, the reaction to the Channel 4 programme, *Queer as Folk*).

Being congruent with homosexuals

Most counsellors believe that they should be non-judgemental and accepting of all their clients, irrespective of ethnicity, creed, gender or sexuality. Most subscribe to the core conditions (Rogers, 1967) and believe that in order to facilitate change – which includes an acceptance of the self – the therapist must openly *be* the feelings and attitudes which are 'flowing in him' in the current counselling situation, without front or façade, and without feigning empathy. Congruence is the personal quality of genuineness and it implies that the counsellor is in touch with his own thoughts and feelings.

In maintaining congruence with homosexual clients the importance of supervision cannot be understated. It is in supervision that the counsellor is given the opportunity to explore his personal feelings about homosexual clients.

Since homophobia is still likely to be influenced by outdated taboos, the counsellor will need to consider her personal beliefs when considering at what level, or whether at all, to counsel young homosexuals. If Christian counsellors are not able to separate their own religious or moral stances from their work and approach their clients in a neutral and value-free fashion, then barriers will get in the way of therapy. The ability to form a therapeutic alliance with gay and lesbian young people will depend not only upon personal skills, but also upon the degree to which religious beliefs and attitudes influence the counsellor.

For a counsellor who may be 'offended' by the gay client's disclosures, so that the feelings 'flowing in him' are condemnatory, or even slightly judgemental, then the therapeutic relationship cannot help but be affected, and empathy will be feigned in a mere pretence of caring. The counsellor should 'stop playing the game' (Masson, 1992: 232) and, perhaps, refer the client on to one who *really can* feel empathy. Gay and lesbian clients have come to the counsellor for a form of support and understanding that they have not found elsewhere. They have not come to receive further prejudice and value-laden 'advice'. If counsellors are unable to encourage autonomy and to help clients accept themselves *as they are*, then they had better refrain from counselling gay clients.

Countertransference feelings of hostility and non-acceptance will impede attempts to ameliorate an adolescent's distress, and there will be no building of self-esteem. In practice, this can leave the young person more anxious than before coming for counselling. All counsellors influence their clients; that is in the nature of their work. Their role is not to change their client's beliefs to conform to their own, but to help *them to arrive at what is right for them* (McLeod, 1993). But how are these values and principles to be applied in the educational setting?

Counselling role

Having due regard to the law, to the BACP *Code of Ethics and Practice* (2000a), and to the principles informing and underlying an agency's statement of aims, there must still be room for ethical judgements and individual decision-making. There is no *direct* law in the UK that prevents a youth counsellor – who will have similar legal latitude to that of the GP and school nurse – from becoming involved in counselling a homosexual young person.

In cases where a school pupil has not 'come out' to his parents, and yet is engaged in an under-age, consenting, homosexual relationship, any support without parental knowledge will pose professional and ethical difficulties for the counsellor in school (DFEE, 2000). After assessing that the client is 'Gillick competent', the counsellor in an independent agency has greater liberty than a school counsellor when working on areas of a client's sexual conduct, even when such conduct is deemed an 'offence' in criminal law. As for school-based practitioners who have a system-oriented counselling role, I think that such a freedom should be granted with legislative support. Teachers are in principle acting on behalf of a 'reasonable parent' – to whom she or he is ultimately accountable – but the school counsellor works within a broader framework.

The school counsellor serving under local educational authority contracts and service conditions is pulled between two obligations:

- loyalty to pupil-clients under codes of confidentiality
- legal obligation *in loco parentis*

There is a need to tilt the balance, and I think this should be towards pupils and students in school, since referral to outside counselling agencies is problematic for young homosexuals in educational settings.

Referral to other agencies

Ethical issues arise in counsellor–client matching in sexual orientation, as in race, gender and ethnicity (Lines, 2000), but, unlike independent counselling agencies, a school will have no choice of counsellors. Inevitably, then, a preference for a gay counsellor to counsel a gay client may require an outside referral. But referral by a school counsellor to outside counselling agencies for homosexual clients without parental consent is problematic and controversial (Hitchings, 1994). Counsellor–client matching in sexual therapy is plagued with boundary difficulties in educational settings in that an angry parent may challenge the counsellor from a perception that she is pushing their son or daughter into a gay sub-culture. Even directing pupils and students to gay help lines and supportive networks, let alone putting them directly in touch with such organizations, may leave the practitioner open to criticism.

But gay and lesbian adolescents need information. In light of the ethical dilemma, it is more advisable to direct a given pupil to where such information on supportive networks can be found, since many homosexuals have had to visit gay clubs for information and companionship (Scher et al., 1987). The school counsellor would do well to set clearly the boundaries of her work at the outset for those pupils contemplating making a self-referral for sexual counselling, and to publicize them in the waiting room and the school prospectus.

BRIEF COUNSELLING FOR HOMOSEXUAL YOUNG PEOPLE

Goal-centred approaches for gay and lesbian youngsters

For pupils and students who are convinced of their homosexual orientation and who approach the counsellor for support in 'coming out' to their parents and/or friends, cognitive-behavioural counselling, solution-focused therapy, the Egan three-stage model and cognitive-humanistic counselling in particular will prove effective. The therapy is clearly goal-oriented and the aim is to help the client gain confidence and find ways to carry out the specified task with a minimum of personal trauma. These approaches are also useful in helping such confident youngsters cope and deal with social isolation, labelling and stigma when personal disclosures to friends have been made public irresponsibly.

> Mark was a bright year thirteen student, popular with the girls but ostracized by the macho-oriented males of his learning group. In GVNQ lessons, his debating skills were excellent, and in this respect he towered above his peers. He sat alone near the front, and appeared detached from all but two girls with whom he regularly conversed. He had ambitions to enter medical school later on. He came for counselling after school when he knew he could find me alone. He informed me straightaway that he was gay – 'I don't know whether you are aware of it but I'm gay.' He had a current relationship with a junior doctor in his middle twenties. His companion had a flat and Mark had often stayed over the weekend, and had sex with him – pretending to his mother that he was staying at the home of a schoolfriend. The relationship had begun a few months earlier, but had become more intense during his final year at school.

In the introductory session, Mark was asked why he wished to disclose to me that he was gay. His reply was that he wanted support in bringing him to the point of 'coming out' to his mother and friends. Egan's (1990) three-stage model was adopted. There were no boundary issues with this aim and no ethical compromises to consider.

A contract of three sessions was agreed upon and the aim was to achieve the goal within two weeks with stage-by-stage tasks. The remaining part of the first session was spent in establishing frank and honest dialogue. His sexual inclination was examined, at his request, to help him assess whether or not he was being exploited, particularly since he was in a relationship with an older man. His preferred scenario – to have his sexual orientation validated and made public within the family – was explored. In respect of the law, Mark was nearly 18, but his homosexual relationship was not his problem; his problem, and his purpose in coming for counselling was to enlist my support in 'coming out' to his mother. Counselling consisted of rehearsing how he might do this and what he might say. He confirmed that he and his partner were practising safe sex. He anticipated that his mother would come round ultimately, for there were already gay role models within the family: his two sisters were lesbians, heterosexual relationships were not the 'norm' for this family. Mark was grateful for the support and terminated his counselling after his goal had been accomplished.

In cases like Mark's, where clients are secretly engaged in homosexual or lesbian activity, it demands considerable courage within a homophobic society for him or her to even approach a straight counsellor to speak over such matters. The school counsellor might be the first person the adolescent has approached to allay his/her feelings of anxiety and confusion, and this calls for great sensitivity. The client will be very anxious about revealing a decision to 'come-out', which often comes without prior warning and with little awareness of how it might be received (Hitchings, 1994).

Admitting one's homosexual inclinations is an early step towards autonomy, and the school counsellor can help in this process, so long as there is no fear of significant 'moral or physical risk', so long as the adolescent is 'Gillick competent'. The counsellor must 'maintain an attitude of respectful, serious attention… no matter how shocking, trivial or ridiculous the patient's productions are':

> Your initial aim is to help the patient to overcome these blocks to open communication. Central to this is your ability to convince the patient that you desire to help him and are competent to do so. To this end, try to act in such a way as to show you are trustworthy, concerned about his welfare, and seeking to understand him. Try to elicit hidden doubts and misgivings and respond accordingly. (Frank, 1986: 16)

Jessica was a year eleven pupil, aged 16, who approached me to help her resolve an inner conflict. She had been in counselling previously for difficulties over her relationship with her mother. She felt at a disadvantage in social relations through what she described as a 'very strict' upbringing. Her mother appeared to counteract every social engagement she had planned at school – going to the pictures, dating boys and going to parties, etc. – with demanding chores at home and baby-sitting. As time moved on in her final year at school, her mother relaxed these responsibilities, and the particular problem she presented in the introductory session had occurred at a party.

She had attended her best friend's sixteenth birthday party and was allowed to sleep over at her house. Some began leaving at a set time and the clearing up was being done when the sleeping arrangements were discussed. There were not enough beds for the group of girls sleeping over, so Jessica agreed to share the double bed with her friend, Sarah. They changed into nightclothes and talked through the early hours about the party and this and that.

Slipping into sleep but still conscious, Jessica became aware of Sarah snuggling up to her back, but still she read nothing into it. She became anxious as Sarah's hand began to stroke her breast, and after being kissed several times on the neck with the soft words, 'I love you Jessica', she became confused. She was dumbstruck and did not know how to respond. She had suspicions that Sarah had had lesbian relations with a mutual friend, by their exclusive conversations and incessant wish to be with each other all the time, often pushing boys away – but how could she respond to this situation? She felt a little nervous. Should she turn and face Sarah, which might lead to more intimate masturbation than she felt ready for, and that she felt sure Sarah wanted. She had some attraction for Sarah but not in a way she felt she wanted to express sexually. Should she spurn her advances and say, 'I'm sorry Sarah but I don't feel the same for you', which would appear rejecting and hurtful. She replied, in a non-committal tone, 'Yes, I know. Good night Sarah.'

They both fell asleep without an escalation of sexual activity, and spoke nothing of the matter the next morning. She came for counselling to help resolve her sexual inclinations – whether she had heterosexual or homosexual urges, or both – and in the light of such feelings arrive at a decision of whether to encourage or discourage any further sexual encounters with open and frank discussion. She also felt ambivalent about coming between Sarah and their mutual friend.

At the close of the third session of cognitive-humanistic counselling (Nelson-Jones, 1999b) she felt she should put a stop to any gestures that would give an impression of anything other than a platonic friendship. Although she recognized within herself a trace of homosexual feelings, she could not be sure that she felt any strong urge to test them out on her best friend. She therefore planned with me how she could speak directly to Sarah and what she might say, in role-play through 'self-talk' exercises (Nelson-Jones, 1996) within a framework of compassion and understanding.

For those who are struggling with bewildering and powerful sexual feelings, who may even regret their desires for same-gender affiliations, goal-centred therapy may not be indicated. For those tormented by homosexual fantasies and urges – to be hugged, kissed, or to engage in mutual masturbation, oral or penetrative intercourse – and who are in conflict with their value system and under social pressure, narrative styles which pay greater attention to 'what we are' within prevailing social attitudes will prove invaluable.

Affirming homosexual orientation with narrative approaches

With sexual mores becoming more relaxed generally but still homophobic, anxiety results for those who are homosexual or bisexual. In the community and in school there is enormous pressure on gay young people who may be accused of being 'queer' or 'perverse'. That prejudice and stigma exist in school goes without saying, 'otherwise, adolescents would simply pair off in social activities as they wish and there would be no occasion to comment' (Harrison, 1987: 226).

Homosexual young people cannot escape from the cultural attitudes underlying censorious narratives that stigmatize their sexual difference as 'deviant'; they will inevitably have cause to hate themselves *because* of their sexuality. According to Friends West Midlands (1993/1994), there has been a significant rise in young callers to the gay and lesbian helpline in recent times (30–31 per cent generally, which is an incremental rise for women from 12 per cent to 36 per cent from 1992 to 1994). These were calls from people already in gay and lesbian relationships who were requesting extensive counselling, but who were unable to find help in school or the community.

The Samaritans inform us that at least two young people between the ages of 15 and 24 commit suicide every day. The suicide rate for young homosexuals is high, particularly for men, and is higher than it is for young heterosexuals. A 1993 survey found that of 416 young people between 15 and 20 years old in the London area, 19 per cent reported a suicide attempt, and a further survey revealed that one in five had inflicted serious self-harm on more than one occasion (Mason, 2000).

> Michelle had persistent dreams of engaging in homosexual acts (never hetero-sexual ones) with her friends in year nine, and when her older brother spread a rumour around the school that she was a lesbian, she felt unable to face people and hold her head up high. Her anxiety was heightened with the realization that her parents would never accept her as having lesbian inclinations. She found the ridicule at home (particularly from older brothers) so unbearable that at one point she contemplated suicide by taking an overdose. Her friends brought her for counselling after seeing her in a 'troubled state'. Her problem was not the acceptance of self, but of being accepted.

Her dreams and poems may or may not have been an indicator of fixed homosexual inclination at her developmental stage, but the effects of unwisely speaking of such dreams, even among sympathetic family members, can be disastrous for social integration. The counselling role was first to affirm the validity of her feelings and desires in a non-judgemental way, then to work on the implications with regard to social relations. How could she convince her parents to at least accept her for what she was?

After initial counselling within a psychodynamic framework (childhood experience and dream analysis), the approach then combined narrative and solution-focused techniques. The miracle question (Davis and Osborn, 2000) prompted Michelle to say, 'I want my friends and particularly my mum and brothers to accept me as I am, whatever I find myself to be.' We attempted to 'externalize the problem' (White, 1989), which we selected as the censorious 'homophobic narrative' itself that had infiltrated the minds of her parents and had altered their consciousness like invading aliens, but though the analogies made us laugh, when we pondered them the model seemed to lack seriousness. We explored sub-plots to her story (Payne, 2000) of 'not being accepted for whom I am', and discovered that her mother had eventually accepted other facets of her personality that she had earlier tried to change, such as her daughter's tastes in music and clothes, preferred foods, friends and places of entertainment, etc. From this we speculated how long it would take for her eventually to come round. This proved helpful and increased her optimism that 'some day she'll accept me for who I am, heterosexual or homosexual'. Realistic goals of confronting her brothers' attitudes and feelings and entrenched homo-phobic prejudices were set, and scaling helped her to reach the point where she could confidently terminate counselling (O'Connell, 1998).

The combined evidence of youngsters feeling stigmatized and needing to talk, together with high suicide rates, suggests that adolescents in schools,

Dominant Narrative	Applied Narrative	Modified Narrative
Homosexual people do dirty sexual things—they are queer.	My parents think I am sexually active in ways they think are 'disgusting'.	I don't know what I want yet sexually, and my parents have ill-founded fantasies over my sexuality; people are ignorant of homosexual lifestyles.
Homosexuality is not 'natural'.	My parents are ashamed of giving birth to someone who is not straight, like them.	I know what my general inclination is by now. It is sad, but I am not responsible for their felt shame.
Homosexual inclination in youth is a phase of being mixed up through the hormones.	My parents can't face the prospect of me being different from them—it suits them to think I'm confused.	I know my wishes and desires in every other respect, why not my sexual preferences?
Homosexuals seek publicity—I don't shout about being straight!	My parents think I am seeking attention; they are embarrassed about people finding out I am gay—I am carrying their prejudice.	The opposite is true for me. I'm struggling to keep my sexual identity a secret—who on earth seeks to be ostracized?

Figure 9.2 *Sean's narrative chart*

particularly boys, are struggling to come to terms with same-gender sexual desires. The professional course has to be one that gives such young people unequivocal support. The school counsellor as a professional is expected to affirm pupil-clients' sexual orientations, to help them *accept themselves*: 'The ethical counsellor must not become the agent of repression, but rather will help the boy understand himself and responsibly manage his sexuality' (Harrison, 1987: 226).

Many pupils become confused over whether their same-gender attractions are sexual or merely the longing for stronger friendship bonding.

Two year nine boys, Paul and Sean, quite independently came for counselling convinced that they were gay, and that they had known it since they were small. Paul had been with a male and a female partner on separate occasions and had strong bisexual urges; Sean felt an irresistible urge to consummate his desires 'when the time was right'. Paul continually, almost obsessively, desired to be in the company of a male friend from another school, yet in the two weeks that followed the session he began dating a girl in his year group. Sean remained resolutely convinced about his inclinations and was in many ways quite brave in warding off occasional insults. His parents were determined to humiliate him and to convince him that he was all mixed up and not really gay at all.

Sean is currently in counselling where narrative questioning, as illustrated in Figure 9.2, is being used to good effect in helping him to combat homophobic pressure.

CONCLUSION

Many pupils in school will be confused about their sexual orientation, but there are others who are very certain that they are heterosexual or homosexual, and some, perhaps, that they have bisexual inclinations. Little prejudice exists over heterosexuality, other than the age of first sexual experience, or what level of intimacy young people should share outside a committed relationship. The most serious issue in school counselling is over confidentiality and the point at which parents should be informed about material shared in counselling that has moral or legal implications. Homosexual inclination and conduct are another matter.

Some parents nursing strong homophobic prejudice try to pretend that their son or daughter is not really gay or lesbian in spite of disclosures to the contrary. They reason that they are just confused through hormonal activity, and thus may be kidding themselves. They are in denial and are certainly not supporting their youngster in the way that is needed.

The counselling of homosexual young people is not easy, and is bound to be controversial in that it invokes strong feelings from parents, feelings of anger, resentment and disappointment, feelings that are as much a problem to the youngster as to the parent or guardian. Education authorities have a responsibility to offer clear guidelines in respect of legitimizing (or otherwise) counselling for pupils/students having homosexual leanings so as to leave practitioners more confident in their involvement. Clients who are really sure of their homosexual orientation will find the stage of 'coming out' to be extremely difficult and threatening, and may seek from the school counsellor support that cannot be found immediately elsewhere. Most adolescents in school – given their age, maturity and opportunity – will not be likely to be practising their homosexuality so much as coming to terms with growing urges and inclinations. Others may move around, flirt and speak as though they are heterosexual through fear of admitting to their homosexual inclinations – to friends and family as well as to themselves. But some will have experimented sexually with same-gender partners to settle their curiosity.

Homosexual adolescents will feel that they are the only people in the world who feel the way they do. If they have no role models within their family or among acquaintances, they need considerable support, for their world is a very lonely one. In light of the high suicide rate among homosexual young people, it is imperative that the school responds to this above all other concerns.

The kinds of cases outlined above need a practitioner who is sensitive and who has examined his own value system and personal prejudices. Counsellors are required to modify their thinking in light of current research, so as to understand the nature of homosexuality generally, and adolescent homosexuality in particular. Affirming models will foster the right therapeutic alliance for meaningful work, so long as homophobic attitudes do not impede progress or stand in the way of a genuine therapeutic alliance. Brief goal-centred counselling is indicated for clients who are at the point of 'coming out', while brief integrative models of narrative therapy may prove helpful for those clients coming to terms with homosexual identities within homophobic communities.

10

SMOKING, DRUGS
AND ALCOHOL MISUSE

Counsellors and psychotherapists have largely been ineffective using traditional approaches with substance misuse ('abuse' is misleading). This is largely due to misconceptions about addiction and addictive behaviour – I use the term 'addiction' to mean the loss of control over personal consumption to the degree that individuals feel compelled to act against their personal codes. One misconception is to view the cigarette, the joint, the pill or the drink as the central problem. A further misconception is to see the motivating factors for change as being merely those issues related to health, and to financial and social hardship. Alcoholics Anonymous (AA) and drug-focused counsellors have begun to recognize the powerful relationships that addicts have with their substances. The medical model aims for total abstinence within a supportive community of 'recovering addicts' (AA, and Narcotics Anonymous) or within a treatment centre (NHS), while the education model favours responsible decision-taking. Both recognize that drugs and alcohol relegate all other concerns and relationships to a very poor second place.

Many teachers, social workers and youth leaders who support families where alcohol is misused are able to describe the dispiriting consequences for children when their parents daily depend on drink. For those who recognize the developmental needs of young people, it is inconceivable that a father would go to the local pub for a pint and miss his son's first school football match. It is, likewise, unimaginable that a mother could leave her young children unattended for a fix of crack cocaine to get through the long night. Yet these are the realities of family life in many troubled communities where high unemployment and low morale are the norm. Therapy with children and adolescents has become confused with providing material and emotional support, rather than teaching them how to cope with alcoholic or drug-dependent parents. Counselling young people in school over smoking, drugs and alcohol misuse involves several activities. These include giving information for responsible decision-taking, a means of regulating intake or maintaining sobriety, and raising awareness of the subtle influences of addictive behaviour.

DRUGS WITHIN WESTERN SOCIETY

Western culture is no different from other cultures in recognizing the pleasures and hazards of chemical substances for altering mood and mind-states, and in setting codes for regulation for personal or collective good. In the UK it is illegal for young people under the age of 16 to purchase cigarettes, and they have to be 18 to purchase alcohol. Unclassified volatile substances that can be inhaled have few statutory regulations other than controlling sale for the purpose of sniffing – where this can be proved. Drug-taking and 'trafficking' are offences that are met with various penalties depending on how seriously they are rated. The 'decriminalization' of cannabis (marijuana) is regularly the topic of political debate. Parental attitudes to alcohol are ambivalent in western society, 'abuse' being defined by degree of consumption, or by the company kept when drinking. For example, for a youngster to drink wine at lunch, or a can of lager at a party, where parents are present is not generally perceived as a problem, but drinking lager on the streets in a group may be regarded as alcohol abuse.

Counselling practitioners are all too aware that some clients entering therapy have been sent by the courts or by school senior staff, which tends to limit clients' motivation for change. The counsellor knows that therapy can never compete with the psychological companionship and the social pay-off that youngsters get from drugs: 'You cannot detox patients and then send them back into deprivation and poverty and expect them to stay free from drugs' (Diamond, 2000: 263). Collaboration with supporting agencies and parents is essential in some cases, and local treatment centres and organizations (such as AA) have much experience from which to draw.

Causal factors of misuse

Both subtle and explicit societal messages may encourage chemical misuse. Pre-adolescent girls are bombarded with images and messages about the 'perfect body' and personality – messages that suggest that the way they are is not good enough. Social drinking for emancipated females (and career-aspiring girls) in the modern workplace represents a shedding of stereotypical taboos as well as abandoning attempts to diet. Teenage boys may suffer from neglect, be short of suitable role models, or may long for physical affection that cultural attitudes largely censor, and chemicals can provide a psychological substitute for the lack of safe touch that boys experience in their lives. Substance abuse can be a way of putting distance between young people and the pejorative messages they receive about themselves from the media.

Smoking may result from modelling behaviour of adults or significant peers in the first instance, but addiction to drugs and alcohol disrupts family life and gives a voice to pain and confusion. Drugs and alcohol can be a way for adolescents to block memories of sexual abuse by anaesthetizing themselves from depression and suicidal feelings. Similarly, young gay clients can use drugs to blunt fears of rejection when they are considering 'coming out'. Drugs may also serve to disguise homosexual desires for those who are struggling to acknowledge their sexuality.

Drug- and alcohol-dependent parents

Many young addicts experimenting with substances are grieving for the loss of mothering and fathering due to their parent's addiction, for alcohol and drugs offer symbolic substitutes. Parents who emotionally abandon their children leave them in roles of responsibility for which they are not ready, leading them to make pseudo-mature decisions over hazardous things such as early sex and drug-taking. The children live in an alcoholic-centred, not a child-centred home, and are expected to parent younger siblings before being ready for parenthood themselves. Children in therapy sometimes feel burdened by guilt when parents blame them for their addiction. Others have low self-worth, and reason 'if they loved me they would stop drinking'. Many can recount times when they have been embarrassed among their friends by their parents' drunken behaviour.

If peers or teachers criticize their parents' drunkenness, children as they get older begin to internalize a sense of shame and embarrassment. Some children blame their non-drinking parent for the other parent's drinking, and many others worry about their parents' health and wellbeing, about whether accidents will befall them while out, or whether they will fall asleep with a cigarette while drunk and cause a fire.

In *Games People Play*, Eric Berne (1968: 64–70) parodies the alcoholic's lifestyle. From a transactional analysis perspective, he describes the supportive characters of the addict's social world. Time and again, I have found the following a common family dynamic. *Alcoholic's* behaviour is reinforced by *Persecutor*, normally the spouse, who serves as 'Parent', and whose role is to give *Alcoholic* a hard time. *Alcoholic* is supported by *Rescuer*, usually a same-gender associate or friend, such as the GP. The pay-off, and point of the game, is not the binge-drinking (which is merely the prelude) but the hangover, for it is within the stage of hangover that players take up their respective roles – 'Feel sorry for me, "Parent" me, I am sick "Child".' In transactional analysis, treatment is through awareness and through getting all parties to stop playing the game. Even children and teenagers play supporting roles as 'Child' or 'Adult', and often in their own behaviour display similar manoeuvres:

> 'See if you can stop me', which involves lying, hiding things, seeking derogatory comments, looking for helpful people, finding a benevolent neighbour who will give free handouts. (Berne, 1968: 70)

RESEARCH ON ADDICTIVE BEHAVIOUR

A decisive question for researchers is why some rather than others having an equivalent genetic predisposition for addictive behaviour fall prey to alcoholism. Biology and cultural factors have a mutual influence upon each other as DNA research points out (Diamond, 2000). The research suggests that all addictions are driven by the 'addiction of control' and the 'management of mood-states' (Knapp, 1996). The addicted have become tired of 'playing by the rules', of complying with social conventions, and seek perpetual pleasure and freedom from pain. The double paradox of being under the control of the very same chemicals that are controlling the person, and as a result suffering hangovers when wanting relief is rarely registered.

Although there may be different causes for the abuse of different substances, there are common factors with much chemical addiction. Three influencing factors appear to over-ride all others: the availability of the substance; the particular nature of parental support; and peer-group influence – though the evidence from research on influencing factors is not wholly consistent.

Modelling behaviour

Research suggests that addiction tends to pass from generation to generation (Diamond, 2000), and that peer-group influence is persuasive. The modelling effects of significant friends are strong in taking up smoking (Hu et al., 1995; Wang et al., 1997), in spite of adolescents recognizing and accepting the health risks involved in becoming a regular smoker. I have found in regular surveys that in a particular environment – such as streets and precinct areas where teenagers hang out – where one teenager of a group smokes, then the majority tend to follow. Smoking serves to cement social cohesion in small groups of young people. The converse is also the case, that whole groups in particular areas can be non-smokers. As mentioned in Chapter 3, identity crisis through adolescence is paradoxical. Teenagers wish to identify with the peer group against their parents in some respects, and yet stand apart from peers in others. In consequence, some youngsters smoke for group identity, while others who smoke alone point to the stress of outside factors (such as school), which suggests that modelling influences are at work whereby teenagers associate a stress-inducing situation with a stress-relieving habit, nicotine becoming a psycho-chemical anaesthetic. The influences are as much parental modelling, then, as significant friendship modelling. In contrast, Geldard and Geldard (1999) recognize that adolescence is a self-assertive phase *en route* to individuation, and that young people are more than capable of making personal decisions within the context of peer pressure.

Adolescence is considered to be the time for the transition from non-smoker to smoker according to research (Geldard and Geldard, 1999), but there is growing evidence that young people, particularly girls, begin smoking before the stress-related transfer to secondary school (ONS, 1998).

Risk-taking behaviour

Geldard and Geldard (1999) have recently reviewed the research on the risk-taking behaviour of adolescents involved in smoking, drinking alcohol, sniffing solvents and taking drugs – marijuana, a variety of pills such as amphetamines, psychotropic substances such as 'magic mushrooms' and LSD and hard drugs such as cocaine and heroin. They argue that it is misleading to link habit-forming addiction with the experimental behaviour of youngsters. As youngsters move from the influence of the home to that of the peer group, they move from safety to the exciting possibilities of expansive experiences, but experimental behaviour does not necessarily become addiction.

The challenge of obtaining the substance is part of the excitement of risk-taking that has appeal for adolescents (like buying cigarettes when under-age). Studies of volatile substance-taking in England, Scotland and the USA (Ives, 1994), highlight the importance of decision-making skills, parental involvement and positive peer influence, for so many of the sniffers who come to be 'lone-sniffers' suffer from low self-esteem. This confirms my own experience through the 1980s and early 1990s when solvent abuse in the local area was rife, and supporting agencies and the police were at a loss as to how to respond to rising rates of glue-sniffing (Lines, 1985).

The counsellor will need to recognize the patterns of individual and group sniffing. Glues and solvents, such as deodorants, butane lighter fuel, 'poppers', cleaning chemicals and the like, are readily available in shops and stores and most shopkeepers will have no hesitation in supplying the commodity on demand. Glue-sniffing has the highest first-use mortality level, though this is more a result of accidents when intoxicated rather than through suffocation (ONS, 1998). Incidents of pupils inhaling butane gas through the nose or mouth have resulted in first-use mortality.

Drugs feed into the sensation-seeking and risk-taking tendencies of adolescents, and research shows that the dominant factor for the increase in drug-taking and drinking is the introduction of substances to friends (Geldard and Geldard, 1999). There are two reasons for this. First, the socializing tendencies of young people put them in touch with those who are all too willing to supply the substances and give them access to whatever they want. Second, the need to be accepted 'by the group' gives them feelings of rejection and isolation if they choose not to identify with what the group sees as acceptable. Naturally, when these factors combine, the risk of addiction is strong. When factors of 'families not abusing drugs themselves', 'friends having no interest in drugs and alcohol', 'restricted access to drugs or alcohol', and 'no psychosocial or school-based difficulties' combine, abstention from alcohol, cannabis and other drugs is more likely (McBroom, 1994). Not surprisingly, academic performance is adversely affected by high drug misuse (Jenkins, 1996).

Insights for therapy

The question of causation is not as important as the question of how to put things right – narrative therapists are more interested in knowing what sort of person has a disease than what sort of disease affects the person (Diamond, 2000). AA regard compulsive drinkers or drug addicts as 'folks looking for a spiritual home who have shown up at the wrong address', suggesting that their addictive behaviour results from vain attempts to satisfy spiritual needs (see Chapter 11).

Young people's substance-abusing habits and journey through recovery have been understood as a rite of passage (White and Epston, 1990), as a phase where a person loses track of time before becoming reincorporated in their social world. Ironically, heroin, mescaline and cocaine are shrouded in mystery, ceremony and ritual that mirror the adolescent's rites of passage. A measured understanding of where experimental behaviour can lead is an important insight for the counsellor of young people over 'safer' drugs such as nicotine, cannabis and alcohol.

Researchers have recognized that professionals 'are losing the war on drugs' (Diamond, 2000). Addicts giving up one addiction often fall prey to another (Knapp, 1996). In light of such a tendency, adult drinkers adopt a bargaining approach to therapy, not aiming for complete sobriety but controlled drinking and regulated consumption. Diamond (2000) has demonstrated the effectiveness of narrative counselling integrated with the 29-step programme of AA, in which the therapist encourages the client to aim for gradual recovery rather than for permanent change. Often clients are asked to refrain from taking drugs before therapy, to keep a behaviour inventory over drinking, or to indulge in a less harmful drug after therapy. This is in order to aid the self-control rather than the therapist-control paradigm where perceptions might suggest an 'all or nothing' remedy (Diamond, 2000). Brief approaches are applicable for younger people (particularly where AA organizations do not exist).

Motivational interviewing (Miller and Rollnick, 1991) addresses addictive behaviour at the point where clients express ambivalent attitudes to habitual behaviour: 'I want to stop, I don't want to stop.' Against therapy that views the client's resistance to give up the habit as pernicious 'denial', MI recognizes ambivalence as the heart of the problem, and through non-judgemental questioning the MI practitioner aims to elicit the motivation for determined change. In light of the fact that young substance abusers are not likely to have incurred serious physical or neuro-psychological damage, and that they are impulsive and risk-taking, conventional MI techniques may need modifying and simplifying (Tober, 1991).

RESPONSIBLE DECISION-TAKING
FOR TARGETED GROUPS

Anxiety is one of the most powerful triggers for drinking: 'It follows then that one of the most difficult tasks facing therapists treating alcoholism is to lessen a person's denial and encourage increased self-awareness and disclosure while they're trying to keep their client's anxiety to a minimum' (Diamond, 2000: 62). Responsible decision-taking helps to remove anxiety in the counselling process.

Drugs policies have tended in recent years to abandon a 'moralizing' and didactic approach in favour of educating young people to make responsible decisions. Although the curriculum on drugs within personal, social and moral education programmes of study is not the focus of this book, the counsellor might at times take on a teaching role with a class or with small groups of targeted individuals. Teaching responsible decision-taking has been demonstrated recently (Winslade and Monk, 1999) by use of the narrative technique of 'interviewing the problem' (Roth and Epston, 1996). Group members are encouraged to take responsible decisions through an exercise in which they are granted a rare opportunity to interview 'Drug' personified – whatever drug has been the central problem for the group.

Targeted group on cannabis

Acting role

Two or three members of the group were prepared by being asked to imagine that they were *cannabis spliffs*, that cannabis has through them become personalized. They were to illustrate the complexity of the problem by indicating the strong appeal and the fun that could be had when under the influence of Drug Cannabis as well as the lows, the depression and the ostracizing effects of becoming addicted. Good acting persuaded the group to befriend Drug Cannabis. Marketing included a typical scenario where Drug Cannabis had given the group 'a good time' at a party, where all were 'stoned' but finally sent home when Debby's parents returned home.

The pros of cannabis misuse

The second stage involved a structured reporter's interview that took place in a press conference. Broadening-out questions illustrated the tactics that Drug Cannabis had used to lure the unguarded into its clutches, such questions as:

- 'What are your favourite tricks of persuasion?'
- 'What hopes and dreams do you offer those addicts who have no future?'
- 'Do you have different tactics with girls than with boys?'
- 'How do you pull mates in and keep teachers and parents out?'

The cons of cannabis misuse

Halfway through, the group were asked to change tack. This was investigative journalism, and they were asked to put hard questions to Drug Cannabis so as not to let Drug Cannabis off the hook. Questions came readily as group members became animated through the apparent neutrality of the counsellor-teacher. Questions drew attention to the demoralizing effects of Drug Cannabis's influence, the manner in which addicts had given up on life, the crime that inevitably results for serious addicts, the subtle spiralling downwards of optimism and the ensuing fracturing of relationships that drugs had brought about.

De-roling and follow-up discussion

After the group had observed the benefits and hazards of Drug Cannabis, and had made notes of the conflicting arguments, the Drugs team de-roled by changing seats and shaking off the Drug-identity; they re-entered the circle for a discussion. As the authors suggest, it is helpful asking each protagonist to say three things that make them different from Drug Cannabis, so as to eliminate a tendency to label individuals (Winslade and Monk, 1999).

The aim is to help the group view people's drug problems from Drug's perspective. The re-storying aspects of narrative therapy continued through the closing follow-up work. This highlighted the methods that successful addicts in recovery have used to 'frustrate the plans of Drug Cannabis to take control of their lives', and the 'devious plans of Drug Cannabis to reassert itself and win back a recovering addict'. Failed Drug Cannabis might be asked to account for his (or her) most embarrassing failure, to expound what form of addict resistance had caused Drug Cannabis to almost give up, or to recount what things Drug Cannabis least liked to hear young people say.

> In our group, Larry and Rob portrayed Drug Cannabis pushing Tom to take a *spliff* for over an hour with continual jibes of 'being scared'. But this had no effect other than that Larry's girlfriend dropped him for 'being a pratt!' – 'Is that the only thing that amuses your tiny mind?'

COUNSELLING SMOKERS

While traditional approaches to addictive behaviour have been largely ineffective, Diamond (2000) illustrates the benefits of narrative

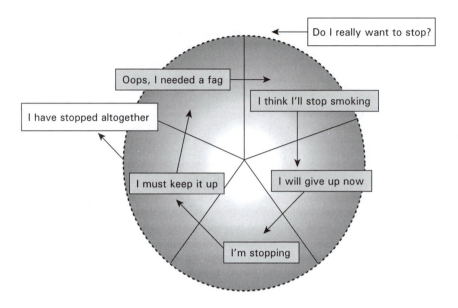

Figure 10.1   *Cycle of change with smoking*

approaches with addicted adults. Brief motivational interviewing (Miller and Rollnick, 1991) and the cycle of change (Prochaska and DiClemente, 1982) have also proved effective with a number of addictive behaviours, including smoking, serious drinking and drug abuse (Devere, 2000). I have found brief integrative models, which utilize aspects of these, to be effective with adolescent smokers. This integrative model is demonstrated with group and individual work.

Because of a lack of resources, group therapy is more productive than individual counselling for those youngsters who really want to stop smoking. In the introductory session, the model for change is described to the group with the diagram in Figure 10.1. The introduction gives an optimistic but realistic outline of the model's therapeutic scope for habit-reduction in three sessions.

I modify the cycle of change model to the stepping on and off a playground roundabout of five sectors (Figure 10.2).

Ground rules are clearly stated to allay the natural apprehension of young pupils over confidentiality. The counsellor is aware of how peer-group associations are formed through smoking habits, how clients generally prefer their parents not to know, and the common use of dinner money to purchase cigarettes during the day.

Change takes place by encouraging members of the group as individuals to step on the roundabout of change of their own volition. The roundabout of change begins with 'contemplation', where engagement or disengagement is discussed through motivational interviewing (MI) and Rogerian therapy. During the group session, each member is asked to

MI for giving up smoking

Figure 10.2   *The roundabout of change*

describe their smoking habit, the degree and frequency of needing to smoke, the where and when and with whom they smoke, its costs each week, their age when starting, and the hold smoking has upon them. This information is not judged from a moral perspective, but serves as baseline data to measure progress and success. An undue stress on journal-recording becomes de-motivating after a short period, since most youngsters cut down in the early stages of drawing their attention to the degree of their habit and its costs, but then find it difficult to maintain the lower smoking rate or give up completely. The advantage of this model for habit-forming behaviour is in offering an effective means of dealing with relapse. It also offers a model that can be applied by the youngsters out of the counselling arena, and this is important for a therapy that largely takes place in the client's social world. If youngsters fail (as most do), then they have a model to which they may return with greater determination later on, rather than one which highlights failure and leaves them feeling permanently labelled 'smoker'. Prochaska and DiClemente (1982) found that most smokers went round the cycle three to seven times before finally quitting for good.

In addition, the first and second sessions focus upon dissonance in a frank and honest manner. 'Cognitive dissonance' is recognized when ambivalence and inconsistency are discussed and when clients acknowledge their irregularities in thinking and behaving. With habitual behaviour, there is often a mismatch between thinking and behaving – believing that smoking is injurious to health while continuing to smoke. Clients who want good health still continue to smoke, albeit reluctantly. Again they may alter their belief, as though in denial, in an attempt to con themselves with shallow arguments, such as those that point to doctors and nurses who smoke, and elderly relatives in their eighties still smoking, etc. They minimize their self-esteem and personal resources by

---

PERSONAL RECORD _____
SAYING GOODBYE TO TOBACCO

1 What is the degree of Cigarette's hold on you?
2 What will you lose by parting with your Fag Buddy?
3 How will you begin to say 'Get lost' to Fag Buddy?
4 When do you wish to be free of 'being under control of Cigarettes'?

Figure 10.3 *Keeping a personal record*

pointing to their lack of will-power and causal circumstances like 'examination pressures' or 'my mother driving me mad'. The dissonance is resolved through MI to alter habitual behaviour, which is what is wanted in reality. Dissonance is thereby weakened through enlightenment over ambivalence, through increased self-esteem, through attributing personal responsibility for behaviour and through increased motivation for change. During this work, I give candidates a self-learning personal record to complete that is written in externalizing language, as shown in Figure 10.3.

I also encourage behavioural imaging exercises.

Stephen, Jackie, Karl, Noel and Naomi were asked to spend a second or two at the point of lighting up and look at the cigarette and ask:

'Do I really need *You* right now?'

I ask them, after a few drags, to stare at the smouldering cigarette and ask themselves:

'Are *You* really helping me?'
'How are *You* taking a hold over me?'
'Why are *You* taking over?'
'Do *You* really make me feel better or am I kidding myself?'

These externalizing questions are designed to weaken dissonance and strengthen resolve.

The second stage involves supporting the client's belief in her ability to change things before converting this to specific, realistic and achievable goals through cognitive-behavioural techniques. Helping clients in the maintenance stage is by recognizing and dealing with relapse, since relapse is part of the process for future change, not failure. Research shows that 90 per cent of those with alcohol problems drink again at some point after treatment, as with smoking and particularly with heroin and crack cocaine (Devere, 2000). Smokers regularly go round the circle four times before stopping smoking for good (ibid.). After relapse, the client may return at any point and step on the roundabout as often as the model proves a useful and motivating tool for long-term change.

The results of group-session work for pupils wishing to give up smoking can vary, depending upon social and personal factors. With this particular group, Stephen cut down to one cigarette a day after twice jumping on the roundabout of change. Jackie hardly modified her behaviour at all, during or after the pro- gramme. Karl and Noel cut down their smoking to one a day during lunchtime, after which they gave up altogether and stepped from the roundabout, having twice dealt with relapse. Naomi reduced her smoking to three a day, then on re-try gave up altogether after going out with a boy who was a non-smoker.

Therapy is not terminated when a goal is reached, since the model serves to empower the individual for future change. Change is not due to the counsellor but to the technique. The timing for change is not restricted to the period of counselling sessions. The advantage of this approach is in its durability and the fact that the roundabout can be imagined and internali- zed. It serves as a permanent model to which to return at later periods when resolve is increased or when social or personal influencing factors have altered.

A second case illustrates the approach applied in an individual case where smoking had become the cause of a more serious relation- ship difficulty.

Erica approached me asking for ideas on how she might give up smoking after a fight with her mother when she was discovered with a cigarette. The key to motivation, however, was not to avoid another fight but to use her money better.

Erica's wish to stop smoking was not for reasons of health or personal image or because the smell of smoke on breath or clothing sometimes affects an ado- lescent's sense of personal attractiveness. She needed to save £30 for a puppy, and by not buying cigarettes she could save £4 each week on top of her pocket money. Her smoking habit, its frequency, her social acquaintances, her mother's attitude to smoking, and other reinforcing factors were explored.

While she would not smoke in front of her mother, she did not feel too intimidated when her mother reprimanded her in the street for 'having a fag in her hand'. Erica was largely unperturbed by this event even though it resulted in a public scene that ultimately put her in care for protection. She felt she needed to smoke more during term-time than in holiday periods. She smoked alone as much as with friends, and all adults viewed her as a strong individual.

On deciding which approach to adopt, the salient factors appeared to be:

- a resolute desire to stop smoking;
- a character of strong ego-strength;
- a clear motive for change;
- a realizable goal within four weekly sessions.

The narrative approach offered some promise, but two elements would not be appealing to Erica. Since she had had some considerable contact with social services (and mistrusted authority figures), a method that relied upon written documents might not have worked. If she wrote a 'farewell' letter to her smoking 'partner' (as illustrated in Diamond, 2000), she might be unsure of the motive for writing such a letter. Written documents might have appeared to Erica to be an unnecessary gimmick, added to which she might have been suspicious as to how they could be used.

Externalizing the problem (White, 1989) of smoking as, for example, an invading enemy, or a disease that might creep up and catch her unawares or force itself upon her while at low ebb, was not found meaningful when first tried, apart from helping her to see herself as a 'non-smoker'. Erica did not feel herself to be 'addicted' to nicotine or to be powerless or out of control, but, on the contrary, to be a person very much in control of most aspects of her life. An integrative narrative approach using techniques of SFT was therefore attempted. The therapy focused on *changing only that which needed changing* (O'Connell, 1998), and it appeared that scaling techniques would help monitor her progress in ceasing to smoke at school.

Baseline data were collected in the first session and this revealed a pattern of smoking around the back of the sports hall with one friend during lunchtime, and smoking alone a further cigarette at the bus stop on the way home. On both occasions, Erica smoked 'because she wanted to', not because of peer influence or social pressure. The counselling aim, therefore, was to further encourage a trait that was already present in her character by restructuring her social habits and routines.

In the second session, we devised an action plan that involved her offering assistance at lunchtimes in a drama production that was scheduled for a month's time, and opening an account with the school bank so as to not support her habit by having spare money from lunch and bus fares with which to buy cigarettes. The third and closing sessions involved monitoring her progress – the money she had saved for her pet and her withdrawal symptoms after giving up.

Scaling techniques proved successful in self-assessment of the wearing-off effect of 'gasping for a fag!' and in terminating our collaborative work: 'On a scale of one to ten – one representing "I'm fully able to go it alone" and ten the sentiment "I am desperate for your support" – what number will you need to have reached before we close counselling?' She said, 'Two'. Over the four-week period, her scaling scores were seven, two, three and two, respectively. Her scaling scores for withdrawal were eight, six, two and one, respectively, where high scores represented maximum temptation to smoke.

Her saving target was also reached by week four, and a follow-up session two months later revealed that she had completely stopped smoking for other benefits than having a puppy – in fact, she bought a walkman instead of a puppy, because her mother wouldn't allow her to have a pet in the house.

BRIEF COUNSELLING FOR DRUG AND ALCOHOL PROBLEMS

'Once an alcoholic always an alcoholic', is one of the mantras that leads AA as well as the medical community to aim for regulation and management of addiction rather than cure. Psychotherapy has largely been unsuccessful with addictive behaviour because of three misconceptions:

> Addicts and alcoholics embrace a lifestyle that avoids pain at all costs, seek immediate gratification, and tend to rely on – put their faith in – chemicals more than people. In other words, for those who are addicted recovery means abandoning the very things that sustain them. (Diamond, 2000: 2)

Traditional psychotherapy can be a *painful and scary business*, requiring a letting go of control. It often offers *no short-term recovery* but uncomfortable feelings, and is based wholly upon *the person of the therapist* to bring clients through. Hence, for adult drug addicts and alcoholics, the three principles of therapeutic change are jettisoned. I think there is more hope for young people.

The cornerstone of change for Diamond (2000) is the recognition of how addicted clients form strong relationships with their addicted substances. Bidding farewell to drug and drink companions through 'externalizing language' and 'parting letters' and documents is the process of recovery and reorientation to life without the drug companion. But I have found MI and the cycle of change, in combination with the language styles of narrative therapy, to be effective with habitual drinking and other drug behaviour for young people. Miller and Rollnick (1991) speak in terms of clients' attachments to addictive behaviours rather than their relationships with substances. The prerequisite of what follows assumes adherence to the BACP *Code of Ethics and Practice* (2000a). The counsellor will have established whether to work on managing the drug or alcohol misuse, or whether to tackle other problems of which the chemical dependency is symptomatic.

It is unusual for school counselling to be offered for very serious drug addiction (heroin and cocaine), since such misuse is likely to have brought the client into conflict with the authorities, calling for exclusion to protect the school's name and members, a prison sentence, or a referral to a drying-out clinic. The higher the tariff of the 'drug–dependency–penal outcome' triad, the less likely it is that group work is indicated over individual counselling. Schools need to protect their image as well as their pupils, and group work indirectly reinforces a social acceptability of drug misuse that senior managers understandably are keen to play down. The behaviour of the seriously addicted is met with greater censure in schools in the current competitive climate than cigarette smoking (perhaps, cannabis) and lighter dependence on low-proof alcohol.

Chris referred himself for support with a growing problem of alcohol addiction to spirits and whisky. His parents were highly tolerant of his drinking and often encouraged him at 14 to drink when they entertained their middle-class friends, which was often. What they didn't know was that Chris was helping himself regularly to an assortment of spirits each afternoon before his parents arrived home from the family business. His 'manly [sic] prowess' was evident when he bragged with his friends at 16 that he could 'drink them under the table' and 'hold his liquor better than anyone'. Rather than revelling in this identity, he was acutely aware of his growing dependency on spirits at the close of school, to 'bury the pressures of the day'. This was a pertinent observation at this time since his father was under a medical consultant for kidney problems, and his mother was becoming more socially embarrassing among his friends by flirting with them after a glass or two of brandy.

The introductory session scanned for a focus of therapy through Egan's three-stage model of brainstorming his preferred scenario (Egan, 1990; Mabey and Sorensen, 1995). He wished to see himself as a 'non-dominated alcoholic', and though the MI technique of 'rolling with resistance' (Miller and Rollnick, 1991) helped to reveal the inner contradiction of Chris's thinking on personal freedom, elements of narrative therapy became the preferred approach. Through 'externalizing language' we reframed his ideal self-concept as the 'Chris who wards off the subtle Demon-Drink who lures him into thinking that mild intoxication removes the pressures of school life'. Chris selected the goal of 'keeping Demon-Drink away' rather than one that validated, through person-centred counselling, his worries over dad's health or mum's social behaviour. Cognitive therapy was not indicated since there was no evidence of cognitive dissonance – he was fully aware of the health risks through his father's worsening condition, and he ceased apportioning blame for his drinking on external circumstances.

The second session, through Egan's framework of goal-setting and action-planning, was wholly dedicated to explaining the cycle of change model. The processes of change – 'contemplation', 'dedication', 'action', 'maintenance', 'relapse' and on to 'contemplation' again, and so round the circle till sobriety was reached – were considered. His motivation for change was high at this point and this indicated that he was at the 'dedication' stage. The roundabout analogy that I customarily use was dropped for the traditional cycle of change diagram, given Chris's intelligence and ability to register diagrams. In spite of moving speedily through the first two sectors of contemplation and dedication, the action stage and, particularly, the maintenance stage had become problematic; it was hardly surprising that relapse occurred within four days and binge-drinking followed for the following three before the next session. This pattern was repeated for each of the next three weeks, and although the binge period was gradually becoming reduced, Chris was becoming demoralized that complete sobriety was evading him.

The fifth and closing session addressed the very real problem of dealing with the negative thinking of relapse behaviour. Statistical information was presented to Chris to help give him a sense of 'normalizing' his experience of relapse. We reapplied the externalizing language of Demon-Drink and we composed a letter to Demon-Drink to help him personalize the problem and give it the gravity it warrants, given the universal influence for destruction that drunkenness has.

Dear Demon-Drink,

You have been my uninvited companion for two and a half years, and I have begun to realize that I am better off without You.

You have fooled me for too long now, into thinking my school problems will go away with your friendship. The next day convinces me You're wrong.

You disguise yourself in many ways, and that gets me angry most. Your velvet feel through sparkling white wine, Your tempting sharpness through claret red, Your enticing fire through whisky and Your social 'respectability' through gin; Your various disguises fool me no longer.

Look what You've done for dad. Look what You're doing to mum. I'm sorry, but I've decided that whatever benefit You've given me, it's time for You to go and trouble someone else instead. I may miss aspects of Your friendship but You will trick me no longer.

With no regrets,

Chris.

Initially, the letter was collaboratively composed for no other purpose than to heighten his motivation for sobriety, but, in view of its forceful effect on his thinking and resolve for complete abstinence the following week, we decided to share the letter in a closing 'witness-audience' meeting with his parents (Payne, 2000; White and Epston, 1990). This session was moving. Both parents began to cry, as their modelling influence on their son's acquired habit became apparent and as their son's determination to 'lead the way' became transparent. Follow-up sessions one and three months later confirmed his ongoing sobriety, with only one confessed relapse after which he re-entered the cycle of change from having internalized the diagram.

CONCLUSION

Drug addicts and alcoholics are unreceptive to conventional psychotherapy in general. They repeat self-destructive behaviour that tests the stamina of therapists, and they continually break vows to give up habits. Young people who experiment with chemicals because of family troubles need to work through their feelings of anger, resentment, rage, despair, powerlessness and dependency in a 'holding' arena. But the 'holding' must be brief, and must aim towards shifting the locus of control from alcohol and drugs (the counsellor too) towards self-regulation.

Herein lies a problem for the young person who has seriously misused drugs and alcohol, and who has become lured into being controlled by chemicals and substances rather than by persons, values and beliefs. This chapter has presented a style of working that shows young clients how they might strengthen their internal locus of self-control in behaviour that is compulsive and habitual.

Some addictions are more serious than others, and the hard-pressed practitioner may need to prioritize resources in favour of attempting to treat more harmful substance abuse. Every client's requirement of counselling support for maintaining sobriety or restricting drug misuse must be honoured under grounds of equal opportunity, which means that therapeutic contracts have to be tailored to suit the educational setting and the time available.

In practice, this favours approaches that are brief with less serious addictive behaviour, such as smoking, cannabis intake and casual drinking, under the group therapy model. More seriously addictive behaviour, however, such as habitual high alcohol misuse, solvent sniffing and illegal-drug misuse – cocaine, heroin, amphetamines, LSD and ecstasy – requires more extensive individual counselling.

An understanding of causal factors only partially aids the practitioner. Abandoning dominant biological and disease metaphors, the narrative approach offers more scope in treating alcoholism and addictive behaviour. Narrative therapy has been applied extensively to addiction to produce positive outcomes. MI integrated with the cycle of change model has similarly proved effective, and when the model is integrated with elements of narrative therapy for pupils in school the results can be remarkable.

The attraction of this approach is that it presents the youngster with a means of recovery that can be internalized and brought into play on future occasions beyond the short-term counselling contract. The approach also presents an optimistic method of dealing with relapse, by reframing the concept of 'failure' and by turning relapse around to serve as a therapeutic tool for continual retrials towards success.

11

LIFE MEANING
AND SPIRITUAL EMPTINESS

In this closing chapter, we enter a minefield of opinion and prejudice. All I can hope to achieve is to open doors of opportunity for practitioners to practise brief spiritual counselling. Defining spiritual counselling requires clear understanding of spirituality, and this involves us with religion and religious practice.

Religion is in decline in western society. There has been a reduction in numbers attending conventional religious services in the UK, Australia and parts of Europe. Congregations tend to be comprised of the elderly, and this puts the future of the Church in doubt. This is not the case, however, with house fellowships and some fundamentalist groups whose numbers appear to be growing. Ethnic minority religious commitment in the UK remains steady, but may soon fall as third-generation children become increasingly westernized (West, 2000).

Dichotomies abound in religion. There is a dichotomy in the rise of social and emotional difficulties in the secular age and the decline of means of resolving them through religion. It is questionable whether the decline of religious solutions is attributable to apathy, since the fall in religious observance has had no substantial impact on numbers having spiritual experiences (Hay, 1982). Hay believes that spiritual experiences are universal cross-cultural phenomena, which affect at least one-third of the population. They invariably bring about an ethical shift in the person concerned.

Another dichotomy concerns people's current interest in spirituality and the lack of emphasis given to spiritual concerns in psychology and psychotherapy (Richards and Bergin, 1997).

There is also a dichotomy in the validity of religion in western thinking. The old certain truths – of what I call the old spiritual paradigm (Lines, 2002) – brought a sense of security and meaning to human existence, but whatever their psychological attractions for personal meaning, they are philosophically untenable for many in the light of modern physics and knowledge. Imprecise definitions of religion and spirituality bedevil understanding (Lines, 2000, 2002). Both involve feelings and the intellect but are not restricted to them. Both can bring peace and contentment, but also trial and pain. I think we could briefly suggest, in spite of overlap, that in general terms religion is about *doing* whereas spirituality is about *being*, since spirituality is more about what we are, and religion's pre-occupation is with what we do.

Pupils and students in school will reflect attitudes that have been shaped and moulded by the decline in institutional religion. This chapter addresses the possibilities of conducting spiritual counselling in an age where traditional religion has begun to wane and become unfashionable in western culture.

SPIRITUALITY IN WESTERN CULTURE

Postmodernity

The old order has to give way to a new spiritual paradigm that is far less certain, more pluralistic, and much more honest (Lines, 2002). Theologians have addressed the problems of postmodern religiosity with renewed constructs, such as the God 'out-there' becoming the God 'within' (Cupitt, 1980). I say 'renewed' because these pictures are not new but are repackaged constructs and emphases that have been around for some time. I have discussed the 'authority' questions of religious theophanies (visions of God) elsewhere (Lines, 1995b), but questions of authenticity suggest that we can measure religious experience objectively, and this 'certainty' has become a deficit discourse for social construction theorists (Gergen, 1996).

The world has radically altered. The new spiritual paradigm has implications for morality. A number of traditional teachings have conflicted sharply with secular morality and have appeared archaic in an age that encourages individual morality in place of precepts handed down from above. The postmodernist ideology abandons authoritarian imperatives, in favour of relative, conditional codes and ethics (McNamee and Gergen, 1992).

Spirituality and psychotherapy

Psychologists and psychotherapists have made reference to spiritual matters. Freud's legacy was a pessimism about the survival of religion and spirituality. He advocated 'the pleasure principle' (Freud, 1963) as the purpose in life, and saw religion as a false explanation ('crooked cure') for those remaining in psychological childhood. By comparison, Jung – with his theories of the 'collective unconscious' and the numinous – left the question open. The immanence of the divine in our nature is an authentic description of the human condition for Jungians. For humanistic psychologists, personal searches for life meaning and subjective experiencing have a higher place than logic. Spiritual matters are more of the heart than of the head, and are about 'wholeness' rather than reductionism. In spite of the current interest in more personal and subjective experiencing, Elkins et al. (1988) have attempted to define and measure spiritual experience. Elkins (1998), further, has portrayed religion in ways that eliminate the 'otherness' aspect of conventional religious encounter, principally through the feminine side of the personality, the arts, the body, psychology, mythology, nature, relationships, and the dark nights of the soul. By contrast, Richards and Bergin (1997) prescribe a confined spiritual strategy for counselling which is wholly theistic – 'God exists' and has created humans, and spiritual forces exert influence in the world.

Several authors have noted the religious and spiritual roots and influences of the founders of psychotherapy (Lines, 2000, 2002; West, 2000). According to West, many therapists believe in transcendence. Freud, Jung and Rogers developed approaches consistent with their cultural and religious origins, and Jung's father was a minister who continued his work as a local priest even after losing his faith (West, 2000).

Gerard Egan (1990) was a Jesuit priest who insisted on the humanistic nature of his basic philosophy, but who strangely made no reference to spirituality or religion in his eclectic three-stage model. In more recent times, Michael Jacobs (1993) has addressed spiritual issues and constructed a psychology of religious belief from theories of developmental stages, Brian Thorne (1998) offers a conservative treatment of spiritual therapy, and William West presents spiritual counselling that is influenced by Quaker spirituality.

Existential therapy

Spiritual counselling has much in common with existentialist therapy. There is recognition in existential therapy that the old world order has gone, and that we must dispense with the traditional picture of God, an Omnipotent Being residing in heaven and ruling over human subjects constantly beset with demonic forces. Every person, for Nietzsche, must stand alone. Existentialism is rooted in the individual's existence (Yalom, 1990). Existentialist philosophers – Kant, Hegel, Keirkegaard and Heidegger – developed a new 'individualist' reality of living within a 'thrown condition', of being-in-the-world, such as it is, and having to face conflict with respect to the self, others and the physical world (McLeod, 1993). Existentialism holds that we have to survive within the givens of birth, freedom, meaninglessness, isolation and death.

Existential therapy subscribes to a range of basic assumptions that help clients to clarify life meanings by confronting paradoxes (van Deurzen-Smith, 1984). Counselling takes place within an assumption that young people can create meaning in their own lives (reaping what they sow), that there is no ultimate chaos or order, and that human nature is intrinsically flexible – there are no givens other than birth and death (Mabey and Sorensen, 1995).

These assumptions are explored in the natural world, the private world, the social world and the ideal world, and it is on this ideal world that spiritual counselling becomes primarily focused. Existential awareness of each person's mortality and finite nature is also drawn out in therapy to offset modern preoccupations that postpone the dreaded day of one's death, and the insular attitude that 'it cannot happen to me' (Nelson-Jones, 1996: 32–6). Effective thinking choices help clients not merely to focus on non-being, but on the quality of living fully in the *present* and on engaging productively in the here and now existence.

SPIRITUAL DEVELOPMENT BETWEEN THE AGES OF 11 AND 18

Cupitt (1980) has asked whether some people have a predisposition to mystical experience, and a similar question has been raised in the context of the religious development of children and adolescents (Goldman, 1964). Goldman reviews the arguments for an 'innate capacity' for religious experience as opposed to William James's (1902) reduction of religious emotions such as religious awe, religious joy and religious love to their natural counterparts: 'Religious love is only man's [sic] natural emotion of love directed to a religious object' (1902: 28). Religion is as much about the intellect as about the emotions, remarks Goldman, but it remains self-evident that 'Some religious experiences are so profound and personal and mysterious that it is doubtful if they are communicable at all, except through the emotional language of the arts' (1964: 2–3). Goldman highlights the compelling importance of the emotions in religious understanding, but also says that 'religious truth must be compelling intellectually', since 'to avoid answering or even raising intellectual problems about religion, is both dishonest and ultimately destructive of religion' (1964: 3). Goldman's interest is in a curriculum-centred linking of religious concepts with adolescent cognitive development, and he feels that 'religious thinking' is no different in mode and method from non-religious thinking (say in mathematical problem-solving).

Religious concepts, such as judgement of right and wrong, 'salvation history', symbolic significance and 'mystery', etc., need to be understood in terms of developmental psychology. Just before puberty and into the phases of adolescent development, the individual is at the stage of formal operational thought, when youngsters are able to integrate thoughts internally, to operate reversal thinking and to co-ordinate information into systems characterized by laws and regulations (Piaget, 1953). As Piaget and associates (Inhelder and Piaget, 1958) suggest, teenagers in school, to varying degree, develop the capacity to think hypothetically and deductively in terms of propositions which may or may not be logically true, and which can be tested out in thought and practice. Reasoning is reversible and logical thinking is possible in terms of symbolic and abstract terms (Inhelder and Piaget, 1958). There are occasions where youngsters, like adults, regress to 'concretization' or 'uni-directional thinking' and egocentricity (Jacobs, 1993), not least in religion (Goldman, 1964).

In addition, adolescents become able to imagine possible and impossible events, to think of a range of outcomes and their consequences, and to act for better or for worse on solutions to problems (Geldard and Geldard, 1999). The social and psychological conflicts of identity formation and individuation were examined in Chapter 3. There is a paradox in youngsters wishing, on one level, to have their separateness and uniqueness (principally from parents) recognized and, on another, needing to conform to peers and to attain 'normalcy'. Similarly, teenagers resist, openly or otherwise, belonging to those religious groups and communities that are important to their parents. So, while adolescents develop the faculty for thinking about other people and seeing issues from other viewpoints, on the psychological level they present as being sometimes reluctant to do so. Peer disapproval may discourage some individuals from attending religious ceremonies, yet, paradoxically, others may boast of their religious affiliations. Thus, social uncertainty co-exists with critical thinking. There is also an impatience to put up with hypocrisy when moralizing adults fail to live up to their own precepts.

During spiritual development in late adolescence, the occult and Satanism become attractive in forming group-identity and peer-bonding, and such interests and allegiances provide opportunities to shock adults and to reject mainstream religion (Geldard and Geldard, 1999). Personalized, as opposed to formal, religion draws teenagers to charismatic sects, particularly if they offer a laudable life meaning and a sense of communal mission. Religious communities become more attractive than individualized self-reflective pursuits of spirituality (Lines, 1995b). Even persuasive fundamentalist sects that draw converts into suicide pacts (such as at Waco, Texas) can have appeal. While symbols and mystery are intriguing for middle adolescents, it is the charismatic preacher who becomes the most persuasive factor for life change and commitment to religious communities, particularly if he or she marginalizes parents for not having sympathy for 'the faith' (Geldard and Geldard, 1999).

Personalized spirituality

Some pupils have an uncanny sense of mystery, and many others believe in paranormal phenomena, even though their rational faculties have been developed in school to accept only what can be demonstrated as true. Mention was made earlier of the comfort young adolescents experienced in having an imaginary companion with whom to share troubles and to whom to turn for safety through times of insecurity and through the long night (Geldard and Geldard, 1999). This experience is not too far removed from the commonly held belief in ghosts. Most people experience déjà-vu, the experience of repeated events, and children, particularly, through the media and cultural small talk, are quite prepared to accept paranormal activities without empirical evidence, such as out-of-the-body experiences (OBEs) and extra-sensory perception (ESP) – telepathy, clairvoyance, telekinesis, premonitions and divining the future (Lines, 1995b; Tart, 1975). Although formal religion holds minimal interest for young people, this is not the case for paranormal phenomena. Biblical stories of God calling men [*sic*], and similar divine appearances in other religious writings are not persuasive or credible to most young people, who feel they belong to a bygone superstitious age, and a particular pre-scientific literary genre.

Studies in the history of religions reveal another form of spirituality that stresses less the notion of a God 'out there' in favour of the divine element within persons, that is far less ontological and more immanent. 'Spirituality within' has become a popular interest in modern times, and is a central theme in Jungian analytical psychology. It sits well with Rogers's 'organismic-self in a state of becoming' and Keirkegaard's 'Be that self which one truly is.' Holistic psychology, which underpins humanistic counselling, affirms a construction of the self that validates spiritual development as much as emotional and intellectual development. Further, I think the relational psychology of Martin Buber (1958) helps us understand the spiritual nature of 'the self' in relation to the personality and society. I have spoken at length elsewhere of the potential of viewing relations – social as well as counselling – through a lens that interprets the natural as the spiritual, so that, in line with the thinking of Buber, I might cultivate a greater sense of 'connectedness' with my fellows and the natural world (Lines, 1995b, 2000, 2002). Self-disclosure forms part of the connecting process with young clients in spiritual counselling.

SPIRITUAL COUNSELLING AND PROBLEMS OF CONGRUENCE

There will be limited scope for counselling on spirituality in view of more pressing socio-emotional difficulties that manifest themselves in public behaviour in school. But some teachers having religious leanings and a desire to help youngsters in non-curricular matters may choose to support pupils with counselling. There is an issue for practitioners motivated by religion, to do with the maintenance of congruence (Lines, 2000, 2002).

Evangelical Christian counsellors are sometimes faced with an ideological conflict when committed to prescribe solutions within a 'saving faith in Jesus' framework. Fundamentalist Christians similarly experience inner conflict in reconciling absolute truth claims with postmodernity and social construction theory (Lines, 1995b, 2002). Some pupils and students may feel the need to break away from the faith of their upbringing, and find a religious counsellor unable to sympathise with their natural feelings of guilt. An alliance may be built upon a relationship that is perceived to be conditional on the client's decision to return to the faith in which they were brought up, yet growth for the client may necessitate a departure from his former religious group, sect or denomination. Alternatively, it may involve a new spiritual direction that produces family tension. In such cases, religious counsellors who have an evangelistic mission to save people may find the work a threat to their own personal belief system which renders their unconscious interventions through countertransference unhelpful.

Countertransference occurs equally with those counsellors who project their own unresolved religious conflicts on to their clients (Lannert, 1991). Research evidence suggests that clients will all too readily adopt the values and beliefs of their therapists, and when a person in authority repeatedly stresses that yellow is not yellow the client will tend to believe it. Spiritual counselling requires a tolerant position of open-ended inquiry about divine dealings with humankind through numerous traditions, some of which may not be ostensibly religious (Elkins, 1998).

Spiritual counsellors should have a genuine interest in philosophy and religion, particularly spirituality in general. Having had a personal religious or spiritual experience will help the counsellor understand those of their clients, so long as such experiences are interpreted within a pluralistic framework. Spiritual counsellors in school who have a religious faith are better equipped to understand the crises that challenge a life in faith of their clients than are those who are agnostic or atheistic (Lines, 2000). The experience of therapy and of faith are linked by common phenomenological principles (Worsley, 2000), and the encountered-journey motif of spiritual counselling that I propose (Lines, 2002) recognizes the 'presence-transcendence' that Rogers (1980) spoke about in his closing works.

In what follows, I present elements of a brief model of insight-based spiritual counselling, in the case of a year eight boy. I am conscious that the medium of writing cannot adequately convey the feelings aspect of what takes place in spiritual counselling. Through the three sessions of brief work, there was felt to be a powerful bond of connectedness, which grew the more we shared each other's worlds. For my part, the age difference between us two became dissolved, as being became joined momentarily with being.

AN INTEGRATIVE STYLE OF SPIRITUAL COUNSELLING

A number of presuppositions are held at the outset of spiritual coun-selling, the rationale of which I cannot discuss here (Lines, 2000, 2002). These presuppositions are as follows:

- I assume that all people have a capacity to be spiritual and to think spiritually, just as they can be emotional in their being and can func-tion emotionally, that spiritual growth is a universal phenomenon (Hay, 1982; Lines, 2000, 2002).
- I assume that brief work can be conducted with teenagers by showing them signposts for spiritual thinking, by suggesting possibilities for experiencing and for exploring pluralistic accounts of life from spiri-tual perspectives.
- I assume that the process of spiritual awakening occurs through Anderson and Goolishian's (1988) conversation metaphor. Life meaning for two people constantly develops through the interchange of ideas that are expressed in an explorative manner. It is not merely the information sharing that gives meaning but, through the conversation, meanings are created from how various nuances are selected and worked upon.
- I assume that in order for effective spiritual therapy to take place, the counsellor must take the one-down stance and engage in dialogue, not as expert but as collaborative fellow-seeker.
- I assume that the process of client self-discovery is enhanced when counsellors begin to disclose material about their own uncertainties. There is no hiding behind masks and no pretence of knowing all the answers. The spiritual counsellor in search of her own life meaning will bring her own unresolved questions to the surface with the client, along with personal paradoxes and inconsistencies in thought, since both parties are engaged on a pilgrimage of self-growth.

Spiritual counselling for Des

Des lost his dad at the close of his first year at secondary school. For two years his father had suffered from an incurable cancer, and during his last three months he was nursed in a hospice. While his mother and sister grieved publicly, Des showed no emotion. At the beginning of year eight, he became very difficult to manage in school. His mother put this down to anger over the loss of his dad. During this period, however, he was not amenable to bereavement counselling. His mother disclosed to me that his father had stopped showing him affection when he entered secondary school because, as he put it, 'Now he has become a man, he doesn't need all that lovey-dovey stuff.' 'Big boys', he said, 'don't need hugging.' Apart from losing his father, then, he had been pushed out emotion-ally and made to feel isolated from the parent who was once his closest ally and support in times of trouble.

Wild and uncontrollable behaviour became the strongest indicator that Des had not adjusted to his loss, and a behavioural programme with built-in incentives had begun to check him moderately for a short while. There are major handicaps in consistent management of behavioural programmes in large comprehensive schools (Lines, 2000), and Des was becoming over-reliant on wayward peers through a lack of suitable adult male role models to take the place of his dad (Biddulph, 1998). Events, however, overtook therapeutic support and time-essential bereavement healing, and Des was sent to a Behavioural Support Unit over the next term to ease the tension between him and some of his teachers.

On his return, Des's self-management and anger control were much improved and he became more amenable to counselling. To further support Des, a range of integrative approaches and techniques that centre on anger-management, effective thinking skills and bereavement counselling could have been used. Although features of these approaches were used in our work, the main emphasis was on enabling healing and readjustment through spiritual counselling. This decision was arrived at after an early assessment had revealed that spirituality was Des's dominant mode of functioning.

In our early sessions, issues kept arising of a religious-spiritual nature and much of his reflective talk was on metaphysical topics and Christian fundamentalist beliefs. Des's mother had become a fundamentalist Christian and was attending Gospel meetings regularly, along with Des's older sister. Des was ambivalent about attending the meetings. Sometimes he would go and get something from the experience and from meeting understanding people, at other times he would prefer to stay in bed, or call for his mates – which carried the risk of leading to deliquency. Des's mother was at times finding Des impossible to manage and keep under control, speaking on occasion of placing him in care. Spiritual counselling is illustrated in Des's case by breaking in to fragments of discourse in order to demonstrate the principles of the conversation metaphor.

Is there a set time to die?

Des:	Some strange things have happened to me [*puzzled look*]. I remember when my dad was very ill, just before he died, he seemed to get better. He was lying in his bed and the cat jumped on to his chest. He didn't like cats, but with the cat on him he began taking deep breaths, and it was as though he came alive again. I think he was dying before that, but something startled him and he seemed to come back to life.
Counsellor:	Strange, isn't it. Do you think dad was meant to die at that time? People say, 'When your time is up, your time is up', as though there is a set time to die. I remember when I was in hospital, there was an old patient in his seventies who had broken his neck and for whom rehabilitation was too much effort. He wanted to die, pleaded with

nurses to let him die, and he eventually willed himself to death. I
wonder if he was deciding when to die? Was he in control?

Des: My dad wanted to die when he did [*resignedly, he glances downward*].
I wasn't there then, but mum said he'd had enough and no longer
wanted to live.

Commentary: The discourse could have dwelt on what Des was judging to
be an almost paranormal phenomenon – a cat compelling dad to breathe
heavily and *causing* him to revive – but such a discussion would have
heightened the importance of irrational explanations. An REBT counsellor
would have disputed 'irrational beliefs' (Ellis, 1987), but the spiritual
counsellor has to view beliefs in a broad and supportive context (Lines,
1999b). Instead, the talk was steered towards the biblical concept of 'For
everything there is a season … A time to be born, and a time to die'
(Ecclesiastes 3: 2). This led to a productive discourse away from the significance of the cat's instinctive action towards an exchange of popular
philosophies of 'time and chance', the injustice of 'innocent suffering' and
'predestination' (Lines, 1995b).

The purpose of my 're-membering' a fellow patient on the ward and
'taking back' his *will to die* had a positive effect (Speedy, 2000). The event
greatly affected my will for recovery as well as underlying the existential experience of choice. Des took up the lead and explored through
sadness his father's volition for recovery or defeat. Pupils at this stage
of intellectual development will not have the reasoning abilities to
debate fully these issues (least of all the interest). But Des, at this point
of his existential dilemma, is being equipped with hooks upon which to
hang notions of more adaptive beliefs till he becomes emotionally able
to accept the finality of death. Des is becoming a mini-philosopher.
Although some people fail to accept the reality of death, and counselling
should challenge this (Nelson-Jones, 1996), there is clear evidence that
young people need metaphysical beliefs early on in the acceptance
process (Lines, 1999b). His remark, 'he seemed to come back to life',
might have been an unconscious wish to over-identify the (supposed)
dying and coming to life again of his dad with Jesus, as the continuing
discourse suggests.

Strange things happen in life – are some events significant?

Des: My dad died when he was 33, the same as Jesus when he was
crucified. When you're dead you stay at 33, the same as Jesus.
You always stay the same age when you're dead, and Jesus'
followers always stay at 33 [*looking up, he spoke with certainty*].

Counsellor: Do you think that is significant, or a coincidence?

Des: I dunno really.

Counsellor: Interesting that, isn't it? When I broke my neck, I was coming on to
forty, which is a generation, a life, so to speak, in biblical days. So my
first life of being able-bodied had then closed, and I'm not sure I will

> survive the second chapter of forty to eighty as a disabled person
> [*spoken in jest, Des laughs along*].
>
> Des: You might do?
> Counsellor: My life in the second chapter has certainly changed.
> Des: Mine too [*said despondently*].

Commentary: Children and young people fall back on metaphysical beliefs at times of loss and trauma, as unstructured interviews with the bereaved have shown (Lines, 1999b). Jacobs (1993) has presented a psychology of religious belief, which promotes belief developmentally from crude metaphysical constructs to advanced coping mechanisms, but adults as well as children oscillate between rational and irrational 'concretized' belief systems in accounting for experience. Des's belief in his dad remaining at the fixed age of 33 at death has no theological or exegetical foundation, yet I felt there was no value in discrediting a belief that a member of Des's Gospel community may have encouraged to give him comfort.

Identifying dad with Jesus was powerful and reassuring at a time when Des's feelings were raw and sensitive, but my disclosure was purposeful in focusing not upon the Jesus–dad identity but on emphasizing significant timings, and living life in a changed relational world. Therapy, from this point on, dwelt upon the productive issues of living in the present and looking towards the future. Adults tend to adopt a 'hurry-up' mentality in social and business activities, which is a disease in modern professional life but which can be addressed with effective thinking skills (Nelson-Jones, 1996). With bereaved youngsters, however, healing cannot be rushed but must occur within 'holding strategies' of understanding and belief systems that provide psychological as well as emotional short-term support.

Do we have the power and choice to determine our futures?

> Des: Mum is angry about me getting into trouble with the police. [*When I
>   formerly counselled Des over delinquent trends, it was as though he was
>   conscious of an internal battle of pulls and pushes, of whether to follow
>   mates whatever the cost, or to do what mum (and God, and, perhaps, dad)
>   said he should do.*]
> Counsellor: It almost seems that you are at a crossroads now [*I felt that he was
>   stuck*]. I don't know whether you understand what I mean by that. It
>   comes from the Bible, and is a saying of Jesus where people are
>   sometimes faced with a choice of going to the left or to the right.
>   Going one way brings trouble, going the other brings success. Is it like
>   that for you?
> Des: I think so in a way [*spoke reflectively*], part of me wants to go where
>   the trouble is because that seems exciting, and another part of me
>   wants to keep out of trouble. Sometimes I go one way, sometimes
>   the other.
> Counsellor: I think many people see life that way when they're young and when
>   you're trying to sort out your friendships. It is a very common
>   experience.

Commentary: The biblical saying of Jesus presents the power of choice starkly and succinctly. It is material which has authority for Des, given his background, and also enshrines Nelson-Jones's (1996) effective thinking skills and accommodates the tendency for youngsters at Des's cognitive stage to switch unconsciously from formal thought to concrete thought and vice versa (Goldman, 1964). Later on, Des will begin to reason that life is not black and white, that there are shades of grey in moral imperatives, but at this point it is more important to help him steer a course towards social conformity rather than rebelliousness. His prime authority-enforcer (dad) had been snatched away from him, which had left him floundering and potential prey to gangs who were heavily into crime.

Des often said that he 'hated himself', which he qualified by saying, 'Mum hates me. No…, well…, she doesn't hate me. She loves me but hates what I do.' This transition in thought, which was developed in counselling, was helping Des move into 'shades of grey' thinking, which encouraged him to form a more positive and self-affirming self-construct. It has always been difficult to keep Des on track. He blocks talk about himself and keeps interjecting with questions about my world, which he asks with a glazed stare of fixed eye-contact. I challenged him with Gestalt-type interventions and he responded with, 'I don't like talking about myself much … Do you drive a Jag?' The healing was going to be slow. While he acknowledged and owned the fact that he was improving, his persona among peers as 'a bit of a trouble-maker' was still over-riding. I closed this session by giving him a handle, for experience had shown that he often reflected outside counselling on the last words spoken in therapy. Utilizing notions of Bible prophecy, which was a major interest of his family, I said, 'You know how parts of the Bible are said to predict the future. I have made a prediction about you. Given a little time, you will come around. You're getting better all the time, and I think you will make it through school.' He left the counselling room musing. I had risen from the one-down position to assume temporarily the stance of prophetic authority-figure for positive reasons.

Is life a series of random events or is there a grand master plan?

Des:	The funny thing is that after my dad had died, his brother died six months later, then his father died. Everybody dies on my dad's side of the family, nobody on my mother's. [*His words were spoken in bemusement more than fear.*]
Counsellor:	You appear to be saying, 'All males die in my family!'
Des:	…Yea [*begrudgingly*].
Counsellor:	Is what you're saying, perhaps, 'When will my time come up?'
Des:	I suppose it is.
Counsellor:	One way of looking at life is like looking at a half-filled glass. Some say, 'The glass is half-empty', and they are what we call 'pessimists', people who look bleakly at the future. Others say, 'The glass is half-full', and they are called 'optimists', people who look to the future with

> promise and hopefulness. Now you have a choice. None of us knows
> how long we shall live or when we shall die, and, as I often say to
> myself when things are not working out well, 'Why worry about
> things you cannot alter? Worry costs energy. Use your energy for
> those things you can affect.'

Commentary: The power of positive thinking is a common counselling strategy for change (Nelson-Jones, 1996). My earlier comments aimed to reach the direct concern from roundabout dialogue. It is possible that my first intervention missed the mark, and, having raised the question, put something in his mind and made links that were not considered, though I doubt it. Cajoling Des to think positively was not to obscure the gravity of his opening observation, but to re-view the facts constructively. If, at worst, Des was reflecting on the possibility of dying by the age of 33, then he could be saying, 'I'll be dead like my dad before reaching 34.' Alternatively, and more optimistically, he could say to himself, 'I can at least live for as long as twenty years from now, which is a lifetime: lots of life to live, lots of fun to be had, lots of things to do.' Biographies of those narrowly escaping death, those having to face terminal conditions or suffering tragedies such as the holocaust, illustrate how altered perspectives affect the quality of living (Frankl, 1959; Lines, 1995a). Depending on the young client's reading level, biographies, or stories within biographies, selectively provided, can be a powerful therapeutic tool for healing.

Theologians such as Michael Goulder and John Hick (Goulder and Hick, 1983) have long wrestled with the ambiguities of 'God of chance or God of providence', and have come up with no conclusive answers other than those of faith. At times, the evidence suggests that God's dealings are capricious, at others that they are designed. It is as possible to argue the case for atheism as to argue for deism. So much depends upon personal opinions. Whatever learning I may have, or however much I have written on theology, Des's views are no less valid than mine. Collaborative therapy facilitates a process of shared self-evaluation.

Is life worth the hassle?

Des:	Have you ever wanted to end your life when you were disabled?
Counsellor:	Yes, there was a time when I wanted to end my life [*I shared the details with him: Lines, 1995a*]. What about you?
Des:	No, I don't think so. I dunno really, perhaps I … I'm scared of nothing.
Counsellor:	So you want to keep on living, and keep improving.
Des:	Yeah, that's it really.
Counsellor:	And teachers tell me you're making remarkable progress since you were very angry, when your dad died.
Des:	Yeah, that's about it.
Counsellor:	And you appear much more able to talk about it. I would like to think you could help others in school having similar experiences. I think

you have a lot to offer. I think, maybe, one day ... Do you think you have a spiritual side to you?

Des: I don't know really. I think we're all here for something, but I don't know what it is though.

Commentary: I had no reservations about making this personal disclosure. Life is a hassle, and there is little point in denying it. My point in answering Des honestly, in relating my suicide wish (Lines, 1995a), was not to model a stance of coming out valiantly on the other side, or to present a crass message of 'carrying on regardless'. Rather, my intention was to register in Des the very real experience of 'dark nights of the soul' (see Elkins, 1998), to share with him that at times we feel that life is not worth the candle, and thereby help him face similar nihilistic thoughts with candour and integrity and without guilt. Youngsters find this thought-identity bonding very reassuring when they have been knocked off course by loss events.

A subtle switch to Des's positive improvements utilizes the solution-focused axiom that *recognizing small changes* and amplifying them in the eyes of the client *helps in motivating the spirit for further improvement*. But this was more than a subtle technique; it carried the thinking into an existential exploration into life-meaning and purpose. Most of the world's great faiths encourage personal missions in life, and this intervention was a ploy to help Des think bigger than the immediate situation – namely to his place in the universe. The point in brief spiritual counselling is not to spell this out in detail, but to prompt early notions for thought and development as life unfolds, to give signposts for journeying.

Are we somehow protected from major hazards – do guardian angels look over us?

Des: I remember another occasion when I was crossing the road. A little boy was sitting on the curb staring at me [*Des, in turn, stares at me*]. It was weird. He sat still and kept staring at me. It was because I kept staring at him that I didn't cross the road just then, and the car missed me. If it weren't for that kid, I would have been run over. When I looked up, the boy wasn't there. It was as though my dad was looking after me in that little kid.

Counsellor: How fascinating [*I felt mesmerized by Des's look*]. Have you ever had other experiences whereby it seems that you are being protected?

Des: Can't think of any ... [*reflective*]

Counsellor: I once had a motorbike accident where I had a lucky escape. I was riding down a steep hill when a car pulled out in front of me. I hit his front wing and flew over the bonnet. A second earlier, I'd have driven into the bonnet and under the front wheels – I'd have been dead. A second later, I'd have crashed into the doorframe – again, I'd have been dead. This accident indirectly turned out to present an opportunity for a change of job, which made me very content. Good fortune

> came from that young man's lapse of concentration on one level, and on another someone [*thing?*] stopped me from a fatality.
>
> Des: I often have dreams about you, about your accident and about other things with you getting better… [*I felt bonded with Des at this point.*]

Commentary: The personal interests and lives of their teachers intrigue pupils, and in the counselling of teenagers therapy can be enhanced with counsellor self-disclosure. Various writers have entered the debate over the merits and short-comings of self-disclosure in adult individual counselling, and authors point out the different practice for different approaches and the various forms of self-disclosure for different therapeutic purposes (Jeffries, 2000). Psychodynamic counsellors refrain from self-disclosure in order to intensify transference, while Rogerian therapists use self-disclosure in order to dissolve it until the feelings are directed toward their true object. Narrative therapists believe that the 'self' is socially constructed. The spiritual counsellor uses self-disclosed events for sharing the philosophies that underlie them.

The idea of guardian angels looking over us is as ancient as religion itself, and there is little advantage in disputing the notion philosophically. I–Thou relations with metaphysical beings like angels do not exist; they are I–It relations (Buber, 1958). Some feel, however, that beliefs in guardian angels can lead to a failure to take responsibility for life and change (Nelson-Jones, 1996), and it is wise to recognize that many youngsters have counter-experiences of dereliction and abandonment. Timely interventions of setting the balance seem appropriate.

The closing statement led us off course to extensive self-disclosure and served to strengthen our therapeutic bond. He was as fascinated with my world as I was with his. Much more is taking place during these interactive moments of communion; there is a meeting of minds, a merging of spirits, an I–Thou encounter (Buber, 1958). When two people engage in each other's phenomenological worlds, there occurs an intimate bridging from person to person, which is almost symbiotic in that the separate identities of each are temporarily lost. The experience is akin to a religious theophany of days gone by (Lines, 1995b, 2002), where the devotee becomes suffused with the deity, the difference being that in collaborative narrative therapy no hierarchical boundaries must exist (Anderson and Goolishian, 1988).

CONCLUSION

Spiritual counselling has parallels in existential therapy and humanistic counselling, along with the conversational metaphor of collaborative therapy. What marks spiritual counselling as different from other phenomenon-based therapies within a postmodern context, is the 'no absolute answers to life's riddles' stance of counselling. Formerly, religion took up the dogmatic-authoritarian narrative of prescribing all the answers, but this is no longer tenable according to social construction theory. Existential counselling takes, I think, a too pessimistic stance, a stance that is not appealing to or motivating for young people. The relational psychology of Buber, particularly its emphasis on a greater sense of connectedness, speaks to the condition of adolescence where human contact, emerging sexuality and peer relations through identity formation are changing the sense of 'self'.

The collaborative emphasis of spiritual counselling requires an element of self-disclosure. This facilitates a joint sharing of ideas and philosophies of personal experience and life meanings within the context of a shared pilgrimage. Change in the life of teenagers is a cause of reflection, and bereavement and personal loss accelerate the process, but change is also a challenge that offers new stimuli, and this makes adolescence an exciting period of development. Life does not stand still, development and growth towards individuation are dynamic processes of social separation and relation-formation, and psychological readjustment. Early familial beliefs and self-constructs will need adjusting to suit the changing world of becoming adult and standing on one's own feet. The journey has no destination except death; the meandering path has many diversions and detours, many junctions and crossroads, and the journey has many breaks for refreshment. The brief spiritual counselling session represents but one opportunity to take a break, re-evaluate the course and seek counsel from a fellow traveller *en route* to finding a preferred 'self'.

REFERENCES

Adams, J. (1976) *Understanding and Managing Personal Change*. Oxford: Martin Robertson.

Adams, S. (1990) 'Child self-protection: concerns about classroom approaches', *Pastoral Care in Education*, 8(3): 3–6.

Ainsworth, M., Blehar, M., Waters, E. and Wall, S. (1978) *Patterns of Attachment: Assessed in the Strange Situation and at Home*. Hillsdale, NJ: Erlbaum.

Alloy, L.B. and Abramson, L.Y. (1982) 'Learned helplessness, depression and the illusion of control', *Journal of Personality and Social Psychology*, 42: 1114–26.

Anderson, H. and Goolishian, H. (1988) 'Human systems as linguistic systems: evolving ideas about the implications for theory and practice', *Family Process*, 27: 371–93.

Arora, C.M.T. and Thompson, D.A. (1987) 'Defining bullying for a secondary school', *Education and Child Psychology*, 4(3): 110–20.

BACP (2000a) *Code of Ethics and Practice*. Rugby: British Association of Counselling and Psychotherapy.

BACP (2000b) *Information Sheet 13*. Rugby: British Association for Counselling and Psychotherapy.

Beck, A.T., Rush, A.J., Shaw, B.F. and Emery, G. (1979) *Cognitive Therapy of Depression*. New York: Guilford.

Berkowitz, D.A. (1987) 'Adolescent individuation and family therapy', in J.C. Coleman, *Working with Troubled Adolescents*. London: Academic Press.

Berne, E. (1968) *Games People Play: The Psychology of Human Relationships*. London: Penguin Books.

Besag, V. (1989) *Bullies and Victims in Schools*. Milton Keynes: Open University Press.

Biddulph, S. (1996) *The Secret of Happy Children*. London: Thorsons.

Biddulph, S. (1998) *Raising Boys*. London: Thorsons.

Bond, T. (1993) *Standards and Ethics for Counselling in Action*. London: Sage.

Bond, T. (1994) *Counselling, Confidentiality and the Law*. Rugby: BAC.

Bowlby, J. (1952) 'A two-year-old goes to hospital: a scientific film', *Proceedings of the Royal Society of Medicine*, 46: 425–7.

Bragg, M. (1999) 'Documentary', June, BBC 2: London: BBC Broadcast.

Brammer, L.M. and Shostrum, E.L. (1982) *Therapeutic Psychology*, 4th edn. Englewood Cliffs, NJ: Prentice Hall.

Buber, M. (1958) *I and Thou*. Edinburgh: T. & T. Clarke Ltd.

Burnham, J.B. (1986) *Family Therapy*. London: Routledge.

Butler, G. and Low, J. (1994) 'Short-term psychotherapy', in P. Clarkson and M. Pokorny (eds), *The Handbook of Psychotherapy*. London: Routledge.

Capey, M. (1998) *Counselling for Pupils and Young Adults: Examples of what LEAs and Schools Provide*. Berkshire: Education Management Information Exchange.

Carkhuff, R.R. and Berenson, B.G. (1977) *Beyond Counselling and Therapy*, 2nd edn. New York: Holt, Rinehart & Winston.

Carr, R. (1994) 'Peer helping in Canada', *Peer Counselling Journal*, 11(1): 6–9.

Casemore, R. (1995) *Confidentiality and School Counselling*.Rugby: BAC.

Catholic Trust Society (undated) *Pastoral Care of Homosexual Persons*. London (pamphlet produced by the Catholic Trust Society).

Clarkson, P. (1994) 'The nature and range of psychotherapy', in P. Clarkson and M. Pokorny (eds), *The Handbook of Psychotherapy*. London: Routledge.

Cohn, T. (1987) 'Sticks and stones may break my bones but names will never hurt me', *Multicultural Teaching*, 5(3): 8–11.

Coleman, J.C. (ed.) (1987) *Working with Troubled Adolescents: A Handbook*. London: Academic Press.

Conger, J.J. (1975) *Contemporary Issues in Adolescent Development*. London: Harper & Row.

Courtois, C. (1988) *Healing the Incest Wound*. New York: W. W. Norton & Co.

Cowen, E.L., Pederson, A., Babigian, H., Izzo, L.D. and Trost, M.A. (1973) 'Long-term follow up of early detected vulnerable children', *Journal of Consulting and Clinical Psychology*, 41: 438–46.

Cowie, H. (1998) 'Perspectives of teachers and pupils on the experience of peer support against bullying', *Educational Research and Evaluation*, 1: 108–25.

Cowie, H. and Sharp, S. (eds) (1996) *Peer Counselling in Schools*. London: David Fulton Publishers Ltd.

Culley, S. (1992) 'Counselling skills: an integrative framework', in W. Dryden (ed.), *Integrative and Eclectic Therapy*. Buckingham: Oxford University Press.

Cupitt, D. (1980) *Taking Leave of God*. London: SCM Press Ltd.

Daniels, D. and Jenkins, P. (2000) 'Reporting child abuse', *Counselling*, 11(9): 551–4.

Davies, G.T. (1986) *A First Year Tutorial Handbook*. Oxford: Blackwell.

Davis, T.E. and Osborn, C.J. (2000) *The Solution-Focused School Counsellor: Shaping Professional Practice*. Philadelphia: Accelerated Development.

DeGaston, J.F., Weed, S. and Jensen, L. (1996) 'Understanding gender differences in sexuality', *Adolescence*, 32: 217–31.

Devere, M. (2000) 'New models: the counselling of change', *Counselling*, 11(7): 412–13.

Diamond, J. (2000) *Narrative Means to Sober Ends*. New York: Guilford.

Dominian, J., Mansfield, P., Dormor, D. and McAllister, F. (1991) *Marital Breakdown and the Health of the Nation*. London: One plus One – Marriage and Partnership Research.

Dryden, W. (ed.) (1984) *Individual Therapy in Britain*. London: Harper & Row.

Dryden, W. and Norcross, J.C. (eds) (1990) *Eclecticism and Integration in Counselling and Psychotherapy*. Essex: Gale Centre Publications.

Dunkley, C. (2001) 'The pain barrier diagram', *Counselling and Psychotherapy*, (12)1: 13–15.

Durrant, M. (1993) *Creative Strategies for School Problems*. Epping, NSW: Eastwood Family Therapy Centre.

Dusek, J.B. (1996) *Adolescent Development and Behavior*. Englewood Cliffs, NJ: Prentice Hall.

Egan, G. (1990) *The Skilled Helper*, 4th edn. Monterey, Pacific Grove, CA: Brooks/Cole (originally published in 1975).

Elkins, D.N. (1998) *Beyond Religion: A Personal Programme for Building a Spiritual Life Outside the Walls of Traditional Religion*. Wheaton, IL: Quest Books.

Elkins, D.N., Hedstrom, L.J., Hughes, L.L., Leaf, J.A. and Saunders, C. (1988) 'Toward a humanistic-phenomenological spirituality: definition, description, and measurement', *Journal of Humanistic Psychology*, 28(4): 5–18.

Elliot, B.J. and Richards, M.P.M. (1991) 'Effects of parental divorce on children', *Archives of Disease in Childhood*, 66: 915–16.

Elliott, M. (1986) *Kidscape Project*, unpublished research. London: The Kidscape Primary Kit, Kidscape, 82 Brock Street, London W1Y 1YP.

Elliott, M. (1990) 'A response to Steve Adams', *Pastoral Care in Education*, 8(3): 7–9.

Ellis, A. (1977) *Reason and Emotion in Psychotherapy*. Secaucus, NJ: Citadel Press.

Ellis, A. (1980) 'Overview of the clinical theory of rational-emotive therapy', in R. Grieger and J. Boyd (eds), *Rational-Emotive Therapy: A Skills Based Approach*. New York: Van Nostrand Reinhold.

Ellis, A. (1983) 'Failures in rational-emotive therapy', in E.B. Foa and P.M.G. Emmelkamp (eds), *Failures in Behaviour Therapy*. New York: Wiley.

Ellis, A. (1987) 'The impossibility of achieving consistently good mental health', *American Psychologist*, 42: 364–75.

Elmore, L.J. (1986) 'The teacher and the child of divorce', paper presented at the Seventh Annual Families Alive Conference, Ogden, UT, 10–12 September.

Epston, D., White, M. and Murray, K. (1992) 'A proposal for a re-authoring therapy: Rose's revisioning of her life and a commentary', in S. McNamee and K.J. Gergen, *Therapy as Social Construction*. London: Sage.

Erikson, E.H. (1956) 'The problem of ego identity', *Journal of the American Psychoanalytic Association*, 4: 56–121.

Erikson, E.H. (1963) *Childhood and Society*. Harmondsworth: Penguin (rev. edn, 1965). London: Hogarth Press, Vintage.

Erikson, E.H. (1968) *Identity: Youth and Crisis*. New York: Norton.

Erikson, E.H. (1980) *Identity and the Life Cycle*, New York, Norton.

Farrell, P. (1999) 'The limitations of current theories in understanding bereavement and grief', *Counselling*, 10(2): 143–6.

Feltham, C. (1997) *Time-Limited Counselling*. London: Sage.

Fergusson, D.E. and Mullen, P.E. (1999) *Childhood Sexual Abuse: An Evidence Based Perspective*. London: Sage.

Forero, R., McLellan, L. Rissell, C. and Bauman, A. (1999) 'Bullying behaviour and psychological health among school students in New South Wales', *British Medical Journal*, 319: 344–8.

Frank, J. (1986) 'What is psychotherapy?' in S. Bloch (ed.), *An Introduction to the Psychotherapies*, 2nd edn. Oxford: Oxford University Press.

Frankl, V.E. (1959) *Man's Search for Meaning*. New York: Washington Square Press.

Freud, S. (1933) *New Introductory Lectures on Psycho-analysis*. London, 1971: Standard Edition 22/Pelican Freud Library 2 (1973): Penguin Books.

Freud, S. (1937) *The Ego and the Mechanisms of Defence*. London: Hogarth Press.

Freud, S. (1963) *Civilisation and its Discontents*. New York: Basic Books.

Friends West Midlands (1993/1994) *Annual Report*. PO Box 2405, Birmingham B5 4AJ.

Geldard, K. and Geldard, D. (1999) *Counselling Adolescents: The Pro-active Approach*. London: Sage.

Gergen, K.J. (1996) 'Postmodern society as a concept', introductory lecture at International Conference for Psychotherapy, Vienna, July, audiotape.

Gergen, K.J. and Kaye, J. (1992) 'Beyond narrative in the negotiation of therapeutic meaning', in S. McNamee and K.J. Gergen, *Therapy as Social Construction*. London: Sage.

Gibran, K. (1972) *The Prophet*. New York: Alfred A. Knopf (originally published in 1923).

Goldman, R. (1964) *Religious Thinking from Childhood to Adolescence.* London: Routledge & Kegan Paul.

Goulder, M. and Hick, J. (1983) *Why Believe in God?* London: SCM Press.

Gregson, O. and Looker, T. (1994) 'The biological basis of stress management', *British Journal of Guidance and Counselling,* 22(1): 13–26.

Hall, A.S. and Fradkin, H.R. (1992) 'Affirming gay men's mental health: counselling with a new attitude', *Journal of Mental Health Counselling,* 14 (3).

Hamilton, C. and Hopegood, L. (1998) *Offering Children Confidentiality: Law and Guidance.* Colchester: Children's Legal Centre, University of Essex.

Harrison, J. (1987) 'Counselling gay men', in M. Scher et al., *Handbook of Counselling and Psychotherapy with Men.* California: Sage.

Hay, D. (1982) *Exploring Inner Space: Scientists and Religious Experience.* Harmondsworth: Penguin.

Herbert, M. (1978) *Conduct Disorders of Childhood and Adolescence.* Chichester: John Wiley & Sons.

Hitchings, P. (1994) 'Psychotherapy and sexual orientation', in P. Clarkson and M. Pokorny (eds), *The Handbook of Psychotherapy.* London: Routledge.

Holland, J. (2000) 'Secondary schools and pupil loss by parental bereavement and parental relationship separations', *Pastoral Care in Education,* 11: 33–9.

Holmes, J. (1993) *John Bowlby and Attachment Theory.* London: Routledge.

Hooker, E. (1985) 'The adjustment of the overt male homosexual', *Journal of Personality Assessment,* 21: 18–23.

Howard, A. (2000) *Philosophy for Counselling and Pschotherapy: Pythagoras to Postmodernism.* London: Macmillan Press.

Howard, K.I., Kopta, S.M., Krause, M.S. and Orlinski, D.E. (1986) 'The close-effect relationship in psychotherapy', *American Psychologist,* 41: 159–64.

Hu, F.B., Flack, B.R., Hedeker, D. and Syddiqui, O. (1995) 'The influence of friends and parental smoking on adolescent smoking behaviour: the effects of time and prior smoking', *Journal of Applied Social Psychology,* 25: 2018–47.

Inhelder, B. and Piaget, J. (1958) *The Growth of Logical Thinking from Childhood to Adolescence.* London: Routledge & Kegan Paul.

Ives, R. (1994) 'Stop sniffing in the States: approaches to solvent misuse prevention in the USA', *Drugs, Education, Prevention and Policy,* 1: 37–48.

Jacobs, M. (1988) *Psychodynamic Counselling in Action.* London: Sage.

Jacobs, M. (1993) *Living Illusions: A Psychology of Belief.* London: SPCK.

Jacobson, E. (1938) *Progressive Relaxation,* 2nd edn. Chicago: University of Chicago Press.

James, W. (1902) *The Varieties of Religious Experience.* London: Fount/Collins.

Jeffries, R. (2000) 'Self-disclosure', *Counselling,* 11(7): 407–11.

Jenkins, A. (1990) *Invitations to Responsibility: The Therapeutic Engagement of Men Who are Violent and Abusive.* Adelaide, Australia: Dulwich Centre Publications.

Jenkins, J.E. (1996) 'The influence of peer affiliation and student activities on adolescent drug involvement', *Adolescence,* 31: 297–306.

Kilty, J. and Bond, M. (1991) *Practical Methods of Dealing with Stress.* Guildford: Human Potential Resource Group, University of Surrey.

Knapp, C. (1996) *Drinking: A Love Story.* New York: Dial Press.

Koss, M.P. and Shiang, J. (1994) 'Research on brief psychotherapy', in A.E. Bergin and S.L. Garfield (eds), *Handbook of Psychotherapy and Behaviour Change,* 4th edn. New York: John Wiley & Sons.

Kramer, S.A. (1990) *Positive Endings in Psychotherapy.* Oxford: Jossey-Bass.

Kübler-Ross, E. (1982) *On Death and Dying*. London: Tavistock.

Lambert, J.L. (1992) 'Implications of outcome research for psychotherapy integration', in J.C. Norcross and M.R.G. Goldfried (eds), *Handbook of Psychotherapy Integration*. New York: Basic Books.

Lambert, M.J. and Bergin, A.E. (1994) 'The effectiveness of psychotherapy', in A.E. Bergin and S.L. Garfield (eds), *Handbook of Psychotherapy and Behaviour Change*, 4th edn. New York: John Wiley & Sons.

Lannert, J.L. (1991) 'Resistance and countertransference issues with spiritual and religious clients', *Journal of Humanistic Psychology*, 31(4): 68–76.

Lazarus, A.A. (1990) 'Why I am an eclectic (not an integrationist)', in W. Dryden and J.C. Norcross (eds), *Eclecticism and Integration in Counselling and Psychotherapy*. Essex: Gale Centre Publications.

Le Count, D. (2000) 'Working with "difficult" children from the inside out: loss and bereavement and how the creative arts can help', *Counselling*, (18)2: 17–27.

Lees, S. (1993) *Sugar and Spice*. London: Penguin.

Lethem, J. (1994) *Moved to Tears, Moved to Action: Solution Focussed Brief Therapy with Women and Children*. London: Brief Therapy Press.

Lewis, J. (1992) 'Death and divorce – helping students cope in single-parent families', *NASSP Bulletin*, 76 (543): 55–60.

Lindsay, W.R. (1987) 'Social skills training with adolescents', in J. Coleman (ed.), *Working with Troubled Adolescents*. London: Academic Press.

Lines, D. (1985) *Counselling Adolescents in Secondary School*. Birmingham: unpublished booklet (dennis@schoolcounselling.co.uk).

Lines, D. (1995a) *Coming Through the Tunnel*. Birmingham: published by the author: (www.schoolcounselling.co.uk).

Lines, D. (1995b) *Christianity is Larger than Fundamentalism*. Durham: Pentland Press.

Lines, D. (1996) 'Early secondary pupils' experiences of name-calling behaviour through a discourse analysis of differing counselling interviews', unpublished dissertation: Westhill College, Selly Oak, Birmingham.

Lines, D. (1999a), 'Secondary pupils' experiences of name-calling behaviour', *Pastoral Care in Education*, 17(1): 23–31.

Lines, D. (1999b) 'Bereavement group therapy in school: the role of a belief in a post-death existence within adolescent development for the acceptance process of loss', *Journal of Children's Spirituality*, 4(2): 141–54.

Lines, D. (2000) *Counselling Approaches for Young People in Secondary School: From Traditional Approaches to Eclectic and Integrative Counselling*. Birmingham: published by the author: (www.schoolcounselling.co.uk).

Lines, D. (2001) 'An approach with name-calling and verbal taunting', *Pastoral Care in Education*, 18(1): 3–9.

Lines, D. (2002) 'Counselling in the new spiritual paradigm', *Journal of Humanistic Psychology* (in press).

Litvinoff, S. (1991) *The Relate Guide to Better Relationships*. London: Vermilion.

Longfellow, C. (1979) 'Divorce in context. Its impact on children', in G. Levinger and O.C. Moles (eds), *Divorce and Separation*. New York: Basic Books.

Mabey, J. and Sorensen, B. (1995) *Counselling for Young People*. Buckingham: Open University Press.

Maher, P. (1990) 'Child protection: another view', *Pastoral Care in Education*, 8(3): 9–12.

Mason, A. (2000) 'A queer law – what counsellors should know about section 28', *Counselling*, 11(3): 138–9.

Masson, J. (1992) *Against Therapy*. London: Harper-Collins.

Matteson, D.R. (1987) 'Counselling bisexual men', in M. Scher et al., *Handbook of Counselling and Psychotherapy with Men*. California: Sage.

May, R. (1969) *Love and Will*. New York: Dell Publishing.

McBroom, J.R. (1994) 'Correlates of alcohol and marijuana use among junior high school students: family, peers, school problems, and psychosocial concerns', *Youth and Society*, 26: 54–68.

McGuiness, J. (1998) *Counselling in Schools: New Perspectives*. London: Cassell.

McLeod, J. (1993) *An Introduction to Counselling*, 2nd edn. Buckingham: Open University Press.

McNamee, S. and Gergen, K.J. (1992) *Therapy as Social Construction*. London: Sage.

Mead, M. (1928) *Coming of Age in Samoa*. Harmondsworth: Penguin.

Mead, M. (1930) *Growing up in New Guinea*. Harmondsworth: Penguin.

Mead, M. (1949) *Male and Female*. Harmondsworth: Penguin.

Meichenbaum, D. (1977) *Cognitive-Behaviour Modification*. New York: Plenum.

Meichenbaum, D. (1983) *Coping with Stress*. London: Century Publishing.

Meichenbaum, D. (1985) *Stress Inoculation Training*. New York: Pergamon Press.

Meichenbaum, D. (1986) 'Cognitive-behaviour modification', in F.H. Kanfer and A.P. Goldstein (eds), *Helping People Change*, 3rd edn. New York: Pergamon Press.

Miller, A. (1978) *Counselling Adolescents: School and After*. London: Faber and Faber.

Miller, S.D., Duncan, B.L., Hubbie, M.A. (1997) *Escape from Babel: Toward a Unifying Language for Psychotherapy Practice*. New York: Norton.

Miller, W.R. and Rollnick, S. (1991) *Motivational Interviewing*. New York: Guilford.

Milner, P. (1980) *Counselling in Education*. Trowbridge: Redwood Burn.

Muncie, J., Wetherell, M., Dallas, R. and Cochrane, A. (eds) (1995) *Understanding the Family*. London: Sage.

Murgatroyd, S. and Woolf, R. (1982) *Coping with Crisis*. London: Harper & Row.

Naylor, P. and Cowie, H. (1999) 'The effectiveness of peer support systems in challenging school bullying: the perspectives and experiences of teachers and pupils', *Journal of Adolescence*, 22: 467–79.

Nelson-Jones, R. (1996) *Effective Thinking Skills*. London: Cassell.

Nelson-Jones, R. (1997) *Practical Counselling and Helping Skills: Text and Exercises for the Life Skills Counselling Model*. London: Cassell.

Nelson-Jones, R. (1999a) 'Towards cognitive-humanistic counselling', *Counselling*, 10(1): 49–54.

Nelson-Jones, R. (1999b) *Creating Happy Relationships: A Guide to Partner Skills*. London: Cassell.

Noonan, E. (1983) *Counselling Young People*. London: Routledge.

Norcross, J.C. and Grencavage, L. (1989) 'Eclecticism and integration in counselling and psychotherapy: major themes and obstacles', *British Journal of Guidance and Counselling*, 17(3): 227–47.

Oaklander, V. (1978) *Windows on our Children: A Gestalt Therapy Approach to Children and Adolescents*. Moab, UT: Real People Press.

O'Connell, B. (1998) *Solution-Focused Therapy*. London: Sage.

O'Hanlon, B. and Wilk, J. (1987) *Shifting Contexts: The Generation of Effective Psychotherapy*. New York: Guilford.

O'Hanlon, W. (1992) 'History becomes her story: collaborative solution-oriented therapy of the after-effects of sexual abuse', in S. McNamee and K.J. Gergen (eds), *Therapy as Social Construction*. London: Sage.

Olweus, D. (1978) *Aggression in the Schools: Bullies and Whipping Boys*. Washington, DC: Hemisphere.

Olweus, D. (1991) 'Bully/victim problems among school children: basic facts and effects of a school based intervention', in D. Pepler and K. Rubin (eds), *The Development and Treatment of Childhood Aggression*. Hillsdale, NJ: Erlbaum.

Olweus, D. (1992) 'Bullying among school children: intervention and prevention', in R.D. Peters, D. McMahon and V.L. Quincy (eds), *Aggression and Violence Throughout the Life Span*. Hillsdale, NJ: Erlbaum.

Olweus, D. (1993) *Bullying at School: What we Know and What we Can Do*. Oxford: Blackwell.

Parkes, C.M. (1986) *Studies of Grief in Adult Life*. Madison: International Press.

Patterson, G.R. (1982) *Coercive Family Process*. Eugene, OR: Castalia Publications Co.

Patterson, G.R. and Stouthamer-Loeber, M. (1984) 'The correlation of family management practice and delinquency', *Child Development*, 55: 1299–307.

Payne, M. (2000) *Narrative Therapy*. London: Sage.

Pechereck, A. (1996) 'Growing up in non-nuclear families', in A. Sigston, P. Corran, A. Labraun and S. Wolfrendale (eds), *Psychology in Practice with Young People, Families and Schools*. London: David Fulton.

Pendergrast, M. (1996) *Victims of Memory*. London: Harper-Collins.

Perls, F.S., Hefferline, R.F. and Goodman, P. (1972) *Gestalt Therapy*. London: Souvenir Press (first published in 1951).

Piaget, J. (1953) *Logic and Psychology*. Manchester: University of Manchester Press.

Pikas, A. (1975) 'Treatment of mobbing in school: principles for and the results of an anti mobbing group', *Scandinavian Journal of Educational Research*, 19: 1–12.

Prochaska, J.O. and DiClemente, C.C. (1982) 'Transtheoretical therapy: toward a more integrative model of change', *Psychotherapy: Theory, Research, and Practice*, 19: 276–88.

Raphael, B. (1984) *Anatomy of Bereavement: A Handbook for the Caring Professions*. London: Hutchinson.

Reid, W. (1996) 'School counselling: a client centred perspective'. Australia: Kids Help Line: www.kidshelp.com.au/school/report.

Rhodes, J. and Ajmal, Y. (1995) *Solution Focussed Thinking in Schools*. London: Brief Therapy Press.

Richards, P.S. and Bergin, A.E. (1997) *A Spiritual Strategy for Counselling and Psychotherapy*. Washington, DC: American Psychological Association.

Rivers, I. (1996) 'The bullying of lesbian and gay teenagers in school: a hidden issue', keynote speech given at the NUT Conference, Birmingham, 7 December. Luton: transcript address: Department of Psychology, University of Luton, Park Square, Luton, Bedfordshire LU 3JU.

Rodgers, B. and Pryor, J. (1998) *Divorce and Separation: The Outcomes for Children*. York: Joseph Rowntree Foundation.

Rogers, C.R. (1967) *On Becoming a Person*. London: Constable.

Rogers, C.R. (1980) *A Way of Being*. Boston: Houghton Mifflin.

Roth, S. and Epston, D. (1996) 'Consulting the problem about the problematic relationship: an exercise for experiencing a relationship with an externalized problem', in M. Hoyt (ed.), *Constructive Therapies II*. New York: Guilford.

Rowe, D. (1996) 'Developing spiritual, moral and social values through a citizenship programme for primary schools', in R. Best (ed.), *Education, Spirituality and the Whole Child*. London: Cassell.

Rowling, L. (1996) 'Learning about life: teaching about loss', in R. Best (ed.), *Education, Spirituality and the Whole Child*. London: Cassell.

Ryle, A. (1990) *Cognitive-Analytic Therapy: Active Participation in Change*. Chichester: Wiley.

Salmivalli, C., Lagerspetz, K., Björkqvist, K., Osterman, K. and Kaukianen, A. (1996) 'Bullying as a group process: participant roles and their relations to social status within the group', *Aggressive Behaviour*, 22(1): 1–15.

Sanderson, C. (1995) *Counselling Adult Survivors of Child Sexual Abuse*. London: Jessica Kingsley.

Schafer, S. (1977) *The Victim and His Criminal*. Reston, VA: Reston Publishing Co.

Scher, M., Stevens, M., Good, G. and Eichenfield, G.A. (eds) (1987) *Handbook of Counselling and Psychotherapy with Men*. California: Sage.

Seligman, S.E.P. and Peterson, C. (1986) 'A learned helplessness perspective on childhood depression: theory and research', in M. Rutter, C.E. Izard and P.B. Read (eds), *Depression in Young People*. New York: Guilford.

Sherratt, E., MacArthur, C., Cheng, K., Bullock, A. and Thomas, H. (1998) *Young People's Lifestyle: Survey 1995–1996 (West Midlands)*. Birmingham: NHS Executive, Birmingham University.

Simpson, J.M. (1995) 'Guidance in Scottish secondary schools: the dichotomy between pastoral care and discipline', unpublished MEd Dissertation: University of Edinburgh.

Skynner, R. and Cleese, J. (1989) *Families and How to Survive Them*. London: Methuen.

Skynner, R. and Cleese, J. (1993) *Life and How to Survive It*. London: Methuen.

Smith, H. (1999) *Children, Feelings and Divorce*. London: Free Association Books.

Smith, M.L., Glass, G.V. and Miller, T.L. (1980) *The Benefits of Psychotherapy*. Baltimore, MD: Johns Hopkins University Press.

Smith, P.K. and Sharp, S. (eds) (1994) *School Bullying: Insights and Perspectives*. London: Routledge.

Speedy, J. (2000) 'White water rafting in cocktail dresses', *Counselling and Psychotherapy*, 11(10): 628–32.

Street, E. (1994) *Counselling for Family Problems*. London: Sage.

Talmon, M. (1990) *Single Session Therapy*. San Francisco: Jossey-Bass.

Tart, C.T. (1975) *Transpersonal Psychologies*. London: Routledge & Kegan Paul.

Thomas, R.M. (1990) *Life-Span Stages and Development*. London: Sage.

Thorne, B. (1994) 'Brief companionship', in D. Mearns, *Developing Person-Centred Counselling*. London: Sage.

Thorne, B. (1998) *Person-Centred Counselling and Christian Spirituality: The Secular and the Holy*. London: Whurr.

Thorne, B. (1999) 'The move towards brief therapy: its dangers and its challenges', *Counselling*, 10(1): 7–11.

Tober, G. (1991) 'Motivational interviewing with young people', in W.R. Miller and S. Rollnick, *Motivational Interviewing*. New York: Guilford.

Tomm, K. (1985) 'Circular questioning', in D. Campbell and R. Draper (eds), *Applications of Systemic Family Therapy: The Milan Approach*. London: Academic Press.

Truax, C.B. and Carkhuff, R.R. (1967) *Towards Effective Counselling and Psychotherapy*. Chicago: Aldine.

Tubman, J.G., Windle, M. and Windle, R.C. (1996) 'Cumulative sexual intercourse patterns among middle adolescents: problem behaviour precursors and concurrent health risk behaviours', *Journal of Adolescent Health*, 18: 182–91.

van Deurzen-Smith, E. (1984) 'Existential therapy', in W. Dryden (ed.), *Individual Therapy in Britain*. London: Harper & Row.

Walters, M. (1990) 'A feminist perspective in family therapy', in R.J. Perelberg and A.C. Miller (eds), *Gender and Power in Families*. London: Routledge.

Wang, M.Q., Fitzheugh, E.C., Eddy, J.M. and Fu, Q. (1997) 'Social influences on adolescents' smoking progress: a longitudinal analysis', *Adolescence*, 21: 111–17.

Watzlawick, P., Weakland, J. and Fisch, R. (1974) *Change: Principles of Problem Formation and Problem Resolution*. New York: Norton.

Webb, S. (1994) *Troubled and Vulnerable Children: A Practical Guide for Heads*. Kingston upon Thames: Cromer Publications.

West, W. (2000) *Psychotherapy and Spirituality*. London: Sage.

White, M. (1989) *Selected Papers*. Adelaide: Dulwich Centre Publications.

White, M. (1995) *Externalising Conversations Exercise*. Adelaide: Dulwich Centre Publications.

White, M. and Epston, D. (1990) *Narrative Means to Therapeutic Ends*. New York: W.W. Norton.

Whitney, I. and Smith, P.K. (1993) 'A survey of the nature and extent of bullying in junior/middle and secondary schools', *Educational Research*, 35: 13–25.

Winslade, J. and Monk, G. (1999) *Narrative Counselling in Schools: Powerful and Brief*. California: Corwin Press.

Wolberg, L.R. (1968) *Short-Term Psychotherapy*. New York: Grune & Stratton.

Wolfe, D.A., Jaffe, P., Wilson, S.K. and Zak, L. (1985) 'Children of battered women; the relation of child behaviour to family violence and maternal stress', *Journal of Consulting and Clinical Psychology*, 53(5): 657–65.

Worden, W. (1984) *Grief Counselling and Grief Therapy*. London: Tavistock.

Worsley, R. (2000) 'Can we talk about the spirituality of counselling?' *Counselling and Psychotherapy*, 12(2): 89–91.

Yalom, I.D. (1990) *Existential Psychotherapy*. New York: Basic Books.

Yerkes, R.M. and Dodson, J.D. (1993) 'The relation of strength of stimulus to rapidity of habit-formation', *Journal of Neurological Psychology*, 18: 459–82 (1908), in D. Childs (ed.), *Psychology and the Teacher*. London: Cassell.

Yule, W. and Gold, A. (1993) *Wise Before the Event: Coping with Crisis in School*. London: Calouste Gulbenkian Foundation.

LEGAL AND DfEE (DFE) DOCUMENTS

Data Protection Act 1984, HMSO.

DFE Circular 5/94/40: 'Education Act 1993: Sex Education in Schools'.

DFEE (1995) Disclosure in Child Abuse: Circular 10/95 Protecting Children from Abuse: the Role of the Education Service.

DFEE (2000) Sex and Relationship Educational Guidance: DFEE 0116/2000.

DH, HO and DFEE (1999) Working Together to Safeguard Children: Department of Health, Home office and DFEE. London: HMSO.

Education (School Records) Regulations 1989. London: HMSO.

Elton Report (1989) *Enquiry into Discipline in Schools: The Report of the Committee Chaired by Lord Elton, R.E.* London: HMSO.

Family Law Reform Act 1987. London: HMSO.

Gillick v. West Norfolk Wisbech Area Health Authority [1986] AC 112, [1985] 3 All ER 402, HL.

HEA (1992) Today's Young Adults. London: Health Education Authority. London: HMSO.

ONS (Office of National Statistics) (1998) *Young Teenage Smoking in 1998: A Report on the Key Findings from the Teenage Smoking Attitudes*. London: ONS.

ONS (Office of National Statistics) (2000). London: ONS.

SED (1968) *Guidance in Scottish Secondary Schools*. Edinburgh: Scottish Education Department.

SED (1976) *Guidance in Scottish Secondary Schools – A Progress Report by HMI*. Edinburgh: Scottish Education Department.

The Children Act (1989), London: HMSO.

The Police and Criminal Evidence Act (PACE, 1984). London: HMSO.

INDEX